# Financial Shenanigans

## Second Edition

## Howard Schilit

**McGraw-Hill**

New York  Chicago  San Francisco  Lisbon  London  Madrid
Mexico City  Milan  New Delhi  San Juan  Seoul
Singapore  Sydney  Toronto

Library of Congress Cataloging-in-Publication Data

Schilit, Howard Mark, 1952-
  Financial shenanigans / Howard M. Schilit.—2nd ed.
    p. cm.
  includes index
  ISBN 0-07-138626-2 (alk. paper)
  1. Financial statements, Misleading.   2. Fraud.   I. Title.
  HF5681.B2 S3243 2002
  657'.3—dc21

                                                           2002002879

# McGraw-Hill

A Division of The **McGraw·Hill** Companies

  13 14 15   DOC/DOC   0 9 8 7 6

ISBN 0-07-138626-2

*Printed and bound by R.R. Donnelley & Sons Company*

This book is printed on recycled, acid-free paper containing a minimum
of 50% recycled de-inked paper.

# CONTENTS

# DEDICATION

To my wonderful parents,
Ethel and Irving Schilit,
who taught me right from wrong
and to speak out when I saw wrong.

# ACKNOWLEDGMENTS

*Teachers and mentors* have played a vital role in my intellectual nurturing. The following will always have a special place in my heart: Louis Geller (Queens College, N.Y.), who taught me my first accounting class; Philip Piaker (Binghamton University, N.Y.), who inspired me to become a professor; and Abraham Briloff (Baruch College, N.Y.), whose impassioned writings about accounting chicanery inspired me to pursue my calling.

*Family* has been my foundation from the earliest days. My siblings, Audrey, W. Keith, and Rob, have provided love, support, and guidance throughout the many years. My wife, Diane, has not only been superlative in her role as a mom and a wife, but also has worked at my side in building an exciting research center. My children, Jonathan, Suzanne, and Amy, have inspired me and kept me feeling young as I approach my fiftieth birthday.

# Preface: Must Be a Sign of the Times

"It is simply a matter of creative accounting," says Matthew Broderick, playing accountant Leopold Bloom in Broadway's new blockbuster musical, *The Producers*. "Under the right circumstances, a producer could make more money with a flop than he could with a hit." Max Bialystock, Bloom's client, sees the potential for solving his own money woes. He raises as much as he can from rich widows to finance a new Broadway musical, *Springtime for Hitler*. He pockets the money and ensures that the show will bomb; in that way, nobody will ask awkward questions about where the money really went. *(BusinessWeek, May 14, 2001)*

Whether in producer Mel Brooks's fictional world played out on a Broadway stage or in the real world played out on Wall Street, creative accounting has often been used to hurt investors. And, in the last decade, it has gotten much worse.

## A Decade of Deceit

In May 1991, while flying over the Pacific Ocean after a visit to Japan, I began writing the first draft of *Financial Shenanigans*. Exactly ten years later, May 2001, while flying home over the Atlantic Ocean, the current edition of the book was born.

The decade began with President George H. Bush in the White House and the economy in a recession. Curiously, ten years later, his son George W. Bush occupies the Oval Office and the economy again is sputtering. During the intervening years, however, Americans enjoyed an unprecedented period of prosperity on both Main Street and Wall Street. Unemployment reached the lowest level in generations and stock market indices seemed to set new records virtually every day. The Dow Jones Industrial Average grew by over 20 percent annually for an unprecedented five straight years—1995 through 1999. That was nothing compared to the technology-heavy NASDAQ index. It jumped 94 percent in 1999 alone.

But beneath the surface and radar of most investors, ominous signs appeared—signs of financial sleight-of-hand and fraud. The decade began with revelations of a massive bank fraud at the Bank of Commerce and Credit International (BCCI). Then reports of fraud at the Phar Mor drug chain, retailer Leslie Fay, and trash hauler Waste Management Inc. The procession kept growing longer and more painful for investors with debacles at the large health maintenance organization Oxford Health, drug chain Rite Aid and the high-flying software firm Microstrategy. Creative accounting of "New Economy" companies made things even worse. Investor losses reached unimaginable levels. In the Cendant fraud alone, the financial settlement reached over $3 billion.

Not surprisingly, among the carnage of investors, some big winners emerged. Securities attorneys representing defrauded plaintiffs in class action lawsuits, and short sellers, betting that these stocks would collapse, made a fortune.

### Some Hopeful Signs Emerge

Some hopeful signs, however, began to emerge by the latter part of the decade. The head of the U.S. Securities and Exchange Commission (SEC), Arthur Levitt, had seen enough to evoke a dramatic response. With missionary zeal, Levitt began a three-pronged strategy to clean up the mess. First, he directed the SEC staff to issue clear guidelines outlining unacceptable accounting practices used in corporate filings. As a result, the SEC published three new Staff Accounting Bulletins (SAB 99, 100, and 101). And noncompliant companies were put on notice to quickly make the necessary changes. Second, the SEC began auditing the auditors (mainly the Big Five accounting behemoths) to ensure their compliance with standards of independence. Third, the SEC began investigating the questionable objectivity of brokerage firm analysts who hype the stock of companies (particularly, those paying lucrative investment banking fees) without performing sufficient objective due diligence.

## My Ten-Year Journey

After completing the 1993 edition of *Financial Shenanigans*, I formed a research and training organization that studies the quality of earnings of companies, stripping away the misleading accounting façade. Our Center for Financial Research & Analysis (CFRA) helps institutional investors, lenders, and others detect early signs of operating problems or accounting anomalies at public companies. Our website (*http://www.cfraonline.com*) contains reports on over 1,500 companies based in North America and Europe and is updated daily.

## Financial Shenanigans (Revised Edition, 2002)

This revised edition of *Financial Shenanigans* uses warning signs at companies CFRA found *before* the stock price collapsed. In contrast, the original 1993 edition of the book primarily focused on case studies from SEC Enforcement Releases and other publicly available material written *after* the stock price had already collapsed.

Fortunately, the analysts at CFRA have mastered the lessons in the original *Financial Shenanigans* in spotting early signs of problems before most investors and lenders. I am confident that you will also become more proficient in finding early signs of financial shenanigans and, consequently, become better investors and more responsible lenders.

A complete summary list of the seven financial shenanigans and the thirty techniques of trickery associated with them can be found on pages 24–25.

**Howard M. Schilit, Ph.D., CPA,** is president of the Center for Financial Research and Analysis (CFRA), a leading independent financial research organization, and is one of today's leading authorities on detecting accounting gimmicks. Dr. Schilit, a former professor at American University, has been quoted or featured in numerous business publications, including *The Wall Street Journal*, *BusinessWeek*, *Fortune*, and *The New York Times*, and has appeared on CNBC, CNN, and other networks. He is also the coauthor of *Blue Chips and Hot Tips*.

# PART ONE
# ESTABLISHING THE FOUNDATION

# 1

# You Can Fool Some of the People All of the Time

Mention the word *whopper* to hamburger lovers and many of them will think of the fast-food giant Burger King. Chapter 1 of this book contains something that is a bit less filling and produces considerably more heartburn—a four-part whopper of financial shenanigans.

## The Whopper, Part I: Cendant/CUC

The Cendant/CUC story begins in the mid-1980s, when the company was called CUC. (Cendant was created in late 1997 with the merger of CUC and HFS.) CUC's business was pretty simple and straightforward: It sold various types of club memberships to consumers. Its accounting, however, was anything but straightforward.

For more than twelve years, until the exposure of the scheme in 1998, CUC's senior and middle management used a variety of clever means to inflate the company's operating income. The fraud only came to light several months after CUC's merger with HFS and the birth of Cendant. (Since the fraud occurred at CUC before the merger, we will refer to the company as Cendant/CUC.) The chronology of events involving Cendent/CUC is outlined in Table 1-1.

Investigators auditing the records found that more than $500 million of bogus operating income had been recorded during the fiscal years ending January 1996, January 1997, and December 1997. Of that amount, more than half—approximately $260 million—had been added to the income of the fiscal year ending December 1997.

Table 1-1. Chronology: Cendant/CUC

| Date | Event |
| --- | --- |
| 1976 | Walter A. Forbes becomes chief executive officer of Comp-U-Card, a reseller of consumer products like washers, dryers, and televisions. |
| 1983 | Comp-U-Card, later renamed CUC, goes public at $1.21 a share, adjusted for later splits. |
| 1983 | Cosmo Corigliano leaves Ernst & Whinney, Comp-U-Card's auditing firm, to join the company as controller. He later says that the fraud had begun by then. |
| 1985 | According to the SEC, management inflates annual profits to meet Wall Street expectations. |
| 1990–1993 | CUC's stock becomes a Wall Street favorite, rising 1,287 percent from the end of 1989. |
| 1994 | Mr. Corigliano becomes chief financial officer (CFO). |
| 1994 | *September:* **CFRA Warning No. 1** |
| 1996 | CUC begins making large acquisitions, which the government now says were needed to help hide fraudulent accounting. |
| 1997 | *January:* **CFRA Warning No. 2** |
| 1997 | *December:* CUC merges with HFS to become Cendant, with Mr. Forbes as chairman. |
| 1998 | *April:* Cendant shares peak at $41.69 the week before the company discloses accounting irregularities. Mr. Shelton, the chief operating officer and number two in command, resigns from Cendant. |
| 1998 | *July:* Mr. Forbes resigns. |
| 2000 | *June:* Mr. Corigliano and two other former CUC accountants plead guilty to fraud. |
| 2000 | *September:* The SEC announces the results of its investigation and charges three individuals with fraud. |

## The Scheme

In the earlier years, management had manipulated profits by using an arbitrary system to determine when to recognize membership sales revenue. Management had also inflated profits by failing to properly account for member cancellations and the related liabilities.

As time went on, however, Cendant/CUC became increasingly dependent on acquisitions and mergers to sustain the scheme. Purchase and merger reserves were intentionally overstated when they were established, and the inflated amounts were later released to boost operating income. When it suited management's purposes, assets were written off against these overstated reserves.

In short, each year senior management would review the *opportunities* for inflating the company's income that were available and would determine how much would be needed from each of these sources that year. The result was an annual "cheat sheet" that assured senior management that that year's results were under control.

## Giving Wall Street What It Wanted

Each fiscal quarter, the reported results just matched the consensus quarterly expectations of Wall Street analysts. The reported operating income was what had been expected, and each major expense bore approximately the same percentage relationship to sales as in the prior quarter. These changes were directed by management through a deliberate, top-down process of "reverse engineering," virtually independent of what had actually transpired.

## Revenue Recognition Tricks

The Comp-U-Card division of Cendant/CUC marketed a number of membership products, with payment terms ranging from twelve to thirty-six months. In many periods, the company failed to amortize solicitation costs from sales over the same period in which it recorded the revenue; it recorded the revenue early and the expenses later. It also had to account for cancellations to sustain the image to investors of steady, predictable growth. Thus, for any given quarter, management would determine the amount of revenue needed and transfer that amount from deferred revenue. Cendant/CUC made fictitious bookkeeping entries, intentionally understating membership cancellation reserves, and occasionally reversing the cancellation reserves or commissions payable directly into revenue or operating expense.

By the mid-1990s, however, opportunities related to membership sales could no longer sustain the scheme. The company's growth requirements forced Cendant/CUC management to look increasingly to another area of opportunity: merger and purchase reserves.

## Manipulating Merger and Purchase Reserves: Turning Unusual Charges into an Ordinary Income Source

By far the largest (in dollar terms) part of Cendant/CUC's games came from merger and acquisition charges and the reversal of these amounts into operating income in later periods.

The company became increasingly acquisitive and engaged in larger and larger deals. Larger mergers provided the opportunity for larger merger reserves, and these large reserves could keep the scheme going for years. In 1996, Cendant/CUC made several acquisitions and established a large merger reserve, and management envisioned that reserve as inflating earnings for years to come. There was just one problem: Cendant/CUC's business was already reeling, and management needed to deplete the reserves much more quickly than it had planned. By 1997, Cendant/CUC was desperate for a major combination, and that desperation led management to renew a previously aborted merger discussion with HFS. By May of that year, those discussions had resulted in the Cendant merger agreement and the possibility of a merger reserve large enough to keep the scheme alive.

## Writing Off Assets against the Cendant Merger Reserve

Another category of reserve-related opportunities was created in connection with the Cendant merger and the December 1997 closing. Immediately prior to the merger, managers implemented a scheme in which impaired assets held by Cendant/CUC were not written off at that time. Then, in connection with the December 1997 year-end close, the managers arranged for millions of dollars of Cendant/CUC's assets to be written off against the reserve of the newly formed company. Overall, the write-off of assets against the December 1997 reserve, and the concomitant failure to recognize certain asset impairments in the proper years, artificially inflated income by $6 million for the fiscal year ended January 1996, by $12 million for the fiscal year ended January 1997, and by $29 million for the fiscal year ended December 1997.

## When the Fraud Broke

On April 16, 1998, just months after the December 1997 merger (and a mere two weeks after the first certified 10-K [see page 48] filing of the newly formed Cendant), the company disclosed the accounting irregularities. The stock price dropped from $35.63 to $19.06. On July 14, there was more bad news: The accounting irregularities were more extensive than had been anticipated, and the company would have to restate the previous three years. The stock took another hit, closing on July 16 at $14.63. It finally bottomed out at $9.00 in the fall of 1998. (See Fig. 1-1.)

## The Charges and Financial Settlements

Before the Enron debacle, Cendant/CUC had been called the biggest accounting fraud ever, with investors having lost a combined $19 billion. Were the scoundrels behind this massive thirteen-year fraud ever brought to justice?

In June 2000, three senior officials pleaded guilty: Cosmo Corigliano, former chief financial officer; Anne Pember, former controller; and Casper Sabatino, former accountant. In his testimony, Mr. Corigliano disclosed something incredible: *The fraud had been going on since 1983, the year he joined the company and it went public.*

In September 2000, the SEC announced the completion of its investigation, charging three individuals with fraud. In February 2001, a federal grand jury in Newark, New Jersey, indicted the

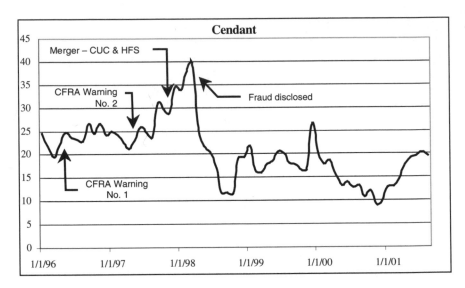

**Fig. 1-1.  Cendant Stock Price, 1996–2001**

three on fraud charges. If convicted, they could spend ten years in prison.

The company also faced massive litigation. Cendant/CUC settled shareholder suits for $2.8 billion, and its former auditors, Ernst & Young (formerly Ernst & Whinney), agreed to pay $335 million to settle litigation. In an unusual turn of events, the company's current management brought a civil action against the auditors, contending that they knew of the fraud and covered it up. The accountants of course deny the allegations.

*Warning Signs and Lessons from Cendant/CUC.*   Cendant/CUC exhibited a number of classic warning signs (see Table 1-2). First, it used aggressive accounting for marketing costs during the earlier years to inflate reported profits. Then, as business started slowing down, it made ill-advised acquisitions of both troubled companies and companies in unrelated fields. The purpose of the acquisitions had nothing to do with business synergies. Instead, the acquisitions created opportunities to take big charges and create reserves. These reserves would then be released into earnings in a later period to artificially inflate earnings. Each of these accounting ploys will be explored in detail in later chapters.

Table 1-2. Warning Signs: Cendant/CUC

| Problem Indicated | Evidence | Shenanigan |
|---|---|---|
| **Aggressive accounting:** Shifted current expenses to a later period | • Cendant/CUC capitalized marketing costs. | No. 4 |
| **Aggressive accounting:** Shifted future expenses to the current period and later released reserves into income | • When it made acquisitions, Cendant/CUC took large restructuring charges to create bogus income. | No. 7 |
| | • In subsequent periods, Cendant/CUC released these reserves into income. | No. 5 |

# The Whopper, Part II: Informix

Since the birth of Hewlett-Packard more than a half century ago, Silicon Valley has received worldwide acclaim for its technological innovations. However, Informix (IFMX), a database management company, has brought Silicon Valley another type of acclaim: the *infamy award for the biggest accounting fraud at a technology company.*

## At First, All Looked Fine

Prior to the quarter ending March 1997, Informix regularly characterized itself in press releases as the fastest-growing company in the database software industry. The company reported 1996 sales of $939 million, up 32 percent from the prior year. And by early 1996, its market capitalization had reached $4.6 billion. But beneath the surface, all was not well.

## How the Fraud Became Known

The first black clouds appeared in early 1997, with the release of the company's fourth-quarter results. In its annual report, IFMX disclosed two disturbing pieces of information: It had begun using barter (*nonmonetary exchanges*) with licensees, and resellers had been unable to find end users (i.e., buyers) for its products. The news proceeded to get worse. One day later, IFMX unexpectedly announced that revenues for the first quarter of 1997 would be $59 million to $74 million below the first quarter of 1996 because purchase commitments from resellers had dried up. Wall Street was totally unprepared for this news, and the company's share price declined 34.5 percent, dropping the market capitalization from $2.3 billion to $1.5 billion (see Fig. 1-2).

About two weeks after the revenue shortfall announcement, the company's auditors learned of potential accounting irregularities relating to certain 1995 and 1996 transactions with European customers. Apparently, the auditors received a tip from a former IFMX employee. A more formal investigation by management and its outside law firm commenced.

By June, the auditors had begun to recognize the magnitude of the fraud. They found evidence of numerous *side agreements* with customers. In one case, the company had granted a customer extended payment terms to late 1998, approximately two years after the sale date. That contradicted the official sales contract, which required payment by November 1997, within the twelve-month period required by accounting rules for revenue recognition. Many

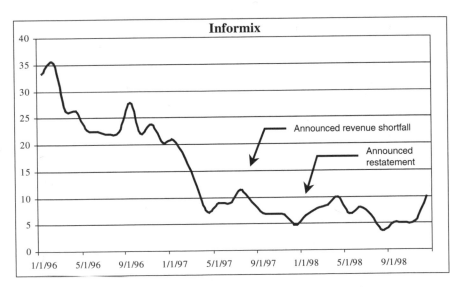

**Fig. 1-2.   Effect of Fraud Disclosure on Informix Stock Price**

of these side agreements essentially allowed customers to void sales. When a new senior management team took over the reins at IFMX, they decided that they had seen enough and made a painful decision. On August 7, 1997, the company publicly announced that it would have to restate the financial statements in question.

Informix and its auditors identified $114 million of accounting irregularities involving more than a hundred transactions, mostly with resellers, in 1995 and 1996. Because the irregularities were so pervasive, the company and its auditors determined that *all such transactions for the three-year period ended in 1996 should be restated* to defer revenue recognition until the resellers resold the licenses to end users.

In November 1997, the company amended its 1996 annual report (Form 10-K) and restated its financial statements for fiscal years 1994 through 1996. Just how large was the three-year restatement? *IFMX had inflated revenue by $311 million (17 percent) and net income by $244 million (1,835 percent)*. Of the $257.3 million of profits reported over the period, only $13.3 million (or 5 percent of the total) was legitimate (see Table 1-3).

The restatements also significantly affected the company's previously reported revenues and earnings for each quarter of 1996 (see Table 1-4).

*Warning Signs and Lessons from Informix.* Informix used a variety of ploys to accelerate revenue and even record fictitious revenue (see Table 1-5). In many cases, the company gave its customers side letters that materially modified the terms of the sale or allowed the customer to nullify the sale. Specifically, the company's

Table 1-3. Informix Reported Net Revenues and Income, 1994–1996

| | Net Revenues (millions) | | | Net Income (millions) | | |
|---|---|---|---|---|---|---|
| | Originally Reported | As Restated | % Over-stated | Originally Reported | As Restated | % Over-stated |
| **1996** | $939.3 | $727.8 | +29% | $97.8 | $(73.6) | +233% |
| **1995** | $714.2 | $632.8 | +13% | $97.6 | $38.6 | +153% |
| **1994** | $470.1 | $452.0 | +4% | $61.9 | $48.3 | +28% |

Table 1-4. Informix Reported Net Revenues and Income by
Quarter for 1996

|        | Net Revenue (millions) | | | Net Income (millions) | | |
|--------|------------------------|-----------|-----------|-----------------------|-----------|-----------|
|        | Originally Reported | As Restated | % Misstated | Originally Reported | As Restated | % Misstated |
| Q1'96  | $204.0 | $164.6 | +24% | $15.9 | $(15.4) | +203% |
| Q2'96  | $226.3 | $159.3 | +42% | $21.6 | $(34.1) | +163% |
| Q3'96  | $238.2 | $187.1 | +27% | $26.2 | $(17.1) | +253% |
| Q4'96  | $270.8 | $216.8 | +25% | $34.1 | $(7.0)  | +587% |

dishonest practices included backdating license sale agreements,
entering into side agreements that granted customers rights to refunds and other concessions, recognizing revenue on transactions
with reseller customers that were not creditworthy, recognizing
amounts due under software maintenance agreements as software
license revenues, and recognizing revenue on disputed claims
against customers.

## The Whopper, Part III: Waste Management

The third member of CFRA's Hall of Shame is the trash hauler
Waste Management, Inc. (WMI). While the perpetrators at Cen-
dant/CUC and Informix magically created revenue out of thin air,
Waste Management's specialty was making expenses disappear.
And no one did it any better. In bringing the first fraud case
against any accounting firm since 1985, the SEC estimated that
WMI's 1992–1996 pretax *profits were exaggerated by an astounding
$1.43 billion.* To settle the lawsuit, the auditor, Arthur Andersen,
agreed to pay a record* penalty (for auditors) of $7 million. That
was only the beginning. Andersen also agreed to pay $220 million
to settle shareholder litigation in the matter.

### Once the Trash King

During the early years of the 1990s, WMI began to dominate the
field of waste management and trash hauling. By 1995, its sales

*While this is a record for an accounting fraud, the amount pales in comparison
to some fines for insider trading. Junk-bond king Michael Milken's $447 million
payment in the 1980s related to an insider trading scandal remains the record.

Table 1-5. Warning Signs: Informix

| Problem Indicated | Evidence | Shenanigan |
|---|---|---|
| **Aggressive accounting:** Recorded revenue too soon or of questionable quality | • IFMX backdated license sale agreements.<br>• IFMX entered into side agreements that granted customers rights to refunds and other concessions.<br>• IFMX recognized revenue on transactions with reseller customers that were not creditworthy.<br>• IFMX recognized amounts due under software maintenance agreements as software license revenues. | No. 1 |
| **Aggressive accounting:** Recorded bogus revenue | • IFMX recognized revenue on disputed claims against customers.<br>• The company purchased computer hardware or services from customers on terms that effectively refunded all or a substantial portion of the license fees paid by the customer.<br>• IFMX paid fictitious consulting or other fees to customers that were to be repaid to the company as license fees. | No. 2 |

exceeded $10 billion. Much of the growth, however, came from acquisitions. Over the period 1993–1995, WMI spent billions acquiring 444 companies. With these acquisitions came the inevitable one-time charges. The special charges became so common that during the seven-year period 1991–1997, WMI took write-offs in six of the seven years, totaling $3.4 billion. In 1997 alone, the special charges amounted to $1.6 billion. Since investors typically ignore special charges in evaluating profitability, WMI appeared to be in tip-top shape. Also, to keep people from asking too many questions about the charges, WMI offset (or "netted") against the write-offs one-time investment gains from asset sales.

## Tricks of the Trade

Another trick that WMI perfected was inflating profits by shifting expenses to a later period. Here's how WMI pulled it off: First, the company moved operating costs like Maintenance and Repair and Interest Expense to the balance sheet as Plant and Equipment. (In fact, WMI admitted that it had misstated its expenses relating to, among other things, vehicle, equipment, and container depreciation; capitalized interest; asset impairments; purchase accounting related to environmental remediation reserves; and other liabilities.) The company then depreciated these costs over forty years. The result was that normal operating costs were expensed over the next forty years. Sweet! The effect this had on the company's stock can be seen in Fig. 1-3.

## Merger with USA Waste Services

As with Cendant, the accounting problems began to surface just after an acquisition. In July 1998, WMI merged with USA Waste Services. The following year, the company initiated a comprehensive internal review of its accounting records, systems, processes, and controls at the direction of its board of directors. As a result of the review, WMI recorded certain adjustments that had a material effect on its financial statements, resulting in a one-time charge of $1.2 billion. The company also reported something even more troubling: *Its internal controls were incapable of providing reli-*

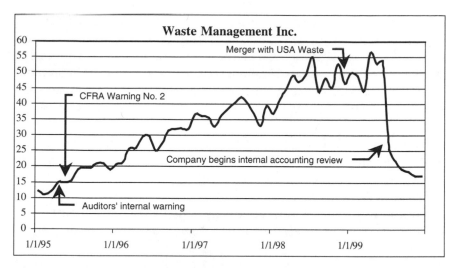

**Fig. 1-3.   Effect of Accounting Tricks on WMI Stock.**

*able information.* Here's how the company described the situation in its September 1999 quarterly report:

> The Company, after consultation with its independent public accountants, has concluded that its internal controls for the preparation of interim financial information did not provide an adequate basis for its independent public accountants to complete reviews of the quarterly data for the quarters in the nine-month period ended September 30, 1999.

## Where Were the Auditors?

The auditors at Arthur Andersen saw evidence of improper accounting, but chose not to push the client too hard. According to an SEC enforcement release, during the years in question, Andersen actually quantified certain misstatements. For example, in its 1993 audit, Andersen quantified current- and prior-period misstatements of $128 million, which, if recorded, would have reduced net income before special items by 12 percent. The partners, however, determined that the misstatements were not material and that Andersen could issue an unqualified audit report on the company's 1993 financial statements.

In 1994, the company continued to engage in the accounting practices that had given rise to the quantified misstatements and other known and likely misstatements. As in 1993, Andersen's practice director, its managing partner, and the audit division head were consulted, and they again concurred in the issuance of a favorable opinion on the company's 1994 financial statements.

Unlike the auditors in the Cendant/CUC and Informix cases, the auditors of WMI apparently knew what was happening and looked the other way. Consider the following internal discussion among the auditors after the 1995 audit and the filing of WMI's 1995 Form 10-K with the SEC. At that time, Andersen prepared a memorandum articulating its disagreement with the company's netting of one-time gains against special charges and failing to disclose this. The memorandum discussed a transaction of 1995 and gains from other transactions in 1996 that were netted without disclosure. According to the memorandum, Andersen recognized that:

> the Company has been sensitive to not use special charges [to eliminate balance sheet errors and misstatements that had accumulated in prior years] and instead has used "other gains" to bury charges for balance sheet cleanups. [Emphasis in original]. . . .
>
> We disagree with management's netting of the gains and charges and the lack of disclosures. We have communicated strongly to management that this is an area of SEC exposure. We will continue to monitor this trend, and assess in all cases the impact of nondisclosure in terms of materiality to the overall financial statement presentation and effect on current year earnings.

Despite its concerns about WMI's use of netting, Andersen did not withdraw its 1995 audit report or take steps to prevent the company from continuing to use this technique in 1996 to eliminate current-period expenses and prior-period misstatements from its financial statements.

## Perhaps Too Cozy with the Auditors

The 1995 internal memorandum was far from unique. Indeed, in every year, the auditors knew of the problems but apparently chose not to push the client too hard. Why? Did the auditors have too cozy a relationship with WMI? Consider the following facts:

- Andersen had been the auditor every year from the time WMI first became a public company in 1971.
- Until 1997, every chief financial officer and chief accounting officer in Waste Management's history as a public company had previously worked as an auditor at Andersen.
- During the 1990s, about fourteen former Andersen employees worked for Waste Management, most often in key financial and accounting positions.
- Between 1991 and 1997, Andersen billed Waste Management corporate headquarters approximately $7.5 million in audit fees. Over this same seven-year period, while Andersen's corporate audit fees remained capped, Andersen also billed Waste Management corporate headquarters $11.8 million in other fees; much of this amount was for tax services, attest work unrelated to financial statement audits or reviews, regulatory issues, and consulting services.
- A related entity, Andersen Consulting, also billed Waste Management corporate headquarters approximately $6 million in additional nonaudit fees. Of the $6 million in fees to Andersen Consulting, $3.7 million was related to a strategic review that analyzed the overall business structure of the company and ultimately made recommendations on implementing a new operating model designed to "increase shareholder value."

*Warning Signs and Lessons from Waste Management.* Most of the inflated profits at WMI resulted from improperly shifting expenses to a later period. Later on, the company would net one-time gains against special charges. See Table 1-6.

## The Whopper, Part IV: Lucent
### The Bigger They Are . . . The Harder They Fall

While what happened at Lucent (LU) is certainly not considered an egregious financial fraud like what happened at Cendant/ CUC, Informix, or Waste Management, it merits a "whopper" la-

Table 1-6. Warning Signs: Waste Management, Inc.

| Problem Indicated | Evidence | Shenanigan |
|---|---|---|
| **Aggressive accounting:** Shifted current expenses to a later period | • WMI improperly capitalized landfill costs, interest expense, and other operating expenses. | No. 4 |
| **Aggressive accounting:** Shifted future expenses to the current period as a special charge | • WMI took special charges in virtually every period. | No. 7 |
| **Aggressive accounting:** Boosted income with one-time gains | • WMI netted one-time gains against special charges. | No. 3 |
| **Weak control environment:** Lack of auditor independence | • WMI had too cozy a relationship with Arthur Andersen. | — |

bel because of the decline in the company's market value. While Cendant's shareholders lost $19 billion, Lucent's investors lost *close to a quarter of a trillion dollars* in value between November 1999 and June 2001 (see Fig. 1-4).

### Those Were the Days that Were

Lucent's story began on a very happy note. From the day that AT&T spun off Lucent in April 1996, its share price appreciated almost 1,000 percent (this is referred to as a ten-bagger) over the next four years. The most widely held stock in America, LU was considered a darling compared to the disappointing AT&T. And for good reason: It produced just what Wall Street wanted—strong, consistent growth in revenue and earnings. By September 1999, operating income had reached $5.4 billion, *tripling* in two short years (see Table 1-7). Moreover, net income had grown more than tenfold during that time period.

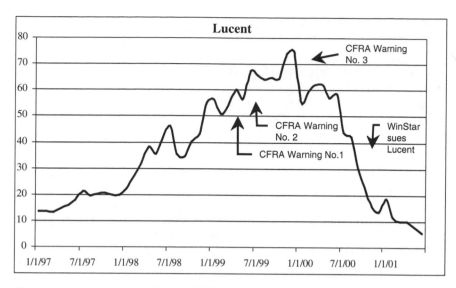

**Fig. 1-4.   Lucent Stock Price, 1997–2001**

Table 1-7.  Lucent Sales and Income

|  | September 1999 | September 1998 | September 1997 |
|---|---|---|---|
| Sales | $38.3 billion | $31.8 billion | $27.6 billion |
| Operating income | 5.4 billion | 2.6 billion | 1.6 billion |
| Net income | 4.8 billion | 1.0 billion | 0.4 billion |

## But All Was Not Well

CFRA became concerned about the situation at Lucent in early 1999, twice warning investors about LU's slowing sales, bloated receivables and inventory, and aggressive accounting (see Table 1-8). Nonetheless, the company continued producing results that were pleasing to investors, and the stock price galloped faster and faster. In November 1999, it peaked at $81.75. On January 6, 2000, CFRA issued a stern warning about a big jump in capitalized software and an artificial boost to income from reversing a restructuring charge. Within a week, the company announced that it would miss Wall Street's earnings estimates for the December 1999 quarter. The stock plummeted 25 percent that day.

Table 1-8. Chronology: Lucent

| Date | Event |
|------|-------|
| 1999 | *February*: **CFRA Warning No. 1** |
| 1999 | *May*: **CFRA Warning No. 2** |
| 2000 | *January*: **CFRA Warning No. 3** |
| 2000 | *October*: McGinn replaced by Henry Schact, Lucent's chairman from 1995 to 1997. The company also cuts the earnings forecast for the first quarter and reports a 22 percent drop in fourth-quarter profits. |
| 2001 | *January*: Lucent announces a $1 billion first-quarter operating loss and a $1.6 billion restructuring charge, including plans to cut 16,000 jobs, or 15 percent of the workforce. |
| 2001 | *February*: Lucent says it is cooperating with the SEC in a probe of previously reported improperly booked sales. |
| 2001 | *April*: Lucent's stock falls to the lowest point in over four years on reports that the company had begun drawing on bank credit lines, suggesting that it might have used much of the $3.8 billion of cash that it had at the end of 2000. The resulting stock decline eliminates virtually all of the gains since Lucent's spinoff from AT&T Corp. in 1996. |
| 2001 | *April*: Lucent says WinStar Communications has defaulted under its vendor financing agreement, a charge that WinStar disputes. Shortly thereafter, WinStar files for bankruptcy protection, blaming Lucent for violating its financing agreement. WinStar also files a $10 billion lawsuit against Lucent, spurring investor concern that other such deals might collapse and cause further damage to Lucent. |

For Lucent shareholders, this was but the first of many disappointments during the next two years. The shareholders witnessed a $250 billion meltdown from the November 1999 pinnacle. With its continued existence very much in doubt, Lucent announced major layoffs and sought a merger partner.

*Warning Signs and Lessons from Lucent.*   Unlike the stories at Cendant/CUC, Informix, and Waste Management, which feature massive fraud, the Lucent story is one of a struggling business that used aggressive accounting for well over a year to camouflage the deterioration. In late 1998, sales slumped, backlog and deferred revenue declined, and receivables and inventory balances shot up. That's when LU's accounting grew more aggressive. Specifically,

Table 1-9. Warning Signs: Lucent

| Problem Indicated | Evidence | Shenanigan |
|---|---|---|
| **Operational problems** | • Sales for the December 1998 quarter grew 5.5 percent, down from 22.8 percent in September.<br>• There was a jump in receivables (days' sales outstanding).<br>• There was a bulge in inventory (days' sales in inventory).<br>• Operating cash flow down. | — |
| **Aggressive accounting:** Recorded revenue too soon | • Lucent restated year 2000 earnings, removing $679 improperly included revenue. | No. 1 |
| **Aggressive accounting:** Reduced liabilities by changing accounting assumptions | • Lucent modified its accounting approach and assumptions for pensions. | No. 5 |
| **Aggressive accounting:** Failed to write down impaired assets | • Lucent reduced the allowance for doubtful accounts and released the previous reserve, despite an increase in receivables of 32 percent.<br>• Lucent reduced the allowance for inventory obsolescence, although the inventory balance increased. The result: lower reported expenses. | No. 4 |
| **Aggressive accounting:** Boosted income with one-time gains | • During fiscal 1998, LU recorded $558 million of pension income—16 percent of earnings for the year. | No. 3 |
| **Aggressive accounting:** Released reserves into income | • LU released $100 million of a previously recorded restructuring reserve, boosting operating income. | No. 5 |
| **Aggressive accounting:** Created new reserves from ten acquisitions | • LU wrote off $2.4 billion (58 percent of the cumulative purchase price) as in-process R & D. This new reserve could later be released into earnings. | No. 7 |
| **Aggressive accounting:** Shifted current expenses to a later period | • LU started capitalizing internal-use software. | No. 4 |

to boost earnings, LU failed to write down impaired assets and began to capitalize certain software costs, changed some pension assumptions and released reserves, and created new reserves related to acquisitions—presumably available to boost future periods' earnings (see Table 1-9). Each of these shenanigans will be covered in later chapters.

## A Look Ahead

Investors in Cendant, Informix, Waste Management, and Lucent paid a heavy price for failing to spot early signs of operating problems that had been camouflaged by financial shenanigans. Fortunately, learning the lessons from these debacles will better arm us to detect similar warning signs today.

Chapters 2 and 3 begin the journey of detecting accounting gimmicks and fraud in financial reports. Part 2 (Chapters 4 through 10) describes seven broad categories and thirty techniques of financial shenanigans.

# 2
# SEEK AND YE
# SHALL FIND

*To strive, to seek, to find, and not to yield.*
ALFRED, LORD TENNYSON, British poet

Financial shenanigans range from benign tricks to outright fraud. They occur at companies of all sizes, from small, unknown firms to the most prominent global ones. This chapter provides some important building blocks for identifying companies that are using accounting tricks. It also provides an important case study showing the very different fates of two companies that employed improper accounting: One company never recovered, and the other bounced back from a "bump in the road" to achieve great success.

Chapter 2 answers the following seven questions about shenanigans:

- What are financial shenanigans, in general?
- What specific techniques are used?
- What are the basic strategies underlying the shenanigans?
- How do the shenanigans relate to one another?
- Should investors be more concerned about certain shenanigans?
- Why do shenanigans exist and where are they most likely to occur?
- What is the profile of a "big" story?

## What Are Financial Shenanigans, in General?

Financial shenanigans are actions that intentionally distort a company's reported financial performance and financial condition. They range from benign (changes in accounting estimates) to egregious (fraudulent recognition of bogus revenue).

## What Specific Techniques Are Used?

The CFRA has identified thirty techniques (grouped into seven categories) that companies use to trick investors and other stakeholders.

---

### SEVEN FINANCIAL SHENANIGANS

*Shenanigan No. 1: Recording Revenue Too Soon or of Questionable Quality*

- Recording revenue when future services remain to be provided
- Recording revenue before shipment or before the customer's unconditional acceptance
- Recording revenue even though the customer is not obligated to pay
- Selling to an affiliated party
- Giving the customer something of value as a quid pro quo
- Grossing up revenue

*Shenanigan No. 2: Recording Bogus Revenue*

- Recording sales that lack economic substance
- Recording cash received in lending transactions as revenue
- Recording investment income as revenue
- Recording as revenue supplier rebates tied to future required purchases
- Releasing revenue that was improperly held back before a merger

*Shenanigan No. 3: Boosting Income with One-Time Gains*

- Boosting profits by selling undervalued assets
- Including investment income or gains as part of revenue

---

- Reporting investment income or gains as a reduction in operating expenses
- Creating income by reclassification of balance sheet accounts

*Shenanigan No. 4: Shifting Current Expenses to a Later or Earlier Period*

- Capitalizing normal operating costs, particularly if recently changed from expensing
- Changing accounting policies and shifting current expenses to an earlier period
- Amortizing costs too slowly
- Failing to write down or write off impaired assets
- Reducing asset reserves

*Shenanigan No. 5: Failing to Record or Improperly Reducing Liabilities*

- Failing to record expenses and related liabilities when future obligations remain
- Reducing liabilities by changing accounting assumptions
- Releasing questionable reserves into income
- Creating sham rebates
- Recording revenue when cash is received, even though future obligations remain

*Shenanigan No. 6: Shifting Current Revenue to a Later Period*

- Creating reserves and releasing them into income in a later period
- Improperly holding back revenue just before an acquisition closes

*Shenanigan No. 7: Shifting Future Expenses to the Current Period as a Special Charge*

- Improperly inflating amount included in a special charge
- Improperly writing off in-process R&D costs from an acquisition
- Accelerating discretionary expenses into current period

## What Are the Basic Strategies Underlying the Shenanigans?

The following are two basic strategies underlying all accounting tricks:

- To *inflate* current-period earnings by *inflating* current-period revenue and gains or by *deflating* current-period expenses
- To *deflate* current-period earnings (and, consequently, inflate future periods' results) by *deflating* current-period revenue or by *inflating* current-period expenses

The first strategy, inflating profits, is intuitive and needs no further clarification. In contrast, the strategy of intentionally making the company look worse than it really is may be confusing. The larger objective of this strategy is to shift earnings to a later period when they will really be needed—in other words, to *inflate tomorrow's profits*. Table 2-1 summarizes the relationship between these strategies and the seven shenanigan tactics.

## How Do the Shenanigans Relate to One Another?

Although all financial shenanigans fit into seven finite categories, there are important connections and intersections among certain of these categories.

For example, Shenanigans No. 1 and Shenanigan No. 5 can be thought of as close cousins. A company that receives an advance payment from a customer for future services and improperly recording revenue immediately has employed both Shenanigan No. 1 (recording revenue too soon) and Shenanigan No. 5 (failing to record or improperly reducing liabilities).

Shenanigan No. 2 is related to Shenanigan No. 6. A company that improperly holds back recording all of today's revenue (No. 6) will invariably record that revenue in a later period (No. 2).

There is also an important connection between Shenanigan No. 5 and Shenanigan No. 7. Consider the following example: A company takes a big restructuring charge (Shenanigan No. 7, shifting future expenses to the current period as a special charge) and in

Table 2-1. Accounting Strategies and the 7 Shenanigans

| | Strategies | | | |
|---|---|---|---|---|
| Accounts | Inflate Current Period | Tactic | Deflate Current Period | Tactic |
| Revenue (or gains) | Recording revenue too soon | No. 1 | Shifting current revenue to a later period | No. 6 |
| | Recording bogus revenue | No. 2 | | |
| | Boosting income with one-time gains | No. 3 | | |
| | Failing to record or improperly reducing liabilities | No. 5 | | |
| Expenses (or losses) | Boosting income with one-time gains | No. 3 | Shifting future expenses to the current period as a special charge | No. 7 |
| | Shifting current expenses to a later or earlier period | No. 4 | | |
| | Failing to record or improperly reducing liabilities | No. 5 | | |

the next quarter releases the reserves with the charge credited (Shenanigan No. 5, failing to record or improperly reducing liabilities).

## Should Investors Be More Concerned about Certain Shenanigans?

Certain shenanigans can be fairly benign, whereas others may be more harmful for investors. In general, shenanigans that inflate revenue should be considered more serious than those that affect expenses. If a company's revenue growth appears solid and its accounting is proper, the company's prospects typically remain strong.

## The Continuum — From Benign to Outright Fraud

Not all financial shenanigans are illegal acts or violations of generally accepted accounting principles (GAAP). They include a broad array of activities that intentionally misreport the financial performance or financial condition of a company. Shenanigans range from the fairly benign (amortizing costs too slowly, a technique under Shenanigan No. 4) to outright fraud (recording bogus revenue, Shenanigan No. 2). Table 2-2 shows the continuum and gives some examples.

## Not Great News for Investors

Not surprisingly, the share price invariably performs poorly after a company begins using financial shenanigans. Moreover, when companies use particularly egregious shenanigans, the stock price decline will generally be steeper and more permanent. There are two obvious reasons for this:

- Generally, companies that use such accounting chicanery are attempting to cover some major operational deterioration in the business. The truth concerning the operating problem will soon become known by investors.
- Such chicanery leads investors to lose faith in management's integrity, causing the stock to remain out of favor for a long time.

# Why Do Shenanigans Exist and Where Are They Most Likely to Occur?

While most people agree that gimmicks can distort financial statements, there are many theories about the reasons why these gimmicks exist. Based on my research, there are three general reasons for shenanigans: (1) It pays to do it, (2) it's easy to do, and (3) it's unlikely that you'll get caught.

## It Pays to Do It

Some managers will resort to accounting gimmicks if they are personally enriched by doing so. Thus, when bonuses encourage

Table 2-2. The Shenanigan Continuum

| More Benign ⟵ | | | ⟶ Most Egregious |
|---|---|---|---|
| 1 | 2 | 3 | 4 |
| Change in accounting estimates | Releasing reserves | Capitalizing operating costs | Including bricks in inventory boxes to trick the auditors who weigh the boxes |

managers to post higher sales and profits and no questions are asked about how those gains were achieved, an incentive for using shenanigans can be created. Unfortunately, misguided incentive plans are not uncommon today in corporations. In explaining why companies use financial shenanigans to manage earnings, Baruch College's Professor Abraham Briloff remarked, "Because it's their report card." Executives like their bonuses and the other perquisites that are tied to reported earnings.

**Be Alert for Misguided Management Incentives.** Like most of us, managers are affected in their behavior by rewards and punishments. Since many companies offer bonuses and stock options based on financial statement measures, executives and managers are motivated to report more favorable financial results. Similarly, if underperforming divisions in companies are threatened with layoffs or lower compensation for their managers, those managers will often search for ways to report stronger results. Because of this pressure to report higher sales and higher profits, managers may be creative in their interpretation of GAAP.

A compensation structure that heavily emphasizes the bottom line creates an environment that sometimes encourages accounting chicanery. Professor Paul Healy of MIT undertook a study to show empirically that management benefited by choosing accounting procedures that produced higher earnings. Healy found a connection between bonus schemes and the accounting choices that executives made. Specifically, he found that executives whose bonuses were already at the maximum level tended to choose accounting options that minimized reported profits, whereas those who had no ceiling chose profit-boosting options. Thus, if no additional bonus is paid once profits reach a certain level, it is not in the executive's interest to have reported profits exceed that amount. In such a case, the manager would be better off deferring any profits above the maximum bonus level to some future period when they might be needed to sustain the manager's own income.

### It's Easy to Do It

Managers select accounting methods (e.g., for inventory valuation or amortization of intangible assets) from a variety of acceptable choices. Thus, depending on the methods selected and the numerous estimates that must be made, a company's reported profit can vary considerably and yet still be in compliance with GAAP.

Honest managers grapple with the many choices and judgments required with the goal of finding accounting policies that portray the company's financial performance fairly. Unscrupulous managers, unfortunately, use the flexibility in GAAP to distort the financial reports.

Indeed, it is surprisingly easy for managers to use accounting gimmicks to manipulate financial statements. This is true for various reasons, including the following: (1) There is substantial flexibility in interpreting GAAP, (2) GAAP can be applied in ways that boost a company's reported profits, and (3) changes in GAAP by the Financial Accounting Standards Board (FASB) often occur long after a deficiency in financial reporting becomes evident.

Unlike tax legislation and the related U.S. Treasury Department regulations, financial accounting standards are fairly broad, and consequently management has considerable flexibility in interpreting them. Thus, decisions on whether to capitalize a cost or categorize it as an expense, or on selecting amortization periods for fixed assets, depend on management judgment.

Furthermore, management can structure transactions or decide when and how to implement new accounting rules to maximize its reporting goals. For example, the use of stock compensation plans (which produce no change in income) as a substitute for other forms of compensation has become increasingly popular at many corporations. Similarly, companies can structure lease agreements to keep the debt off their books (e.g., using an operating lease approach).

**Question Overly Liberal Accounting Rules.** Because management has substantial control over the numbers that are reported, consider whether the accounting policies selected are overly aggressive. Consider various accounting policies of a company, such as inventory method, amortization period, and revenue recognition policy. Further, consider any changes in accounting policies and the reasons cited for them.

Beyond the realm of ethics, judgment plays an especially important role in the banking and insurance industries. Bankers use judgment in determining whether and when to write off loans that may not be repaid. If they are slow to recognize problem loans and fail to write them off, the bank will continue accruing interest on shaky loans. The result is an overstatement of assets, interest income, and profits on the bank's financial statements.

**Watch for Poor Internal Controls.** In addition to taking advantage of the flexibility of GAAP, management may have little difficulty distorting financial reports if the company has weak internal controls. Such controls relate to the organizational structure and to corporate procedures for safeguarding assets against losses and ensuring the reliability of financial records for external reporting purposes. Strong controls (i.e., checks and balances) tend to reduce the temptation for management to engage in shenanigans. If safeguards and controls are lacking, however, unethical employees may engage in shenanigans with impunity. While independent auditors scrutinize the adequacy of these controls, it may be difficult for readers of financial statements to ascertain whether the controls contain weaknesses.

## It's Unlikely That You'll Get Caught

Just as some people cheat on their tax returns because they think they won't get caught by the IRS, companies may use accounting tricks because they believe that they won't get caught by auditors or regulators. Unfortunately, for the reasons outlined below, they are usually right. And, even when they are caught, the penalty is often too little, too late.

**Note that Quarterly Financial Statements Are Unaudited.** Investors and bankers who rely on quarterly financial statements and press releases on financial performance may believe that those reports have the blessing of an independent CPA. Unfortunately, that's not usually true. Only the annual financial statements of publicly held companies must be audited; quarterly statements need not be. Moreover, most companies are privately held and are rarely audited by an outside CPA. When companies use accounting tricks on unaudited financial statements, there is little risk that they will be caught. As a result, investors must be especially careful when reading quarterly financial statements.

## What Types of Companies Are Most Likely to Use Shenanigans?

While it is relatively easy for managers to use shenanigans and there is only a moderate chance of their getting caught, most companies *do not* intentionally distort their financial reports. Unfortunately, since you never know in advance which companies *do* publish misleading information, it is prudent to be a bit suspicious of all companies and to search for early warning signs of problems. Such signs often include (1) a weak control environment (i.e., lack of independent members on the board of directors or lack of a competent/independent external auditor), (2) management facing extreme competitive pressure, and (3) management known or suspected of having questionable character. Be particularly alert for these factors in the following types of companies: fast-growth companies whose real growth is beginning to slow, basket-case companies that are struggling to survive, newly public companies, and private companies.

The growth of all fast-growth companies will eventually slow considerably. At that point, managers may be tempted to use accounting gimmicks. Investors and lenders should be alert for shenanigans in all such companies. At the other extreme, managers of very weak companies might be tempted to use accounting tricks to deceive the outside world into thinking that their companies' problems are minor. Investors and lenders should be particularly alert when a company may not be in compliance with bank lending covenants on such financial measures as minimum net worth and working capital. Many newly public companies whose shares are first issued through an initial public offering, or IPO, have never been audited before and may lack strong internal controls. Shenanigans may be prevalent. Finally, private companies, particularly those that are closely held and have not been audited, are more likely to use shenanigans.

## What Is the Profile of a "Big" Story?

As indicated earlier, some accounting tricks are considered fairly benign and others are lethal. Knowing the difference between the two is essential. The story of two companies, AOL and Medaphis, provides an example of this.

### AOL: An Interesting Story

Back in 1994, AOL was far different from the media giant AOL Time Warner of today. In fact, there were real doubts that AOL would survive against its larger and more formidable competitors of that era, CompuServe and Prodigy.

AOL needed sizable capital infusions from investors, but it had one glaring problem: It was spending considerably more than it was receiving from subscribers. That fact would have been clear to investors had AOL used more conventional accounting.

Specifically, in 1994 AOL decided to exclude current marketing costs in calculating its profit—an unusual and aggressive policy. Instead of immediately expensing these costs, AOL shifted them to the balance sheet (as an asset) and charged them off in future periods. Table 2-3 shows the resulting effect on AOL's revenue, income, and profits.

By the following year, profits were becoming more elusive and AOL's accounting became even more aggressive. The company began amortizing marketing costs over eighteen months, rather than twelve. The shine started coming off AOL in 1996, and the

Table 2-3. AOL Revenue ($ in millions)

|                                            | 1996     | 1995     | 1994     | 1993     |
| ------------------------------------------ | -------- | -------- | -------- | -------- |
| Revenue                                    | 1,093.9  | 394.3    | 115.7    | 52.0     |
| Operating income                           | 65.2     | (21.4)   | 4.2      | 1.7      |
| Net income                                 | 29.8     | (35.8)   | 2.2      | 1.4      |
| Total assets                               | 958.8    | 405.4    | 155.2    | 39.3     |
| Deferred subscriber acquisition costs      | 314.2    | 77.2     | 26.0     | —        |

share price sagged. With rapid growth of the number of sub-scribers, AOL's infrastructure proved to be inadequate to meet customers' needs. The result, not surprisingly, was massive sub-scriber defections. In fact, during the March 1996 quarter, net ad-ditions to AOL's subscriber base were virtually zero. The company again started tinkering with its accounting for marketing costs, pushing out the amortization period from eighteen to twenty-four months.

Those who had been bullish on AOL apparently had seen enough, and they dumped the stock, cutting the share price from a (pre-split) high in May 1996 of $75 to only $25 in September (see Fig. 2-1). The very survival of the company was now being de-bated. On top of the soft subscriber growth, investors worried about the impact on future earnings of amortizing the $385 million of marketing costs that AOL had shifted to future periods.

In October 1996, management announced a bold plan to turn the company around. The plan included a scheme to write off the $385 million of marketing costs as a one-time, nonrecurring (and to be ignored) restructuring charge.

Over the subsequent months and years, AOL's business strengthened, making it the dominant Internet data provider. In-vestors have been richly rewarded, as the share price has appre-ciated almost twentyfold off its 1996 low. AOL used its richly val-ued stock to acquire Netscape and its nemesis CompuServe. Finally, in 2000, AOL swallowed media giant Time Warner.

**Justice Is Not Always Swift in Coming ... and May Arrive Too Late.** For years, AOL inflated earnings by aggressively deferring the marketing expenses related to sending out millions of com-

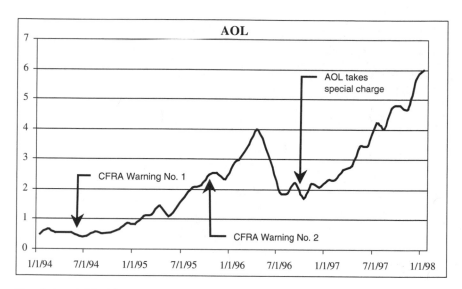

**Fig. 2-1.   AOL Share Price, 1994–1998**

puter disks to potential customers. That enabled AOL to look more profitable than it really was, helping it issue securities to raise cash and to make the acquisitions that fed its growth.

Although AOL's accounting transgressions failed to derail its aggressive plans, the regulators finally caught up with it. On May 15, 2000, AOL submitted to an SEC settlement (without admitting or denying any wrongdoing), paid a $3.5 million fine, and restated its former income to losses. The company was home free.

*Warning Signs and Lessons from AOL.*   CFRA issued three separate warnings (June 1994, October 1995, and June 1996), focusing on AOL's aggressive and unusual accounting for marketing costs (see Table 2-4). Instead of charging those costs against income immediately, AOL pushed them to future periods, thereby inflating current-period income. Finally, in 1996, AOL changed to the more conservative approach of expensing such costs. In so doing, it also wrote off the previously deferred costs as a "special charge." As a result, future-period operating income received a boost from the exclusion of the already written off amortization costs.

Table 2-4. Warning Signs: AOL

| Problem Indicated | Evidence | Shenanigan |
|---|---|---|
| **Aggressive accounting:** Capitalized normal operating costs | • AOL capitalized marketing costs as "deferred subscriber acquisition costs." | No. 4 |
| **Aggressive accounting:** Amortized costs too slowly | • Stretched out amortization from twelve to twenty-four months. | No. 4 |
| **Aggressive accounting:** Shifted future expenses to the current period as a special charge | • AOL changed the accounting for marketing costs and wrote off the $385 million of deferred subscriber acquisition costs as a one-time nonrecurring charge. | No. 7 |

## Medaphis: A Big Story

In April 1995, a CFRA analyst (electronically) searched through financial reports for any mention of "unbilled revenue"—a tip-off that aggressive revenue recognition was going on. That's when Medaphis Corporation (MEDA), a medical information company, first came to our attention. Based on its 1994 filing, the company would book 100 percent of a contract as revenue, although it had collected only 15 percent of that amount from the customer. CFRA calculated that of the $17.2 million of profit reported, only $3.1 million (or 18 percent) was appropriate.

After the release of our April 1995 report to investors, the share price declined markedly as a result of the accounting concerns (see Fig. 2-2). Almost immediately thereafter, eight brokerage firms published harsh rebuttals to CFRA's warnings, helping the share price recover. By year-end, the share price had increased by another 25 percent. On March 20, 1996, it reached an all-time high of $53.25, giving the company a market value of $3.5 billion.

Medaphis had reported impressive growth during the period 1993 to 1995. Revenue for 1995 hit $467.7 million, up almost 50 percent from the prior year. Operating profits raced ahead 65 percent, hitting $75.2 million during 1995 (see Table 2-5). However, in June 1996, one year after our first warning, we noticed a more

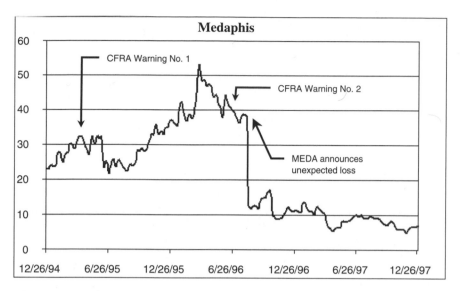

**Fig. 2-2.  Medaphis Stock Price, 1994–1997**

troubling sign. Specifically, MEDA had recorded as part of its revenue $12.5 million that represented its share of the earnings from an investment partnership. Investment income is certainly nice to have, but it should not be included as part of revenue. After the CFRA analyst restated the reported revenue and operating income by excluding the investment gains, the results were shocking— MEDA's operating profits were off 37 percent.

Two months after CFRA's second warning to investors was issued, MEDA shocked the markets by announcing a big unexpected loss. The company said that it was having problems with a major European contract and was reporting a loss on that contract, which involved designing and installing a computerized accounting system. The stock price (which had peaked in March at $53.25) melted down, falling 60 percent to $14.25 on volume of more than 42 million shares, well over half the 71 million shares outstanding.

Over the coming months, the news got worse. On October 22, when Medaphis reported a far larger loss than it had forecast in August, the stock fell 38 percent from its already depressed level. Medaphis also announced that it would restate earnings for the fourth quarter and full year of 1995. The restatements were nec-

Table 2-5. Medaphis Operating Profits, 1994–1996

|  | Quarterly ($ in millions) | | |
|---|---|---|---|
|  | March 1996 | March 1995 |  |
| Revenue | 136.6 | 110.1 | +24.1% |
| Operating income | 24.0 | 18.2 | +31.9% |
|  | Annual ($ in millions) | | |
|  | December 1995 | December 1994 |  |
| Revenues | 467.7 | 319.1 | +46.6% |
| Operating income | 75.2 | 45.6 | +64.9% |

essary because of improperly recorded revenues booked in connection with a major license agreement executed in December 1995 and other unspecified transactions. These agreements had side letters relieving the customer of obligations under the agreement. The restatement reduced reported fourth-quarter 1995 operating results from a net income of approximately $4 million to a loss of $1.1 million *for the quarter* (a shocking 120 percent reversal). In a similar vein, the previously reported loss of $3.4 million for full year 1995 more than doubled to a restated loss of approximately $8.5 million. By March 1997, the stock had reached a low of $3 and MEDA's auditors were questioning whether the company could continue as a going concern. The company's accountants said that they did not expect the company to generate enough cash to pay off its debt.

*Warning Signs and Lessons from Medaphis.* While Medaphis's revenue and earnings growth *was* impressive, most of it was coming from the company's rapid acquisition program, not from organic growth. Since 1988, the company had made approximately fifty acquisitions, with the pace accelerating in more recent periods. In the March 1996 quarter alone, MEDA had announced six new acquisitions. In addition, CFRA found a number of other concerns related to operational deterioration and very aggressive accounting practices. (Reports were published in April 1995 and

June 1996.) Evidence of the operational problems included an enormous operating cash flow deficit, bulging *unbilled* receivables, and deteriorating operating margins. Telltale signs of aggressive accounting included shifting certain operating costs to future periods by capitalizing software costs and including in revenue certain investment gains from a joint venture (see Table 2-6).

Table 2-6. Warning Signs: Medaphis

| Problem Indicated | Evidence | Shenanigan |
|---|---|---|
| **Aggressive accounting:** Recorded revenue too soon | • MEDA used percentage-of-completion accounting, thereby recording revenue before the product was shipped.<br>• There was a big increase in unbilled revenue. | No. 1 |
| **Aggressive accounting:** Recorded investment income as revenue | • MEDA included in March 1996 revenue $12.5 million of net earnings from a joint venture. | No. 2 |
| **Aggressive accounting:** Capitalized normal operating costs | • During 1995, MEDA capitalized $33.5 million (52 percent of pretax earnings), up an astonishing 423 percent from 1994. | No. 4 |
| **Aggressive accounting:** Amortized costs too slowly | • MEDA lengthened the amortization period from five to seven years in 1995. | No. 4 |
| **Operational problems** | • MEDA's cash flow from operations was deteriorating.<br>• MEDA's margins were deteriorating.<br>• MEDA had made acquisitions of troubled companies. | — |
| **Aggressive Accounting:** Shifted future expenses to the current period as a special charge | • MEDA recorded a $25 million restructuring charge and created reserves. | No. 7 |

Particularly troubling was the ploy related to inflating revenue. During the quarter ended March 1996, MEDA and a German telecommunications company signed an agreement to provide systems integration and workflow engineering systems and services over a multiyear period.

### Comparison of AOL and MEDA—Why Did AOL Recover and MEDA Not?

The MEDA vignette illustrates a most egregious accounting transgression: recording bogus revenue. By including in revenue the proceeds from an investment, the company hid from its investors a substantial revenue slowdown (revenue grew 12 percent rather than the reported 24 percent) and deteriorating operating margins. Once the truth was revealed in August 1996, investors fled. In contrast, despite AOL's aggressive accounting practice of pushing expenses to a later period, its revenue was solid and was reported accurately. After a rocky period in 1996, AOL's share price recovered its loss and went on to greater heights. MEDA had a very different fate: Its share price continued falling, only bottoming out at a level 90 percent off its high. Today MEDA is part of Atlanta-based Per Se Technologies.

## A Look Ahead

Chapter 3 discusses the publicly available sources of information that can be used to begin the investigation.

# 3

# SEARCHING FOR SHENANIGANS

*Detection is, or ought to be, an exact science, and should be treated in the same cold and unemotional way.*

*When you have eliminated the impossible, whatever remains, however improbable, must be the truth.*
SIR ARTHUR CONAN DOYLE
Author and creator of Sherlock Holmes

Sherlock Holmes and other good detectives search for clues, examine all the evidence, and deduce what actually happened. Similarly, successful investors, lenders, and analysts read financial reports and other information, searching for clues and deducing how the company actually performed in the past and how it is likely to perform in the future. This chapter describes the process of evaluating financial evidence.

An essential skill for analysts is the ability to detect early signs that companies are using financial shenanigans to camouflage problems. This chapter discusses the sources of information analysts use (see Table 3-1), including database searches that enable them to systematically hone in on the problems.

## Living a Dream—and a Nightmare

Imagine living the American dream during the Internet era. You and your college buddy form a software company. For the first few years you work around the clock, but you take virtually no cash compensation. Instead, you reward yourself and your valued employees with stock and stock options. You begin meeting with investment bankers to plan your much anticipated initial public offering (IPO). Then it happens—the bankers successfully peddle your shares to the public. You now have your first millions. But that's only the beginning. The share price of your (now public) company begins to levitate, appreciating more than 1,000 percent. You are one of the wealthiest people in America and you are not even old enough to run for the presidency. The media treat you like royalty.

That was the real-life dream of MicroStrategy's (MSTR) founder, Michael Saylor. Founded in 1989, MSTR went public in 1998. At that time, Saylor's stock was worth over $200 million. That was only the beginning of an incredible odyssey. In the last four months of 1999, the share price began to rise dramatically, from $20 to over $100 (see Fig. 3-1). Over the next ten weeks, the stock reached the stratospheric price of $333. Michael Saylor's net worth reached an almost inconceivable $14 billion; he was the richest person in the nation's capital.

Then the dream turned into a nightmare of epic proportions. In March 2000, MSTR disclosed to investors that its financial reports contained accounting irregularities. The financial reports for the years 1997 to 1999 had to be restated, resulting in massive losses

Table 3-1. Sources of Information

- Press releases
- SEC filings
- Company interview
- Commercial databases (screening)

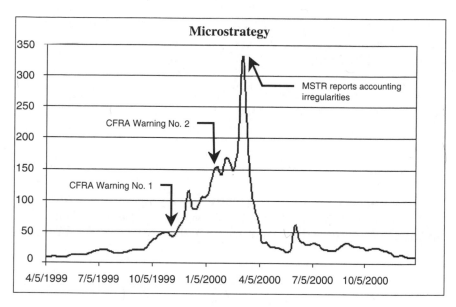

**Fig. 3-1.  Microstrategy Stock Prices, 1999–2000+**

rather than the previously reported profits. Shocked investors started dumping the stock, dropping the share price $140 the day the news broke. That was only the beginning. The once $333 stock didn't bottom out until it reached $1.75 in March 2001.

## What Led to the Collapse?

In early March 2000, only weeks after the auditors at PricewaterhouseCoopers (PWC) had blessed MSTR's 1999 financial reports, contained in the prospectus for a proposed stock offering, *Forbes* magazine questioned the company's accounting.

PWC conducted an internal investigation and concluded that the company's audited financial reports were false and misleading. The auditor's swift about-face, an extremely rare event, sent the share price into a free fall.

## The Punishment

In addition to watching their net worth dwindle by billions, senior management had to disgorge $10 million of improper gains from stock sales and pay a fine of $1 million. That was a pittance compared to the fines paid by the auditors to settle the litigation: those fines totaled $55 million.

*Warning Signs in Press Releases.*   On October 5, 1999, MSTR announced in a press release that it had signed a deal with NCR Corporation. The following month, the CFRA warned investors about an unusual revenue-generating transaction that was first disclosed in that press release. In the release, MSTR described a $52.5 million licensing agreement and a partnership with NCR Corporation. Under the agreement, MSTR invested in an NCR partnership and NCR returned the favor and purchased MSTR's products. We refer to that practice as a "boomerang." As the press release put it,

> Under the terms of the partnership, NCR signed a $27.5 million OEM {Original Equipment Manufacturer} agreement for MicroStrategy's entire suite of Intelligent E-Business products. ... The agreement also includes several ongoing royalty streams associated with the reselling of MicroStrategy's products and personal information services. In addition, MicroStrategy has chosen to purchase an NCR Teradata Warehouse worth $11 million to power the Strategy.com network.
>
> As part of the OEM agreement, NCR will become a master affiliate of Strategy.com. As a master affiliate, NCR will join the network, sell Strategy.com affiliations, and sell MicroStrategy products and services. As part of the agreement, MicroStrategy will provide NCR's future OLAP technology. MicroStrategy has agreed to purchase NCR's TeraCube business and all related intellectual property in exchange for $14 million in MicroStrategy stock.

Initially, Wall Street seemed concerned about CFRA's warnings, and the share price fell 10 percent. However, investment bankers and analysts at Merrill Lynch, who were helping MSTR float a secondary stock offering, issued a stern rebuttal of CFRA's warning. This seemed to alleviate investors' concerns, as the stock price strengthened and began to rise rapidly.

### It's Déjà Vu All Over Again

By the time CFRA issued its second warning in late January 2000, the share price was approaching $100, double the price at the time of our November warning. Again, we found an unusual disclosure about revenue recorded from a new joint venture partner in a press release issued by the company. The facts are quite similar to those in the NCR ploy, with a press release issued a week after the quarter closed. The other player this time was Exchange Application, Inc., and the press release (excerpts from which are shown below) was dated January 6, 2000. However, MSTR, curiously, recorded the revenue in December 1999.

> Under the terms of the agreement, Exchange Applications will pay MicroStrategy an initial $30 million fee, payable through a combination of cash and Exchange Applications stock, of which approximately one-third will be recognized by Micro-Strategy as revenue during the fourth quarter of 1999. In addition, MicroStrategy can earn up to an additional $35 million for future eCRM applications over the next two to three years.
>
> As part of the agreement, Exchange Applications will become a master affiliate of Strategy.com. As a master affiliate, Exchange Applications will join the network, sell Strategy.com affiliations, and sell MicroStrategy products and services.

### Press Releases Were the Key

The MSTR story underscores the fact that important information may be contained in corporate press releases. The auditors at PricewaterhouseCoopers missed the problem and certified that the financial reports could be relied upon. Yet investors who read MSTR's press releases in October 1999 and January 2000 would have seen the warning signs.

## The "Pro Forma" Game

As the MSTR example illustrates, disclosures contained in press releases can provide useful information for investors. One problem, however, is the occasional attempt to obfuscate the truth by using a new metric called *pro forma* earnings. This measure removes from net income items that management believes are not related to the company's normal recurring business. Traditionally, pro forma numbers were provided to give investors an idea of what the earnings of a completely new business or the business that would result from a merger would look like.

Recently, some companies have issued press releases that contained misleading earnings, using the pro forma metric. They have whimsically excluded expenses that really are related to the company's normal recurring business. For example, some companies have excluded such costs as stock-based compensation and amortization expense in computing pro forma earnings.

This subjective approach to accounting and financial reporting can turn losses into profits. That's just what happened at Computer Associates International (CA), whose accounting was challenged in an April 2001 story in *The New York Times.* By changing the terms of its software sales and how it accounts for them, CA reported 42 cents of pro forma earnings per share in the final quarter of last year, versus a 59-cent loss under GAAP. Company officials say that the new presentation is actually more conservative and that the purpose of the change was not enhancing growth.

Similarly, giant telecom carrier Qwest Communications International Inc. reported $2 billion in quarterly earnings before interest, taxes, depreciation, and amortization, or EBITDA (one version of pro forma), in a January 2001 press release. Shareholders had to wait weeks to find out, in a footnote to the annual results, that according to GAAP rules, Qwest had actually lost $116 million.

### SEC Not Amused by Pro Forma Chicanery

The SEC has taken note of these schemes. In a March 2001 speech, the agency's chief accountant, Lynn Turner, attacked company disclosures that appeared to "turn straw into gold." He described how the fixation on corporate profits has led companies to move from reporting EPS (earnings per share) to creating the turbocharged pro forma EBS—Everything but the Bad Stuff.

## Mr. Buffett Says It Best

Investment guru Warren Buffett (chairman of Berkshire Hathaway) has poked fun at the managements that create pro forma metrics by comparing this practice to someone who first shoots an arrow and then, after seeing where it is headed, draws the bull's-eye on the target. Similarly, management first decides what it would like to highlight and then comes up with a descriptor. *It's pretty difficult to lose that game.*

Table 3-2 shows the enormous difference between the actual GAAP-based earnings and the inflated pro forma earnings recently reported by various technology companies. JDS Uniphase (JDSU), for example, actually lost $1.13 per share, yet in its pro forma disclosure, JDSU reported profits of $0.14 per share. That's some difference!

# Gathering Financial Data

The main source of financial information on public companies is found in documents filed with the SEC. The financial shenanigans discussed in Chapters 4 through 10 can be detected in SEC filings. These filings fall into two broad categories: regular and irregular. All companies regularly file annual (Form 10-K and the proxy) and quarterly (Form 10-Q) reports. In addition, companies are required to file when specific events occur, such as when insiders sell stock (Form 144), when additional stock or debt is offered to

Table 3-2. Comparison of Pro Forma and GAAP Results of Selected Companies (March 2001 Quarter)

| Company | Pro Forma | GAAP | Difference |
| --- | --- | --- | --- |
| JDS Uniphase | $0.14 | −$1.13 | 1.27 |
| Checkfree | −0.04 | −1.17 | 1.13 |
| Terayon | −0.43 | −1.01 | 0.58 |
| Amazon.com | −0.22 | −0.66 | 0.44 |
| PMC-Sierra | 0.02 | −0.38 | 0.40 |
| Corning | 0.29 | 0.14 | 0.15 |
| Qualcomm | 0.29 | 0.18 | 0.11 |
| Cisco Systems | 0.18 | 0.12 | 0.06 |

the public (Registration S-1 or S-4), and when other special events occur (Form 8-K).

---

**A SUMMARY OF CORPORATE FILINGS**

I. Regular Filings

    **A. Annual**

| | |
|---|---|
| Form 10-K[1] | All publicly held companies report detailed financial results to the SEC on an annual basis using Form 10-K. This report, audited by an independent accountant, is due 90 days after the close of the fiscal year. |
| Annual report | Publicly held companies generally report their financial results to their shareholders once a year in an annual report. This report, a condensed version of Form 10-K, contains the basic financial statements, the accompanying footnotes, a report by an independent CPA, and a letter from the company president. |
| Proxy | A proxy statement is mailed to stockholders in connection with the annual stockholders' meeting. This document explains proposals to be voted on by shareholders, including such routine items as the reappointment of the company's accounting firm. More important, it contains information about management compensation, management stock options, special deals for management and directors, related-party transactions, and changes of auditors. |

## B. Quarterly

| | |
|---|---|
| Form 10-Q | Publicly held companies must file quarterly reports within 45 days after the close of each quarter using Form 10-Q. This report, which is far less detailed than Form 10-K, is *not* audited by a CPA. It contains a balance sheet, a statement of operations and cash flow, footnotes, and management discussion and analysis. |
| Form 8-K | Using Form 8-K, a company must inform the SEC of special events, including changes in control of the company, the acquisitions, dispositions, auditor changes, the resignation of directors, and bankruptcy. These reports are due within 15 days after the occurrence of the event, except in the case of auditor changes, which must be reported within 5 days. |
| Form 144 | Insiders must register whenever they buy or sell stock. |
| Registration | Whenever a publicly held company plans to issue securities, it must first file a registration statement, including a prospectus and exhibits, with the SEC (using Form S-1 or Form S-18 for initial public offerings). The prospectus describes the company's background, financial performance, and future plans. It is a detailed business plan; it provides many valuable clues that can be used for predicting a company's future performance. |

[1]Publicly held companies must file a Form 10-K, an annual shareholders' report, and a proxy. They have some flexibility concerning what to disclose in each one, so readers should view these three filings as an integrated document. A typical Form 10-K contains the following sections: Audited Balance Sheet, Statement of Operations, Cash Flow Statement, Footnotes to the Financial Statements, Management Discussion and Analysis, Auditor's Report, and Liquidity Position and Capital Expenditures.

### Finding Data on Non-U.S. Companies Creates Challenges

Foreign companies that are not traded on U.S. stock exchanges have less stringent reporting requirements. Such companies rarely file quarterly results, and the annual report (Form 20-F) is due 180 days (rather than the 90 days for U.S. companies) after year-end. However, foreign companies typically report their results on their Web sites at least semiannually.

## Beginning the Search for Financial Shenanigans

With these documents in hand, you are ready to begin the search. So, where should you start? Interestingly, you should *not* begin with the balance sheet, statement of operations, or statement of cash flows. (Chapter 12 discusses how to find shenanigans in these financial statements using a case study on MiniScribe Corporation.) Instead, your search should begin with the accompanying information, such as the auditor's report, proxy statements, footnotes to the financial statements, the letter from the president, management discussion and analysis (MD&A), and Form 8-K filings. Table 3-3 lists what you should look for in this material.

Table 3-3. Using the Documents to Find Shenanigans

| Where to Look | What to Look For |
|---|---|
| Auditor's report | Absence of opinion or qualified report |
| | Reputation of auditor |
| Proxy statement | Litigation |
| | Executive compensation |
| | Related-party transactions |
| Footnotes | Accounting policies/changes in those policies |
| | Related-party transactions |
| | Contingencies or commitments |
| President's letter | Forthrightness |
| MD&A | Specific concise disclosure |
| | Consistency with footnote disclosure |
| Form 8-K | Disagreements over accounting policies |
| Registration statement | Past performance |
| | Quality of management and directors |

## The Auditor's Report

Since the auditor has spent weeks reviewing the financial records and searching for accounting tricks, first read the auditor's opinion and see what he or she has to say. Generally, this letter contains a "clean" opinion. However, if the auditor has a strong reservation about the company's financial condition or the fairness of its financial statements, he or she will generally "qualify" the report.

**Watch for Qualified Opinions.** Investors should be cautious about investing in any company that receives a qualified opinion—especially if it is a "going concern" qualification. That was the opinion that auditors Ernst & Young gave on Carolco Pictures' 1991 financial statements. Ernst & Young indicated "substantial doubts" about the movie company's ability to continue as a going concern after it posted a loss of $265 million. A going concern qualification warns investors and others that the company is experiencing major financial difficulties.

**Be Wary When No Audit Committee Exists.** Another warning sign for investors is the absence of an audit committee composed of outside members of the board of directors. This committee serves as a buffer between management and the independent auditor. While companies that are listed on the New York Stock Exchange are required to have audit committees, there is no such requirement for the majority of publicly traded companies. Investors should be concerned if (1) no audit committee exists, and/or (2) members of the audit committee appear not to be independent of management.

## Proxy Statements

Although proxy statements are separate from the annual report, investors should consider them an integral part of the financial report. Astute investors read the proxy statement to search for important information that is not included in the financial reports, such as special compensation "perks" for officers and directors, and also lawsuits and other contingent obligations facing the company. One such investor, Hugo Quackenbush, senior vice president of Charles Schwab & Co., describes proxy statements as follows:

> They are like a soap opera in black and white. Management has to disclose all the stuff they don't want to and investors can get more of the texture and flavor of a company reading the proxy statement than the glossy annual report.

## Footnotes to the Financial Statements

Appended to the financial statements are footnotes. They provide the reader with a wealth of information for assessing the financial condition of a company and the quality of its reported earnings. Specifically, the footnotes detail such matters as accounting policies selected, pending or imminent litigation, long-term purchase commitments, changes in accounting principles or estimates, industry-specific notes (e.g., unbilled receivables for a government contractor), and segment information showing which operations are healthy and which are not.

Many analysts agree that the information in the footnotes is actually more important than what is shown on the financial statements. Columnist Kenneth Fisher, for example, wrote in *Forbes:*

> The back of the report, the footnotes is where they hide the bad stuff they didn't want to disclose but had to . . . they bury the bodies where the fewest folks find them—in the fine print.

Table 3-4 gives criteria for evaluating a company's accounting policies, whether they are conservative or aggresive.

**Favor Companies with Conservative Accounting Policies.** Footnotes can provide signs of "creative" accounting or gimmicks. Some footnotes should lead you to question not only the validity of the financial statements, but also the integrity of management. Companies that fail to use conservative accounting methods may be demonstrating a lack of integrity in their financial reporting process. Indeed, many analysts place a premium on companies that use conservative accounting policies. In searching for excellent companies, for example, the widely respected analyst and shenanigan buster Thornton O'glove offers the following advice:

> Look for companies that use very conservative accounting principles. In my experience, if a company does not cut corners in its accounting, there's a good chance it doesn't cut corners in its operations. You know you've got your money with a high quality management.

**Be Alert for an Aggressive or Inappropriate Inventory Valuation.** The selection of an inventory valuation method, which can substantially affect a company's reported profits, often indicates the degree of conservatism of a company's accounting policies. The most popular methods are last-in, first-out (LIFO) and first-in, first-out (FIFO). LIFO charges the latest inventory costs as an expense first; conversely, FIFO charges the earliest costs first.

During inflationary periods (i.e., when inventory costs are rising), the difference between LIFO and FIFO can affect profits substantially. Under these circumstances, LIFO generally produces lower reported profits for a company than does FIFO (this also

Table 3-4. Evaluating Accounting Policies

| Accounting Policies | Conservative | Aggressive |
|---|---|---|
| **Revenue recognition** | After sale, when risk has passed to buyer | At sale, although risk remains |
| **Depreciation choice** | Accelerated over shorter period | Straight-line over longer period |
| **Inventory method** | LIFO (assuming prices are rising) | FIFO (assuming prices are rising) |
| **Amortization of goodwill** | Over a shorter period | Over 40 years |
| **Estimate of warranty** | High estimate | Low estimate |
| **Estimate of bad debts** | High estimate | Low estimate |
| **Treatment of advertising** | Expense | Capitalize |
| **Loss contingencies** | Accrue loss | Footnote only |

results in lower taxes and therefore in higher cash flows). FIFO undervalues the rising costs of inventory and produces a higher level of reported profits. Thus FIFO is often considered a more aggressive inventory valuation technique.

**Consider Pending or Imminent Litigation.**   In addition to searching the footnotes for nonconservative accounting principles, note any pending or imminent litigation. (The litigation footnote is usually less informative than a company's response to item 3 on Form 10-K.) Such litigation may have serious consequences for a company's future operations.

**Question Long-Term Purchase Commitments.**   As well as letting investors know about litigation, footnotes also can alert them to long-term purchase commitments. Buried in the footnotes of Columbia Gas Systems' first-quarter 1991 10-Q was notification that the company had a long-term commitment to purchase natural gas at inflated prices. Investors who noted this footnote and understood its significance should have been nervous. The company had signed a long-term contract in early 1991 (during Operation Desert Storm in Kuwait), when gas prices were at their highest. Since Columbia's customers were not locked into buying this high-priced gas, investors should have concluded that the company would be unable to sell it at a profit. Sure enough, Columbia was unable to sell the gas, and in April 1991 it filed for bankruptcy. In subsequent lawsuits, investors and lenders alleged that Columbia had misled them by failing to disclose a substantial contingent liability.

**Watch for Changes in Accounting Principles.**   As indicated earlier, management has substantial flexibility in choosing accounting principles, and that choice generally affects a company's profits. Investors and lenders should thus take note whenever a company changes accounting principles for no apparent reason. Such changes can also sometimes signal bookkeeping games to boost weak financial statements.

Slowing down a company's depreciation schedule or changing its depreciation method can dress up earnings quite nicely. In 1988, according to stock analyst David Healy, General Motors was able to post record earnings directly because of its decision to liberalize its accounting policies. Healy calculated that about $1.8 billion of GM's $4.9 billion in profits came from such tricks: $790 million from changing its depreciation period for plant assets from 35 to 45 years, $480 million from changing its accounting for pensions, $217 million from changing its inventory valuation policies, and $270 million from changing its assumptions about the residual value of cars leased out by the company.

### The Letter from the President

After reading the footnotes, you should turn to the front of the annual report, where you will be greeted with a picture of and some words from the president. Sometimes the president announces some recent event that will significantly hurt the company's future performance. But don't count on it. The tone of this letter is almost invariably upbeat—regardless of the real conditions. In a recent study intended to identify the words used most frequently to disguise the fact that a company is in serious trouble, Professor Martin Kellman found that no word is more ominous than *challenging*. His interpretation of "challenging": "Your company has lost money, is losing money, and will continue to lose money." His recommendation: "If the C-word appears in any form three or more times in the front pages of any annual report—sell immediately!"

> The first four months of 2001 were extremely challenging as we went from year-over-year bookings in excess of 70% in November, to 30% negative growth within a span of months.— John Chambers, CEO of Cisco Corporation, May 2001

**Read the Letter from the President with a Grain of Salt.** Many professional analysts agree that the letter from the president is used to bias the reader into thinking that the company is doing better than it really is. Thornton O'glove describes the president's letter this way:

> It is designed to serve as a veil for the striptease—namely, to offer a hint of what is underneath, to indicate shape and form but not to permit too much insight.

O'glove also suggests reading the president's letter for the previous three or four years to determine how earlier predictions turned out. Like O'glove, Raymond DeVoe (an analyst with Legg Mason Wood Walker, Inc.) has made a hobby of perusing annual reports and their letters from the president. DeVoe has developed a way of translating what the president is really saying. Here are a few of his "translations" of presidential declarations:

ANNUAL REPORT: "Your company is now poised for significant earnings growth."
(TRANSLATION: "We lost so much last year and wrote off everything possible, so earnings couldn't get much worse.")

ANNUAL REPORT: "These results were somewhat below the projections that management had announced publicly during the quarter."
(TRANSLATION: "We lied.")

ANNUAL REPORT: "The quarter's earnings contained a substantial contribution from a settlement arising from the involuntary termination of operating equipment."
(TRANSLATION: "If the plane hadn't crashed, we would have been in the red. Fortunately, only one was killed, and the insurance company paid off a helluva lot.")

While most letters from presidents are short on informative disclosure and long on fluff, Warren Buffett's letter stands out for its candor. Buffett often uses his letter to discuss mistakes that he has made and to reflect on important issues of the time. Of particular interest in his 1992 letter was his criticism of the financial shenanigans used in the insurance industry to prop up earnings. He stated:

Loss-reserve data for the [insurance] industry indicate that there is reason to be skeptical of the outcome, and it may turn out that 1991's ratio should have been worse than was reported. In the long run, of course, trouble awaits managements that paper-over operating problems with accounting maneuvers. Eventually, managements of this kind achieve the same result as the seriously-ill patient who tells his doctor: "I can't afford the operation, but would you accept a small payment to touch up the X-rays?"

**Focus on Management and Its Estimates.**   Reading the president's letter is a good way of assessing the integrity of management. Things to look for:

- Does management cast a rosy glow on unfavorable developments?
- Has there been a significant turnover of high-ranking managers from year to year? (That could be a tipoff to corporate turmoil.)

## Management Discussion and Analysis

If the information in the president's letter lacks substance, try reading the section in the annual report and Form 10-K entitled "Management Discussion and Analysis." This section requires management to discuss specific issues on the financial statements and to assess the company's current financial situation, its liquidity, and its planned capital expenditures for the next year. This section is also a good place to learn about management's candor. If the company is clearly having financial difficulties, the MD&A section should level with the readers and not try to avoid or sugarcoat the problem.

## Form 8-K

After you have reviewed the company's annual report (and Form 10-K), scan the SEC Web site, http://www.sec.gov, to learn whether there have been any recent Form 8-K filings for the company. Besides telling investors about major acquisitions or divestitures by the company, Form 8-K highlights any changes in auditors. Changes could offer clues to financial shenanigans, especially in those cases in which the auditors may have been fired because they found some problem that they were unwilling to suppress.

A company that fires its auditor because of a disagreement over financial principles and then shops around for a new auditor that is more agreeable to its interpretation of GAAP has engaged in what is known as "opinion shopping." To prevent this practice, the SEC requires a company that changes auditors to file a Form 8-K, notifying the commission of the termination and giving the details of any accounting disagreements. Unfortunately, few disagreements are ever actually disclosed in these filings.

### Form 144: Insider Stock Transactions

Management and directors must notify the SEC of their intention to purchase or sell company stock. Substantial insider sales might indicate impending problems at the company.

### Company Interview

After you have thoroughly read and analyzed the company's SEC filings, consider interviewing a senior financial executive at the company. Typically, the chief financial officer (CFO) would be the first choice. Others who may be helpful are the head of investor relations, the corporate comptroller, and the treasurer. Since these companies are publicly held, their officers expect telephone calls from investors concerning issues raised in SEC filings.

During the course of the interview, you have a wonderful opportunity to not only gather specific factual information, but also assess the "tone" of senior management through the way they address your concerns.

**Fair Disclosure (FD) Guidelines.** Private discussions with analysts and investors have become somewhat less open since the SEC issued new guidelines called Regulation FD. These guidelines were issued because certain professional investors and brokerage firm analysts were being given information before other investors or information that was not available to other investors.

While Regulation FD may cause companies to not answer all your questions, it should help individual investors in two ways: Big investors will no longer be able to obtain information before the rest of us, and companies will probably send out more frequent and more complete press releases to ensure compliance with full and fair disclosure.

### Commercial Database

Financial analysts use commercial databases to screen for companies exhibiting certain warning signs. CFRA's analysts use

Compustat (a division of Standard & Poor's) and Lexis/Nexis (a division of Reed Elsevier).

Chapter 11, "Database Searches," focuses on specific screens used to detect operating and accounting problems.

## A Look Ahead

Chapters 4 through 10 formally introduce the seven major shenanigans (and thirty techniques) that companies use to distort financial reports. Each chapter also provides strategies for detecting such tricks.

# PART TWO:
# THE SEVEN
# SHENANIGANS

# 4

# SHENANIGAN NO. 1: RECORDING REVENUE TOO SOON OR OF QUESTIONABLE QUALITY

Perhaps the most common financial shenanigan related to revenue recognition is recording revenue too early—either before the earnings process has been completed or before an unconditional exchange has occurred. Accountants use the term *front-end load* to describe revenue recorded too soon.

## Six Techniques

Chapter 4 describes six techniques. The first three involve recording revenue too soon.

1. Recording revenue when future services remain to be provided
2. Recording revenue before shipment or before the customer's unconditional acceptance
3. Recording revenue even though the customer is not obligated to pay

The last three techniques involve recording revenue of questionable and inflated quality:

4. Selling to an affiliated party
5. Giving the customer something of value as a quid pro quo
6. Grossing up revenue

Some of these techniques are relatively benign, whereas others are far more egregious. Table 4-1 outlines this continuum.

*Guiding Principle: Revenue should be recorded after
the earnings process has been completed and an
exchange has occurred.*

---

Accounting Capsule

## The Correct Way to Record Revenue

- Sell product to an unaffiliated customer and give no financial incentives ("bribes") as a quid pro quo.
- Deliver the product in accordance with the contract terms and receive unconditional acceptance from the customer.
- Confirm that the customer is responsible for paying (i.e., there is no seller financing) and has the wherewithal to pay.
- Record as revenue *only* the net proceeds received from customers.
- Provide all services required under the contract.

---

The first technique described in this chapter involves recording revenue before the seller has completed all the terms of the contract, so that future obligations remain.

Table 4-1. Revenue Recognition Continuum

| More Benign $\longleftarrow$ | | | $\longrightarrow$ | Most Egregious |
|:---:|:---:|:---:|:---:|:---:|
| 1 | 2 | 3 | 4 | 5 |
| Recording too soon | | Questionable amount | | Bogus revenue |

# Technique No. 1: Recording Revenue When Future Services Remain to Be Provided

**Growing Old Gracefully: You Can't Change the Inevitable.**   Like most middle-aged men, I enjoy playing basketball and other sports with my 18-year-old son, Jonathan. Until a few years ago, Jonathan was unable to win our competitive games. Recently, I challenged him to a 100-yard race, my specialty from high school days. The first race ended with Jonathan slightly ahead. I argued that we needed a rematch because of my slow start. The second race ended with Jonathan in the victor's circle again and me lying on the ground in pain, having just blown out my knee.

As companies grow older, their sales growth naturally slows, as well. Some companies gracefully accept the slowing growth, while others try to deny the inevitable.

Software maker Transaction Systems Architect (TSAI) apparently was experiencing slowing sales in late 1998. It had always used conservative accounting. Specifically, it had recorded revenue only when customers were billed over the five-year license agreement. Then TSAI suddenly changed its accounting. Apparently to cover up a sales slowdown, during the December 1998 quarter, TSAI began recording almost the entire five-year revenue immediately.

Changing the method of revenue recognition to hide the problem would be akin to me running 50 yards and Jonathan running 100 yards and me claiming victory.

**Change in Revenue Recognition Hid the Problem—Temporarily.**
TSAI was able to hide the business problem for a while because investors did not have an apples-to-apples comparison until a year later. (Companies typically do not restate prior financial reports to reflect a change in accounting.) The day of reckoning finally came in the December 1999 quarter, a full year after the accounting change. Revenue in that quarter was down 20 percent from the December 1998 period. By early 2000, investors had finally learned the truth—and the stock price collapsed (see Fig. 4-1, which charts the stock price of TSAI during this period).

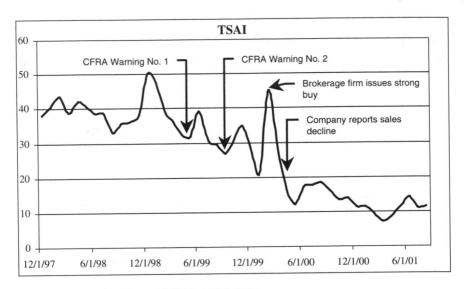

**Fig. 4-1.  Stock Price of TSAI, 1997–2001**

Table 4-2. Year-over-Year Growth in Licensing and Total
Revenue, Quarter and Six Months Ended 3/99, Adjusted to
Exclude Impact of Change in Revenue Recognition

| ($ millions, except %) | 3 months, 3/99, Reported | 3 months, 3/99, CFRA-Adjusted | 6 Months, 3/99, Reported | 6 Months, 3/99, CFRA-Adjusted |
|---|---|---|---|---|
| License revenue | 50.6 | 36.2 | 96.6 | 78.0 |
| Growth, year-over-year | 26% | (10%) | 23% | 0% |
| Total revenue | 87.0 | 72.6 | 173.0 | 154.4 |
| Growth, year-over-year | 21% | 1% | 23% | 10% |

Without the change in revenue recognition, TSAI's licensing revenue would have declined materially. As shown in Table 4-2,
TSAI's license revenue would have declined 10 percent without
the accounting change, whereas with the accounting change, the
company reported a 26 percent increase in license revenue. Moreover, without the accounting change, TSAI would have reported
no growth at all in licensing revenue during the six months ended
March 1999.

By changing to a new method of revenue recognition, the company obtained an artificial revenue boost of $14.4 million for the March quarter. Moreover, by recognizing future-period revenue too early, as it apparently did, it depleted the pool of revenue available for recognition in future periods.

**Warning Signs and Lessons from Transaction Systems Architect.** By the first quarter of 1999, signs of problems at TSAI had become obvious. In May, CFRA issued the following warnings: The change in revenue recognition camouflaged a sales slowdown, and the decline in cash flows from operations (CFFO) and the enormous increase in long-term receivables suggested operational problems (see Table 4-3). We warned at the time that the change in revenue recognition was nothing more than a short-term artificial fix.

**Watch for CFFO Lagging behind Net Income.** One common sign of aggressive revenue recognition is when cash flow from operations (sometimes called operating cash flow) starts to materially lag behind reported net income. That's just what happened at TSAI in March 1999. As shown in Table 4-4, CFFO lagged behind net income by $9.5 million in March 1999, whereas it exceeded net income in the 1998 period. Moreover, CFFO repre-

Table 4-3. Warning Signs: TSAI

| Problem Indicated | Evidence | Shenanigan |
|---|---|---|
| **Aggressive accounting:** Recorded revenue too soon | • TSAI changed its method of revenue recording to accelerate future years' service fees earned into current period. | No. 1 |
| **Operational deterioration** | • There was a big jump in receivables, particularly long-term receivables.<br>• There was a sharp drop in CFFO.<br>• Revenue growth was sluggish. | — |

Table 4-4. Cash Flows from Operations
(CFFO) versus Net Income (NI) — March
Quarter, Year-over-Year

| ($ millions) | Q2, 3/99 | Q2, 3/98 |
|---|---|---|
| CFFO | 1.4 | 9.4 |
| NI | 10.9 | 8.3 |
| CFFO—NI | (9.5) | 1.1 |
| CFFO/NI | 13% | 113% |

sented only 13 percent of net income in the March 1999 quarter,
compared to 113 percent of net income in March 1998.

**Watch for a Jump in Long-Term Receivables Versus Revenue.** A
second warning sign for investors was the substantial increase in
TSAI's receivables, particularly the long-term receivables. Normally, receivables are collected within a month or two after the
sale is recorded. Long-term receivables are those that are due *more
than one year from the sales date.* The presence of a large and growing balance of long-term receivables suggests very aggressive accounting: Revenue is being recorded more than a year before the
customer is required to pay. During the nine months ended September 1999, while sales grew modestly and the currently due
billed receivables declined by 24 percent, the long-term receivables
grew by 3,200 percent. By September 1999, the long-term installment receivables represented an astonishing *29 percent of revenue,*
compared to only 1 percent of revenue in the December 1998 quarter (see Table 4-5).

**The Young and the Restless: Pyxis**

It's not only aging companies with slowing sales that feel the need
to fiddle with recognition policies. Young and small companies
dreaming of the golden initial public offering (IPO) can be
tempted to change their method of revenue recognition to give the
appearance of turbocharged revenue.

That's apparently what happened at medical-equipment maker

Table 4-5. Receivables in Days' Sales Outstanding, Based on Quarterly Revenue

| ($ millions, except DSO in days) | Q4, 9/99 | Q3, 6/99 | Q2, 3/99 | Q1, 12/98 | Q4, 9/98 |
|---|---|---|---|---|---|
| Revenue | 92.6 | 89.1 | 87.0 | 86.1 | 79.3 |
| Current billed receivables | 50.6 | 57.1 | 61.2 | 66.4 | 58.1 |
| Accrued (unbilled) receivables | 41.9 | 39.2 | 40.0 | 34.0 | 33.0 |
| Long-term installment receivables | 26.9 | 13.0 | 9.3 | 0.8 | 2.1 |
| Total receivables | 119.4 | 109.2 | 110.5 | 101.2 | 93.1 |

Pyxis, Inc. (now a division of Cardinal Health) just before its 1993 IPO.

PYXS typically leased its product to hospitals over a five-year period. At first, like TSAI, it received cash and recorded rental income over that period. In 1991, the period right before its IPO, however, PYXS changed to a more aggressive method of accounting for its leases: It recorded most of the revenue immediately, rather than over the five-year period. As a result of the accounting change, PYXS recorded sales of $13.4 million, up from $344,000 in 1990. The 1990 revenue using the more aggressive accounting method would have been $2.1 million, an increase of 410 percent over the reported revenue under the more conservative accounting.

**You Have to Eventually Pay the Piper.**   The change in revenue recognition at TSAI and PYXS boosted near-term earnings, but it created enormous problems for the future. By recognizing virtually all of the revenue from the entire five-year contract in the first period, the company created two major problems for itself. First, because legitimate future-period revenue had been shifted to the present period, that revenue was no longer available to be counted in that future period. Second, the comparables became an enormous challenge. That is, moving $1 million into an earlier period made it more difficult for the company to actually achieve superior growth over the bogus (and inflated) sales.

**How Did Pyxis Play Out?**   In March 1994, CFRA warned investors about an imminent sales growth slowdown. By summer, PYXS had announced the inevitable sales slowdown, with the share price losing one-third of its value. The stock price never recovered to the pre-report level. In May 1996, Cardinal Health acquired Pyxis.

---

**RED FLAG!**

**Watch for Changes to More Aggressive Revenue Recognition Policies**

---

## Technique No. 2: Recording Revenue Before Shipment or Before the Customer's Unconditional Acceptance

Risk must pass from seller to buyer before revenue can be recorded. Occasionally, companies record revenue before the product is shipped or before it is unconditionally accepted by the customer. Among the tricks to watch for are recording revenue before shipment, shipping goods too soon or of the wrong type, and recording revenue when the customer (or consignee) can still return the goods.

*Guiding Principle: Generally, product must be shipped to the customer and approved before the period closes.*

### Recording Revenue Before Shipment

There are two strategies for recording revenue before shipment. One is using percentage of completion (POC) accounting, and the second is using "bill and hold" revenue recognition.

Under *POC accounting,* revenue is recorded during the production period, before the product is shipped to the customer. However, POC applies only to companies with very long production periods, like aerospace manufacturers. The amount of revenue recognized under POC is subject to various estimates; as a result, POC creates opportunities for financial shenanigans. Here are some specific tricks:

- *Using POC when it is not permissible.* Service companies typically are not eligible to use POC, since their projects are shorter-term. Companies that sell products with short (less than one year) production cycles also should refrain from using POC.
- *Being too aggressive in applying POC.* A symptom of using POC improperly would be a large increase in unbilled receivables when sales and billed receivables are growing more moderately.

Consider the Belgian software maker Lernout & Hauspie (LHSP). In 1998, when sales grew 113 percent (from $99.4 million to $211.6 million), unbilled receivables jumped 220 percent (from $8.2 million to $26.4 million). Interestingly, several years later the share price collapsed when evidence of a massive accounting fraud was disclosed. A lesson from the LHSP case is that the fine line between aggressive accounting and accounting fraud may be crossed at any time. Evidence of aggressive accounting should be considered a harbinger of bigger problems to come.

Even when it is appropriate for companies to use POC, incorrect estimates and bad luck can lead to inflated revenue and earnings. That's just what happened at Raytheon (RTN). It recorded revenue for several years based on its estimates of costs and expected unit sales. When it became clear that the revenue from the contract would materially lag behind the original estimates, Raytheon announced that the previously reported revenue was too high and took a one-time charge.

Under *bill and hold accounting*, a customer agrees to a future purchase and future payment. The product remains with the seller until the agreed-upon date, and the obligation to pay is deferred until shipment. The seller continues to hold the product in inventory, but it records the sale even though the customer will not receive the product until a later period. Generally, the customer is not obligated to pay until the product is shipped in that later period.

Sunbeam (SOC) began using this ploy in November 1996. Anxious to extend the selling season for its gas grills and to boost sales in CEO Al Dunlap's "turnaround year," the company hoped to convince retailers to buy grills nearly six months before they were needed. In exchange for major discounts, retailers agreed to purchase merchandise that they would not physically receive until months later and would not pay for until six months after billing. In the meantime, the goods would be shipped out of the grill factory in Neosho, Missouri, to third-party warehouses leased by Sunbeam, where they would be held until the customers requested them.

Nonetheless, Sunbeam booked the sales and profits from all of the $35 million in bill-and-hold transactions. When outside auditors later reviewed the documents, they reversed a staggering $29 million of the $35 million and shifted the sales to future quarters. In doing the audit, Arthur Andersen questioned the accounting treatment of some transactions. But in almost every case, it concluded that the amounts were "immaterial" to the overall audit. Sometimes detecting signs of aggressive accounting is close to impossible. In the case of Sunbeam, it required nothing more than reading the revenue recognition footnote in the company's 1997 10-K:

> The Company recognizes revenues from product sales principally at the time of shipment to customers. In limited circumstances, at the customers request the Company may sell seasonal products on a bill and hold basis provided that the goods are completed, packaged and ready for shipment, such goods are segregated and the risks of ownership and legal title have passed to the customer. The amount of such bill and hold sales at December 29, 1997 was approximately 3% of consolidated revenues.

---

**RED FLAG!**

**Key Warning Sign of Improper or Aggressive Accounting: When "Unbilled Receivables" Grow Substantially Faster than "Billed Receivables."**

---

## Recording Revenue at Shipment, but Before the Customer Expected the Goods

Typically, companies record revenue at the point of shipment. Two tricks used to inflate revenue are to (1) ship goods before the customer expected delivery and (2) stretch out the quarter end date.

**Watch for Early Shipping, Before the Sale Occurs.**   The fiscal quarter is coming to a close, and profits are sagging. What can a company do? Why not simply start shipping out merchandise and recording revenue, thereby boosting sales and profits? Merchandise is rushed out of the warehouse to customers toward the end of the year (even before the sales have taken place), and sales revenue is recorded. Since under this method revenue is recognized when an item is *shipped* to retailers or wholesalers, some manufacturers may be tempted to keep shipping their products during slow times—even if the retailers' shelves are overstocked. Automobile manufacturers have been doing this for years, thereby artificially increasing their sales.

By shipping the product late in a quarter, rather than during the following quarter when the customer expects to receive it, a seller can improperly record revenue too soon.

Consider the high-flying technology company Datapoint Corporation and its slowing business during 1981. It recorded revenue when products were shipped to distributors. When the distributors had less business, Datapoint was asked to curtail the high shipping volume. In fact, because Datapoint had shipped so much to the distributors in earlier periods, their warehouses were overflowing. The distributors then contacted Datapoint again, this time asking the company to suspend all shipments. Datapoint had a problem: It needed a place to ship its products in order to record revenue and keep profits flowing. That was no problem for this clever management team. They simply leased a warehouse and shipped the goods there. In essence, they shipped the goods to themselves.

Another way to record revenue too soon is to ship goods before the customer expects them. Specifically, goods may be shipped before the sale is consummated, or the seller may simply stretch out the quarter end date to inflate revenues. Other tricks are backdating contracts or extending the quarter by changing the end date in order to record future sales in the current period.

**Watch for Backdating Contracts.**   As the end of each quarter neared, Informix sales personnel routinely rushed to conclude as many transactions as possible in order to meet their revenue and earnings goals for that quarter. In numerous instances, however, they were unable to complete negotiations and obtain signed license agreements from customers prior to quarter-end, as required for revenue recognition under GAAP. The company had a written policy that revenue on license agreements should not be recognized unless the agreements were signed and dated before quarter-end. Nevertheless, signing license agreements after quarter-end and then backdating them to make it appear that they had been executed prior to quarter-end was an accepted practice. In at least one instance, the company recognized revenue on an agreement that was not signed until approximately one month after the end of the quarter. By engaging in this conduct, the former management and others fraudulently inflated quarterly and annual revenues and earnings.

**Watch for Changes in the Quarter End Date.** To make up for a revenue shortfall, Sunbeam changed its quarter end date from March 29 to March 31. (Sunbeam will be featured in Chapter 10.) The two additional days permitted Sunbeam to record another $5 million in sales from its operations and $15 million from the newly acquired Coleman.

Informix also played this game of accelerating revenue by stretching out the end of a quarter. The change resulted in an additional two days of operations for the first quarter of 1998 as compared to the previous year. The impact on the company's financial statements was to increase license revenue by $11.4 million, or 8 percent.

## Recording Revenue Upon Shipment, Even Though the Customer Can Return the Product

**Determine Whether the Buyer Is Likely to Return the Goods.** Many businesses permit the buyer a "right of return" if it is not satisfied with the goods. That is true, for example, for companies that sell consumer goods (such as appliances and automobiles). As another example, publishers generally sell books to bookstores on a right-of-return basis (the books can be returned if they are unsold). Thus, even though a publisher has made a sale to the bookstore and there has been an arms-length exchange, it would be inappropriate for the publisher to record all the revenue (since some books will surely be returned).

If a customer chooses to return the product, the seller has recorded revenue prematurely. Among the tricks to watch for are delivering an incorrect product to customers or counting as revenue on sales of products that are likely to be returned.

Whereas it's clearly improper to ship products to yourself, as illustrated in the Datapoint case, or to backdate contracts, as Informix did, many companies properly ship their product and give customers a right of return. Generally, revenue should not be recorded until the return period has lapsed, unless the seller can reliably predict the amount of the returns and account for them accordingly.

**Watch for Companies That Record Revenue When a Right of Return Exists.** This could be a company with a legitimate sale, but the company may be aggressive in recording revenue and failing to account for the likely customer returns.

---

Accounting Capsule

## Sale with Right of Return

In some industries, it is common practice for customers to be given the right to return a product to the seller for a refund or a credit. However, when companies experience a high ratio of returned merchandise to sales, the recognition of the original sale as revenue is questionable. The Financial Accounting Standards Board has issued authoritative guidelines (SFAS 48) on revenue recognition when a right of return exists. Typically, if the customer can return the product and either the seller cannot determine the amount of returns with reasonable certainty or other important contingencies exist, revenue recognition should be deferred until the cash is actually received.

---

**Watch for Sales with Right of Return.** The SEC found that $24.7 million of Sunbeam's 1997 fourth-quarter sales to distributors were subject to a right of return. In addition, SOC offered discounts, favorable payment terms, and guaranteed markups. These "sales" were without economic substance.

Sometimes companies intentionally ship out the wrong product, knowing full well that it will be returned. That's what happened at Informix.

**Be Alert for a Failure to Deliver a Usable Product.** At the end of the fourth quarter of 1996, Informix (IFMX) recorded a $9.2 million sale but failed to deliver the required software code prior to year-end. Then, in January 1997, IFMX delivered a "beta" version of the software code that did not function with the hardware. It took Informix another six months to deliver usable software code. As a result, IFMX recorded revenue in the first quarter rather than the third quarter of 1997.

Still another technique for prematurely recording revenue at point of shipment involves consignment sales. With such sales, the products are shipped to an intermediary, or consignee, who must find a buyer. If the manufacturer, or consignor, records revenue when products are sent to the consignee and before a buyer is found, this would be recording revenue prematurely. Thus, no revenue should be recorded when a consignor ships product to a consignee. One company that failed to account for consignment sales was Sunbeam; it recorded $36 million in guaranteed and consignment sales in 1997.

## Technique No. 3: Recording Revenue Even Though the Customer Is Not Obligated to Pay

A key requirement for revenue recognition is that the financial burden has shifted from the seller to the customer. Problem signs to watch for include the seller providing financing to customers, the seller offering customers extended payment terms, and customers who lack the capacity to pay and/or whose financing is uncertain.

**Watch for Seller-Provided Financing.** To accelerate revenue in recent years, a number of high-tech companies have begun lending money to customers to pay for their products. In moderation, vendor financing is a sound selling technique; when it is abused, it's a dangerous way to do business. Among telecommunication equipment suppliers, the amount of financing provided to customers should have made investors nervous. At the end of 2000, these suppliers were collectively owed as much as $15 billion by customers, a 25 percent increase in a single year. Effectively, they were buying their own products with their own money, exaggerating the size and sustainability of their sales and earnings growth.

---

Accounting Capsule

## Rules for Software Companies

The ability to recognize revenue for a software license sale under GAAP depends, in part, on whether the related fee is fixed, and a fee is presumed not to be fixed if it is due more than twelve months after delivery of the software. GAAP thus requires restricting the initial revenue recognition from a software license sale to only those payments due within twelve months, with deferral of revenue recognition for payments due beyond twelve months.

---

**Watch for Companies Offering Extended Payment Terms, Particularly on New Products.** During the September 1995 quarter, Chicago-based software seller System Software, Inc., started offering customers *extended payment terms up to 14 months* on its new product. By doing so, the company pushed future-period sales into the current period, artificially inflating revenue and profits.

Informix routinely recognized revenue on reseller software license purchase commitments that included payment terms that extended beyond twelve months. To do so, the company used third-party financing to accelerate cash receipts to within twelve months of the sale.

---

Accounting Capsule

## Rules for Creditworthiness of Customer

Under GAAP, revenue cannot be recognized "until persuasive evidence of the agreement [with the customer] exists and an assessment of the customer's creditworthiness has been made."

---

**Watch for Customers Who Lack the Wherewithal to Pay.** In connection with transactions with newly established or undercapitalized resellers, former sales managers at Informix pressured the European finance staff to disregard the company's policy for assessing customer creditworthiness. As a result of these revenue recognition practices, the company improperly recognized revenue in 1996 of at least $3.3 million in the first quarter, $9.1 million in the second quarter, and $8.2 million in the third quarter.

**Watch for Customers Whose Financing Is Uncertain.** A sale might be contingent on either the customer's receipt of funding from third-party sources or the customer's subsequent resale of the product to a third party; in either case, no revenue should be recorded at the time of sale. There are many examples of companies that recorded revenue even when important contingencies existed that should have raised doubts about whether the buyer would pay.

**Check Whether the Buyer Has Financing in Place.** When a sale depends on the buyer's receiving financing, revenue should not be recorded until the financing is in place. This is common in real estate transactions, in which the sale depends on the buyer's ability to obtain a mortgage.

One company that failed to wait for financing commitments was Stirling Homex Corporation, a manufacturer of completely installed modular dwelling units. Stirling sold homes to low-income buyers who had limited resources, most of whom obtained financing through the U.S. Department of Housing and Urban Development (HUD). Stirling improperly recorded revenue when HUD signed a preliminary commitment of funding, rather than waiting for the final approval. As a result, Stirling recorded revenue for certain customers who ultimately failed to receive financing; and the financial statements that portrayed Stirling as a healthy, prosperous company with increasing sales and earnings, in reality, covered up the company's serious business and financial problems.

The first three techniques discussed in this chapter help companies record revenue too soon. The remaining techniques raise questions about the quality of the revenue reported. Doubts about the quality of revenue should be raised when sales are to an affiliated party; the customer receives something as a quid pro quo for the sale; and the seller records sales revenue at an inflated amount.

## Technique No. 4: Selling to an Affiliated Party

Whenever the buyer has some other affiliation with the seller, the quality of the revenue becomes somewhat suspect. Thus, a sale to a vendor, a relative, a corporate director, or a business partner raises doubt as to whether the transaction can be considered *at arm's length.* Was a discount given to the relative? Was the seller expected to make future purchases from the vendor at a discount? Were there any side agreements requiring the seller to provide a quid pro quo? A sale to an affiliated party may be entirely appropriate. The question raised, however, concerns the appropriate amount to be recorded. Watch for revenue from strategic partners or other affiliated or related parties.

### Doubts Arise When a Company Sells to a Strategic Partner

Unusual transactions with strategic partners muddy the waters and may give the company an opportunity to obtain an artificial boost to revenue and earnings. Consider the example of Sabratek (SBTK).

SBTK, a seller of medical equipment, had entered into strategic partnerships with several entities in recent years. One such agreement obligated SBTK to pay up to $7 million for a 15-year technology license for the use of the partner's software and to bundle that software with SBTK's own product.

SBTK generates revenue by selling its products to third parties. Historically, SBTK has also provided its partners with loans, recording a note receivable in connection with this financing transaction. In addition, SBTK *licensed its own products to its partners, recording a note receivable in connection with its recognition of licensing revenue.* Also under the agreement, SBTK had the option to purchase its partner.

## Two-Way Transactions with Strategic Partners Raise Questions

A two-way transaction means that you both buy from and sell to the same party. Questions should be raised about the quality of the revenue recorded on such transactions. Consider the following examples.

*Healtheon/WebMD (HLTH),* a Web-based information provider, signed a five-year alliance with Microsoft. Healtheon must pay Microsoft $162 million in license fees over a five-year term, while Microsoft must pay Healtheon the first $100 million of revenues from advertising on Microsoft's three health care channels.

*MicroStrategy (MSTR)* and Exchange Application (EXAP) announced a licensing agreement under which EXAP was to purchase MSTR software, MSTR was to purchase EXAP software, and together they would develop future software. In connection with this agreement, MSTR recognized approximately $10.0 million of licensing revenue during the December 1999 quarter. EXAP recorded revenue of $4.5 million (34 percent of expected total revenue) of sell-through license revenue from MSTR.

## Technique No. 5: Giving the Customer Something of Value as a Quid pro Quo

If, as a condition of making a sale, the buyer receives something of value from the seller (in addition to the product), the amount of revenue recorded becomes suspect. This may involve a barter exchange, offering the customer stock or stock warrants, or investing in a partnership with the buyer.

### Barter Transactions with Vendors Can Artificially Boost Reported Revenues

Software seller Broadvision (BVSN) boosted its sales by *classifying as revenue the value of concessions obtained* through a barter transaction with a vendor.

Prior to the June 1998 quarter, BVSN was obligated to make royalty payments to a vendor based on a percentage of "product revenues." During that quarter, however, the royalty agreement was modified such that BVSN agreed to provide the vendor with *software* in exchange for a reduction in future royalty payments due to the vendor through 2001. In addition, the vendor agreed to provide BVSN with certain internal development rights. BVSN recognized revenue of $1.31 million (9 percent of total revenue for the quarter) from this transaction. *A modification in payment terms to the vendor would not be considered a revenue-generating transaction with a customer.*

### Giving the Customer Stock or Stock Warrants as an Inducement Raises Questions

In February 2001, the *Wall Street Journal* provided an interesting account of how Broadcomm (BRCM) inflates future-period revenue related to some of its acquisitions. Before making an acquisition, BRCM encourages the target company to have substantial purchase commitments in place from customers. To entice the (future BRCM) customers to make those commitments, stock warrants are given as a quid pro quo. After the merger closes, BRCM records the revenue and the customer receives BRCM stock. From the following illustration, you will see the interesting accounting used by BRCM.

Assume that the purchase commitment is for $1,000,000 and the stock warrants given totaled $250,000. After the merger, BRCM records $1,000,000 in revenue and assigns $250,000 to goodwill on the balance sheet, to be *amortized against earnings over the next 40 years.* That's right—the revenue is recognized immediately, yet the stock given as a condition for the sale is pushed into this 40-year "black hole." Without doubt, the more conservative accounting treatment would be to report net revenue of $750,000. That is what the customer is really paying.

## Technique No. 6: Grossing Up Revenue

Some New Economy companies have stretched the limits on appropriate revenue recognition by recording an amount far in excess of the service fee. Consider Priceline.com (PCLN) and Papa John's International (PZZA).

PLCN could be considered a modern day matchmaker. It contracts with airlines, hotels, and others to find customers for their excess capacity. For its efforts, PLCN pockets the difference between the amount received from the actual customer and the amount that PLCN pays to the airline or other supplier.

Consider the following example. PLCN sells a $160 airline ticket to a customer for $200, keeping the $40 spread as its fee for the matchmaking service. What is PLCN's revenue for providing this service—$40 or $200? PLCN records the "grossed up" amount of $200, raising questions about the quality of its reported revenue.

PCLN should not include amounts owed to its airline and hotel partners in its revenue line item (nor in its cost of operations line), since these costs are merely a pass-through and serve only to boost the company's revenue base. It appears that PCLN serves merely as an intermediary and should record as revenue only the fee for providing the service to both the customer and the supplier.

PZZA sells pizza mainly through franchises. One service provided to the franchises was securing for them commissary products and the equipment needed to make and sell the pizza. PZZA would purchase these items, mark them up around 10 percent, and sell them to the franchises. Curiously, PZZA included these pass-through reimbursable costs as revenue. During the first nine months of 1995, PZZA recorded $171.8 of revenue, including pass-through costs of $78.7 million. In other words, by grossing up its revenue to include the pass-throughs, PZZA artificially inflated its revenue by 84.6 percent (reporting $171.7 million rather than $93.1 million).

## A Look Ahead

Chapter 5 discusses a more egregious revenue trick: recording bogus or fictitious revenue.

# 5

# SHENANIGAN NO. 2: RECORDING BOGUS REVENUE

Before relying on representations in financial reports, successful investors first ascertain whether those reports tell the company's economic story fairly and completely. In one sense, investors are like art dealers, trying to separate the real thing from fakes. Without sufficient training and a keen eye, identifying a fake may be difficult, as the following story by Arthur Koestler in *The Act of Creation* illustrates:

> After purchasing a canvas signed "Picasso," an art dealer traveled all the way to Cannes, where Picasso was working in his studio, to discover whether it was genuine. Picasso cast a single look at the canvas and announced, "It's a fake."
>
> A few months later the dealer bought another canvas signed "Picasso." Again he traveled to Cannes; and again Picasso, after a single glance, grunted: "It's a fake."
>
> "But cher maître," expostulated the dealer, "it so happens that I saw you with my own eyes working on this very picture several years ago."
>
> Picasso shrugged: "I often paint fakes."

One example of a "fake" on financial statements is fictitious revenue. This chapter describes five specific techniques that create fictitious revenue:

1. Recording sales that lack economic substance
2. Recording cash received in lending transactions as revenue
3. Recording investment income as revenue
4. Recording as revenue supplier rebates tied to future required purchases
5. Releasing revenue that was improperly held back before a merger

*Guiding principle:* Revenue should be recorded after the earnings process has been completed and an exchange has occurred.

## Technique No. 1: Recording Sales that Lack Economic Substance

One popular technique for recording bogus revenue is to concoct a scheme in which the company sells a product to a customer, yet the customer has no obligation to keep the product or pay for it. Such a transaction is said to lack economic substance. How can you trick the auditor into believing that the transaction is legitimate? Just draft a normal sales contract signed by the parties and have a separate "side agreement" hidden from the auditors that *modifies the sales contract.*

**Be Alert for Side Agreements.** A side agreement typically changes some important terms in the sales contract. For example, such an agreement may allow customers to return goods at any time for a full refund.

At Informix, side letters were rampant. Salespeople and managers often entered into these agreements in order to "park" software licenses with resellers and thereby accelerate revenue recognition. These salespeople and managers sometimes entered into side agreements because they were unable to complete transactions with identified end users by the end of the period in which they wished to recognize revenue. On other occasions, they entered into such agreements because they needed additional revenue but had not yet found end users who were prepared to pur-

L

chase software licenses. Table 5-1 lists a number of terms found
in these side agreements.

Notwithstanding the resellers' inability to sell a substantial
amount of the licenses they had committed to purchase from Informix, to inflate the company's 1995 and 1996 revenues and earnings, Informix employees repeatedly induced the resellers to agree
to quarter-end purchase commitments by entering into a variety
of side agreements.

**You Scratch My Back and I'll Scratch Yours.** At the end of the
fourth quarter of 1995, an Informix reseller was reluctant to make
any further purchase commitments—until IFMX made it an offer
it couldn't refuse. The reseller, also a computer equipment distributor, agreed to an additional $2.5 million commitment only *after
Informix agreed to a $2 million purchase* of computer hardware, in-
cluding obsolete equipment.

Here's another financial shenanigan used by Informix. Under
pressure to find additional revenue to meet third-quarter sales
goals, IFMX employees asked a reseller to purchase $3.9 million
of software licenses for its internal use. The reseller agreed to this

Table 5-1. Terms of Side Agreements with Informix — Biggest
Silicon Valley Fraud of the 1990s

- Allowing resellers to return unsold licenses and receive a refund
  or credit
- Committing the company to use its own sales force to find customers for resellers
- Offering to assign future end-user orders to resellers
- Extending credit terms beyond twelve months
- Committing the company to purchase computer hardware or
  services from customers under terms that effectively refunded
  the license fees paid by the customer
- Diverting the company's own future service revenues to customers as a means of refunding their licensing fees
- Paying bogus consulting and other fees to customers to be repaid to the company as license fees

proposal only on the condition *that Informix pay back the license fees through a software maintenance outsourcing agreement*—a boomerang!

## Side Letter at HBO & Co.

Just as at Informix, side letters provided a convenient tool allowing health care information company HBO & Co. (HBOC—later merged with McKesson) to record revenue from activities that lacked economic substance. When the SEC and prosecutors brought fraud charges against former employees of McKesson/ HBOC, they cited extensive use of these side letters to change the terms of contracts on which revenue was booked.

**Once Considered a Star among Stars.**   Before anyone knew of the fraud, Wall Street for a long time had had a love affair with HBOC. Why not? It had become a market leader in its industry, with 1998 revenue exceeding $1 billion. The stock price had responded to the company's reported stellar performance, with the market capitalization jumping from about $100 million in 1991 to more than $13 billion. HBOC ranked second among Standard & Poor's 500 companies in stock performance, appreciating almost 1,400 percent in a recent five-year period. It ranked first among Georgia public companies in 1996 and 1997, as measured by the *Atlanta Journal-Constitution.*

And senior executives at the company were rewarded with enormous compensation packages. Charlie McCall, the CEO, took home a compensation package valued at $52 million in 1997 and owned shares worth more than $120 million.

**McKesson's Surprise Just After the Marriage.**   This impressive growth made HBOC an attractive merger candidate for a slower-growing partner. In January 1999, McKesson, a San Francisco health products distributor, bought HBOC for $14 billion. This turned out to be a colossal mistake. On April 28, 1999, when the results of the year-end audit were announced, the company did not receive the standard clean bill of health. Instead, the auditors found that $42 million in sales had been improperly recorded and that sham deals had been used to inflate profits. The stock immediately dropped almost 50 percent, from $65 to $34, wiping out $9 billion of value in a day (see Fig. 5-1). When McKesson's auditors completed a more comprehensive evaluation several months later, they found that the cancer was much deeper. Three years of HBOC's results were bogus, and the restatement wiped out over $325 million of revenue. More than fifty shareholder suits were filed. The aftershocks were still being felt at McKesson a year later; with the weight of the enormous litigation exposure, the share price bottomed out at $17.

**The Schemes to Trick Investors.**   The way the scheme worked was this: Software contracts between HBOC and hospitals would be signed, but the sales representative and the hospital customer would often agree to a "side letter" that stated a contingency for the sale, such as hospital board approval. Revenue was recorded at that point, although under GAAP, sales cannot be recognized until all contingencies are satisfied.

Another ploy used by HBOC was to back-date hundreds of sales contracts. For example, on April 5, 1999, almost a week after McKessonHBOC closed its 1999 fiscal fourth quarter, computer

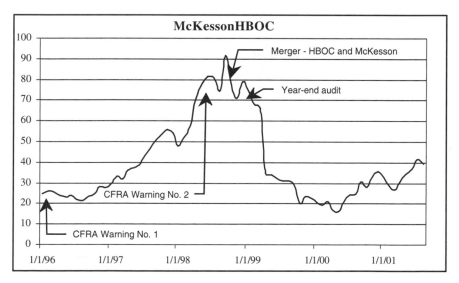

**Fig. 5-1**

hardware maker Data General (now part of EMC) suddenly agreed to buy $20 million of HBOC software in a deal that was backdated to March 31, 1999. The deal, which made up 17 percent of HBOC's software revenues for the quarter, helped the company beat Wall Street forecasts of $0.62. Without the deal, HBOC would have missed its estimates.

In return, Data General simultaneously received a contract to sell $25 million of hardware to McKessonHBOC, plus a *side letter* that allowed it to return the software. (This deal was particularly unusual because Data General, a hardware manufacturer, apparently had little use for software.)

HBOC also got the Internet health company WebMD to backdate to December 31, 1998, a $5 million software sales contract that was actually signed on January 7, 1999. And guess who negotiated the backdated contract on behalf of WebMD? HBO's former president Jay Gilbertson, who had left HBO to become WebMD's president and chief operating officer. It's a small world we live in!

**The Punishment.** HBOC's former co-presidents, Jay Gilbertson and Albert Bergonzi, have been charged with fraud and face up to ten years in prison if convicted. In September 2000, the U.S. Attorney's office in San Francisco filed a seventeen-count indictment (revised in 2001) alleging that senior executives inflated HBOC's revenue by more than $270 million between December 1997 and April 1999.

According to Helaine Morrison of the San Francisco office of the SEC, "This is one of the largest financial reporting frauds ever, both in terms of the scope of the scheme and the impact on innocent investors."

**Comparison with Cendant/CUC Fraud.** There are a few striking similarities between HBOC and Cendant/CUC: The core business was slowing; the firm acquired troubled companies; the firm took aggressive write-offs to create sham reserves and later released those reserves into income; and the fraud became known shortly after a major acquisition closed.

**Warning Signs and Lessons from McKessonHBOC.** Like Cendant/CUC and Medaphis, HBO moved to an aggressive acquisition strategy when its business started to struggle. Another similarity was that it started using aggressive accounting for revenue to maintain the appearance of fast growth.

A particular concern was the growth in HBOC's unbilled receivables. Such receivables, the level of which HBOC fails to delineate in its public filings, arise because the company employs the percentage of completion (POC) method of accounting for certain portions of its revenues. See Table 5-2 for a more detailed list of HBOC's aggressive accounting policies.

### Contingent Sales at Bausch & Lomb

Another instance of a well-known company creating bogus revenue in order to trick investors was cleverly uncovered by the media. In its December 19, 1994, issue, *Business Week* exposed a variety of accounting shenanigans at Bausch & Lomb related to "contingent sales" by its contact lens division.

Specifically, late in 1993, Bausch & Lomb summoned its thirty-two independent contact lens distributors to a meeting at the company's Rochester, New York, headquarters. They were given a list of lenses to buy—up to two years' inventory—at prices 50 percent higher than Bausch & Lomb had charged three months earlier. And, the lenses had to be bought by December 24, the date Bausch & Lomb closed its 1993 books.

The distributors purchased close to $25 million of goods during that frantic period in 1993, boosting Bausch & Lomb's U.S. contact lens sales 20 percent, to $145 million, and providing half the division's $15 million in earnings for the year.

This activity came back to haunt the company. In June 1994, Bausch & Lomb announced that "high distributor inventories" in its contact lens and sunglass business would severely hurt 1994 results. The stock slid from $50 to the low $30s.

Company executives promised that the distributors wouldn't have to pay for the lenses until they were sold and said that final payments would be renegotiated if the program flopped. But ten months after the sale, Bausch & Lomb had collected less than 15 percent of the money. Some distributors never paid a dime.

Table 5-2. Warning Signs: McKessonHBOC

| Problem Indicated | Evidence | Shenanigan |
|---|---|---|
| **Aggressive accounting:** Recorded revenue too soon | • HBOC used percentage-of-completion accounting, therefore recording revenue before product was shipped.<br>• There was a big increase in unbilled receivables. | No. 1 |
| **Aggressive accounting:** Recorded sales that lacked economic substance | • HBOC backdated sales contracts.<br>• HBOC engaged in boomerang sales with Data General.<br>• HBOC engaged in a boomerang sale with WebMD; a former HBO executive was now president of WebMD.<br>• HBOC engaged in contingency sales with side letters. | No. 2 |
| **Operational problem** | • Receivables, particularly unbilled receivables, were soaring.<br>• Operating cash flow was deteriorating.<br>• There were concerns about the IMNET acquisition.<br>• There were concerns about US Servis, Inc. | — |
| **Control environment concerns:** Insiders exiting | • HBOC engaged in related-party transactions.<br>• Insiders were selling stock. | — |
| **Aggressive accounting:** Failed to write off impaired assets | • Although HBOC accounts receivable soared 60 percent in fiscal 1996, the allowance for bad debts declined by 1.0 percent. By reducing the reserve, HBOC understated operating expenses. | No. 4 |
| **Aggressive accounting:** Shifted future expenses to the current period as a special charge | • HBOC recorded a $136.5 million nonrecurring charge in fiscal 1995. The reserve created opportunities to artificially inflate future-period profit. | No. 7 |
| **Aggressive accounting:** Released questionable reserves into income | • In the June 1998 quarter, HBOC released $3 million from a 1997 special charge. | No. 5 |

## Technique No. 2: Recording Cash Received in Lending Transactions as Revenue

Never confuse money received from your friendly banker with money received from a customer. The bank loan must be repaid and is considered a liability. In contrast, money received from a customer in return for a service rendered is yours to keep and is considered revenue. Apparently, Xerox failed to understand the distinction between a liability and revenue.

### Financial Reporting Tricks at Xerox

The financial media scored another coup by exposing accounting shenanigans at Xerox (XRX). In a February 6, 2001, *Wall Street Journal* piece, it was reported that XRX had engaged in a variety of financial reporting tricks over the previous three years. Among other things, Xerox was charged with:

• Recording revenue from the sale of "future" receivables to a lender
• Improperly recognizing revenues from its leasing operations by booking up front those lease payments attributable to future supplies and services
• Boosting short-term results by overstating the value of future payments from leases originated in developing countries
• Failing to write off mounting bad debts and improperly classifying transactions in its Mexico operations, which resulted in $119 million in charges in the second and third quarters of fiscal 2000

Several class action lawsuits were filed against the company. Meanwhile, Xerox shares fell from as high as $62 a share during the class action period (February 15, 1998, and February 6, 2001) to just $4.43 a share (see Fig. 5-2), resulting in hundreds of millions of dollars in losses to class action members. The company's accounting practices are now the subject of a Securities and Exchange Commission (SEC) investigation.

On June 16, 2001, Xerox issued a statement about the "irreg-

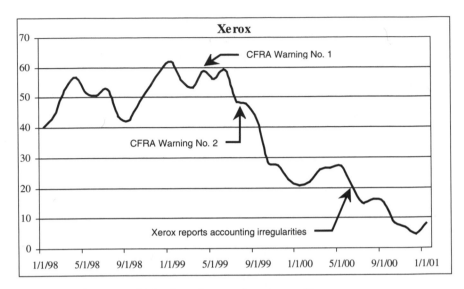

**Fig. 5-2. Xerox stock during class action proceedings.**

ularities" in Mexico, falsely portraying them as an aberration perpetrated by rogue executives. Independent auditor KPMG did give Xerox a sharp slap on the wrist, saying that the company had run afoul of generally accepted accounting principles. As a result, Xerox adjusted its consolidated financial statements for the previous three years, reducing its shareholders' equity by $137 million and its tangible net worth by $76 million. The restatement related to three main areas: the charge for the Mexican scandal, which Xerox had spread over three years, rather than taking it all in 2000; a mistaken application of expenses to a $100 million liability linked to the purchase of 20 percent of Xerox's U.K. operations by Rank Group in 1997; and "misapplications" of U.S. accounting rules on lease modifications and residual values.

### Financing Transactions at Livent

Toronto-based show producer Livent also provides an excellent example of the confusion between a financing transaction and legitimate revenue.

In 1996, Livent negotiated the "sale" of an interest in the production rights to *Show Boat* in Australia and New Zealand for a $4.5 million fee. However, this was really a financing transaction; Livent had orally promised to repay the fee advanced for the production rights, plus 10 percent interest. The agreement called for the lender to "recoup by December 31, 2000 all capital together with interest accrued monthly at the rate of 10% per annum." As a result of this concealed arrangement, Livent improperly recorded the present value of the fee, $4.2 million, as revenue in fiscal 1996.

### Question Advances Received from a Partnership that Are Classified as Revenue

Molten Metal and Lockheed Martin formed a partnership to perform research and development on waste technology. Lockheed provided the funding, and Molten performed the research. Molten received $14 million from the partnership in 1994–1995 and recorded that amount as revenue. Molten was still essentially a development-stage company; it derived virtually none of its revenue from actual sales to unaffiliated customers. The $14 million received from Lockheed should have been considered a distribution or loan from a partnership to fund the research, not revenue.

## Technique No. 3: Recording Investment Income as Revenue

Nonrevenue sources of cash flow may include asset sales and other investment income. It would be improper to record either of these types of cash flow as sales revenue, since neither of them resulted from selling a product or serving a customer. Gains from asset sales and other investment income certainly belong in net income, but they do not belong in revenue.

In Chapter 2, you were introduced to Medaphis. MEDA's major accounting transgression was to improperly include in revenue its $12.5 million share of the profits from an investment joint venture. Under the equity method of accounting for investments, if the investor has at least a 20 percent stake, its proportionate share of

the profits should be included as nonoperating investment income, not as revenue. The misclassification resulted in sales being
overstated by 10 percent and, more important, operating profit
being inflated by 108 percent. In addition, when the report was
restated, the company's operating margin (operating profit as a
percentage of sales) dropped to 9.3 percent from the originally
reported 17.5 percent (see Table 5-3).

Similarly, movie theater giant Cineplex Odeon hid problems
from investors in 1989 by including in revenue one-time investment gains from selling off a production company. Had Cineplex
Odeon been more forthcoming, investors would have noticed that
it had a $14.5 million operating loss; instead, they were fed the
bogus results of $48 million operating income. Ouch!

## Technique No. 4: Recording as Revenue Supplier Rebates Tied to Future Required Purchases

Occasionally, a company will agree to overpay for inventory today, provided the vendor rebates that excess charge with a cash
payment in a later period. Recording that rebate as revenue is
improper. Instead, it represents an adjustment to the cost of the
inventory purchased.

### Question How Retailers Account for Returned Goods

Retailers periodically receive cash refunds (or credits) from suppliers and other vendors for inventory purchases that the retailer
has returned. The proper accounting treatment for such refunds
is to record a purchase return—not sales revenue. However, sometimes retailers overstate their sales by recording as revenue the
credits received from suppliers for misshipments. For example, the
SEC charged that L.A. Gear improperly classified as income $4.7

Table 5-3.  Medaphis—March 1996

| ($ in thousands) | Reported | Correct Amount | % In- flated |
|---|---|---|---|
| Sales | 136,582 | 124,082 | 10.0 |
| Operating profit | 24,021 | 11,521 | 108.0 |
| Operating margin | 17.5% | 9.3% | 88.2 |

million in one-time vendor credits (for supplier misshipments and other sourcing troubles) that it had not actually collected.

More recently, Sunbeam used this ploy to inflate revenue. In 1997, it agreed to make substantial future purchases (probably at an inflated price) if the vendor would give SOC an immediate "rebate." SOC recorded the rebate as revenue. The proper accounting treatment for rebates is to adjust the inventory to reflect the lower cost of the product.

## Technique No. 5: Releasing Revenue That Was Improperly Held Back Before a Merger

Inflating revenue right after the closing of an acquisition is a pretty simple trick: Once the merger is announced, instruct the target company to hold back revenue until after the merger closes. As a result, the revenue reported by the newly merged company improperly includes revenue that was earned by the target company before the merger.

Consider the 1997 merger of 3Com (COMS) with U.S. Robotics (USRX). Because the two companies had differing fiscal year-ends, a two-month "stub period" was created just before the closing. Apparently, USRX held back an enormous amount of revenue so that it would be available to COMS after the merger closed.

It appears that COMS may have included in its August 1997 quarter revenue that USRX deferred during the stub period. Here's the "smoking gun": USRX reported a minuscule $15.2 million of revenue for the stub period (approximately $7.6 million per month), a tiny fraction of the company's recent sales level (see Table 5-4). During the March 1997 quarter, in contrast, USRX had recorded $690.2 million (or approximately $230 million per month). Rather than recognizing the revenue during the normal course of business, USRX apparently held back well over $600 million.

Table 5-4. Sales, USRX ($, in millions)

| Two Months ended 5/97 | Q2, ended 3/97 | Q1, ended 12/96 | Q4, ended 9/96 | Q3, ended 6/96 |
|---|---|---|---|---|
| 15.2 | 690.2 | 645.4 | 611.4 | 546.8 |

## A Look Back — and Ahead

Chapters 4 and 5 addressed techniques for inflating revenue. These tricks include:

- Recording revenue when future services remain to be provided
- Recording revenue before shipment or before the customer's unconditional acceptance
- Recording revenue even though the customer is not obligated to pay
- Selling to an affiliated party
- Giving the customer something of value as a quid pro quo
- Grossing up revenue
- Recording sales that lack economic substance
- Recording cash received in lending transactions as revenue
- Recording investment income as revenue
- Recording as revenue supplier rebates tied to future required purchases
- Releasing revenue that was improperly held back before a merger

Chapter 6 shows how one-time gains, even if properly recorded, may create distortions in financial reports.

# 6

# SHENANIGAN NO. 3: BOOSTING INCOME WITH ONE-TIME GAINS

When a magician wants to make a rabbit appear out of thin air, he may use a special potion, tap a wand, or say the magic word *abracadabra*. Not to be outdone, managers have their own way of creating something from nothing when it comes to profits. Managers don't need special props, though, and they don't need to use special words like *abracadabra*. All they need to know are a few easy-to-use techniques:

1. Boosting profits by selling undervalued assets
2. Including investment income or gains as part of revenue
3. Reporting investment income or gains as a reduction in operating expenses
4. Creating income by reclassification of balance sheet accounts

## A Healthy-Looking Company Was Very Sick

Boosting profits with accounting tricks and one-time gains may make managers happy, but investors and lenders who rely on the misleading financial reports that result aren't always so thrilled. Such reports often present an image of a healthy company when in reality the opposite is true. For example, consider how investors in and lenders to The Charter Company must have felt in 1983 when, shortly after reporting a $50.4 million profit, the company filed for bankruptcy. Were there no warning signs in the financial statements that the reported profits were misleading?

To answer that question, we have to take a closer look at the company's 1983 statement of operation. In doing so, we can see that while the bottom line was favorable, most of the company's income was derived from nonoperating activities. If an analyst had adjusted net income to exclude all nonrecurring or nonoperating items, the company would have looked quite sick. In fact, as shown in Table 6-1, Charter lost over $64 million from its normal recurring operating activities.

As The Charter Company's unhappy investors and lenders learned, one must be alert for one-time techniques used by management to boost weak profits. This chapter describes various accounting gimmicks that involve using one-time gains or activities not directly related to a company's core business to inflate profits.

*Guiding Principle: Investors should be alert for one-time gains or income from noncore activities that camouflage a company's deteriorating core business. However, such one-time gains accruing to an otherwise healthy business should be of little concern. Table 6-2 shows a continuum of one-time gains, from benign to egregious.*

Table 6-1. Charter Company Losses

| ($ millions) | |
| --- | --- |
| 1983 reported *income* from continuing operations | $50,382 |
| Subtract: | |
| Change in estimate of asset | 3,003 |
| Liquidation of LIFO layers | 12,803 |
| Gain from contract renegotiation | 33,600 |
| Gain on exchange of investment | 17,125 |
| Equity in earnings in excess of dividends | 105,447 |
| Add: | |
| Write-down of refinery | 49,428 |
| Write-down of tanker | 7,772 |
| Equity in net losses in affiliates | 12,511 |
| Adjusted *loss* from recurring operations | $(64,396) |

## Technique No. 1: Boosting Profits by Selling Undervalued Assets

One technique that may be used to increase a company's income is to sell assets that have appreciated at prices above their cost (or book value). If such assets are on the books at unrealistically low values, the resulting gain from their sale will be quite substantial. Consequently, investors and lenders should look very critically at nonrecurring gains resulting from the sale of undervalued assets—especially if the sale makes no readily apparent economic sense.

Undervalued assets on the balance sheet are most common in the following situations:

- A company acquired assets in a business combination that was accounted for as a pooling of interest.
- A company acquired real estate (or other investments) years ago, and it has appreciated considerably in value.

### Watch for the Sale of Pooled Assets Acquired in a Business Combination

When a company is acquired in a *pooling-of-interest* (or "pooling") transaction, its assets are recorded on the combined company's balance sheet at their book value at the time of the combination. (The pooling method generally applies when no cash is paid—that is, when there is simply an exchange of stock.)

If the acquired company's assets had been purchased years earlier, their book value may be substantially less than their current market value. That sets the stage for an accounting trick: selling off those assets at their fair market value and recording an instant gain. By selling such assets—which have not increased in value since the acquisition—a company releases "suppressed profits" that were created as a result of its having initially recorded the assets at far less than their fair market value.

Just imagine: If you pay $100 million for a company with $5 million of net assets, $95 million of this cost will not appear on your balance sheet. The result is that the cost of the acquisition is greatly understated (this explains in part why so many mergers have poor outcomes). Understating the cost means that returns to

Table 6-2. How Companies Create One-Time Gains

| More Benign<br>1 | 2 | 3 | 4 | Most Egregious<br>5 |
|---|---|---|---|---|
| • Recording gains from overfunded pension plans | • Recording gains from selling deflated assets<br>• Selling assets after write-off | • Including investment gains as an offset to operating expenses | • Changing pension assumptions<br>• Creating income by reclassifying investments<br>• Changing assumptions on deferred taxes | • Including investment gains in revenue |

capital after the merger are artificially inflated. This suits those who are keen on pushing for mergers, including top managers who have little else to show as achievements, but is grossly misleading and unfair to investors.

---

Accounting Capsule

## The Meaning and Significance of Suppressed Profits

Gains are reported whenever a company sells assets at prices that exceed their original cost. When assets are held for several years, it is natural that their value will increase and that gains will be reported when they are sold. However, if recently purchased assets are recorded at less than their true fair market value (as is the case for assets acquired through a pooling of interest), the company will report a "windfall" gain when those assets are sold. Thus the sale of assets recorded at artificially low amounts enables a company to record a gain by releasing suppressed profits.

---

Accounting Capsule

## Sale of Assets Acquired in a Pooling Transaction

As an example of a business combination accounted for under the pooling method, assume that a company acquires another company by exchanging stock with a market value of $1 million (but a book value of $200,000). The company holds this new business for one year, then sells it for $1.1 million. Clearly, the company's economic gain is $100,000. Because of a quirk in GAAP, however, the company would report a gain of $900,000 —which includes the suppressed profit received by initially recording the asset for less than its fair market value of $1 million.

Until 2002, the pooling method was perfectly acceptable under GAAP. However, investors and lenders should discount profits and gains that resulted from selling assets that had been recorded at less than fair market value (and which, consequently, had an inherent suppressed profit at the time they were acquired).

**Cisco Systems.** The accounts of networking giant Cisco have been analyzed by Professor Abraham Briloff in *Barron's*. In the fiscal year ending June 2000, Cisco bought twelve other companies for a total cost of $16 billion, paid for with its shares. Five of these purchases, worth $1.2 billion, were not regarded as significant enough to even be taken into account in restating the company's profits. The other seven companies, for which Cisco paid $14.8 billion, were shown as costing just $134 million. Thus, thanks to pooling, $16 billion of acquisitions were shown as costing only $134 million, creating suppressed profits of $15,866 billion. The performance of Cisco's stock is shown in Fig. 6-1.

---

Accounting Capsule

## New Accounting Rules on Pooling and Goodwill

In June 2001, the Financial Accounting Standards Board issued Statements of Financial Accounting Standards (SFAS) No. 141, "Business Combinations," and No. 142, "Goodwill and Other Intangible Assets," effective for fiscal years beginning after December 15, 2001. Under the new rules, goodwill (and intangible assets deemed to have indefinite lives) will no longer be

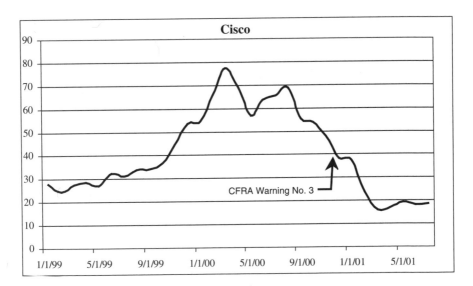

Fig. 6-1

amortized but will be subject to annual impairment tests in accordance with the statements. Other intangible assets will continue to be amortized over their useful lives. Also, pooling-of-interest will no longer be permitted. The illustrations of one-time gains from pooling, however, still offer important lessons. Watch for companies recording assets at unrealistically low amounts and later reaping windfall gains when selling those assets.

---

**General Electric.**   General Electric (GE) was able to use the pooling method to help boost its profits when it acquired Utah International in 1976 by exchanging stock worth approximately $1.9 billion. GE recorded Utah's assets at their book value of $547.8 million, thus suppressing about $1.4 billion in value. The unrecorded asset value would be reported as a gain when GE sold those assets. In addition, even if the assets were not later sold, their below-market valuation allowed GE to understate its expenses (cost of sales and depreciation) and thereby overstate net income.

## Watch for Gains from the Sale of Undervalued Investments

Assets such as real estate and other investments may have been acquired years ago at much lower prices and will provide a company with instant profits when sold. Assume, for instance, that a developer acquires land for $200,000 and that the land appreciates over time to $2 million. The land is then transferred to a corporation for development. Since the owners are the same, the land will be recorded at its original cost of $200,000. If the land is then sold, the $1.8 million in suppressed value will be reflected as earnings of the new entity, creating the impression of a successful operation.

It is important to note that recording gains from the sale of assets that have appreciated in value is perfectly acceptable under GAAP. Nonetheless, investors should be especially critical of companies with weak operating profits that continually try to prop up net income by selling undervalued assets, particularly when the sale comes at the end of a quarter or year.

## Technique No. 2: Including Investment Income or Gains as Part of Revenue

As illustrated in the account of The Charter Company debacle, whenever a company has one-time income, GAAP requires that it be separated on the financial statements from income that stemmed from ordinary continuing operations. Analysts should be particularly alert when nonoperating gains are included in sales revenue or in operating income—either as sales revenue or as a reduction of an operating expense. Boston Chicken, franchiser of the Boston Market restaurant chain, camouflaged its deteriorating business by including, in revenue, interest income and various fees charged to the franchisees.

### Boston Chicken—Touted as the Next McDonalds

The story begins in October 1993 with one of the decade's most memorable and successful IPOs. Merrill Lynch, the lead investment banker, helped Boston Chicken (BOST) raise close to $1 billion in funds from stock and convertible debt offerings over the next few years. Investors referred to BOST as the next McDonalds.

There was, however, one small problem: The company was losing money in its core business, restaurant sales and franchise fees. All of its profits were coming from interest income and various service fees charged to franchisees. BOST noted in its 1996 annual report that "the financed area developers have incurred, and will continue to incur, substantial net losses during the Company's expansion phase—which is anticipated to result in negative net worth." The losses in question grew to $156.5 million in 1996 from $149.1 million during the prior year.

**Recycled Capital Magically Turned to Income.**   BOST raised capital (equity and debt) from the market and lent the money to franchisees, many of whom had some affiliation with the executives and directors. BOST then received money back from the franchisees in the form of interest income and other forms of revenue. Ominously, this ancillary revenue and income was becoming the predominant portion of the company's reported operating income.

In fact, such income was bundled with restaurant sales revenue, making it difficult for individuals to detect the problem.

**How Did It Play Out?**  The company's December 1996 10-K disclosed losses from operations totaling $156 million (see Table 6-3). Over the next three months, the stock price collapsed (see Fig. 6-2), and BOST eventually filed for bankruptcy in October 1998. Ironically, McDonalds bought some of the company's assets and has successfully relaunched the Boston Market division.

*Warning Signs and Lessons from Boston Chicken.*  Boston Chicken cleverly hid signs that its business was deteriorating by including in revenue noncore sources of income. As shown in Table 6-4, the company reported that 1996 pretax income doubled to $109.9 million, yet CFRA calculated that it had actually lost $14.7 million on its core operations. (We define income from core operations to include revenues from company-operated stores and from royalties and initial franchise and area development fees, but *not* from activities such as interest, real estate, and software fees. Expenses deducted include cost of products sold, salaries and benefits ex-

Table 6-3. Boston Chicken, 1993–1997

| ($, in thousands) | Dec. 1993 | Dec. 1994 | Dec. 1995 | Dec. 1996 | Dec. 1997 |
|---|---|---|---|---|---|
| Revenue: | | | | | |
| Company stores | 29,849 | 40,916 | 51,566 | 83,950 | 261,077 |
| Royalties & franchise-related fees | 11,551 | 43,603 | 74,662 | 115,510 | 117,857 |
| Interest income | 1,130 | 11,632 | 33,251 | 65,048 | 83,434 |
| Total revenue | 42,530 | 96,151 | 159,479 | 264,508 | 462,368 |
| Costs & expenses: | | | | | |
| Cost of products | 11,287 | 15,876 | 19,737 | 31,160 | 94,736 |
| Salaries & benefits | 15,437 | 22,637 | 31,137 | 42,172 | 109,424 |
| General & administrative expenses | 13,879 | 33,027 | 41,367 | 99,847 | 292,534 |
| Provision for loan loss | — | — | — | — | 128,000 |
| Losses of area developer | — | — | — | — | 49,352 |
| Total | 40,603 | 71,540 | 92,241 | 173,179 | 674,046 |
| Operating income | 1,927 | 24,611 | 67,238 | 91,329 | (211,678) |

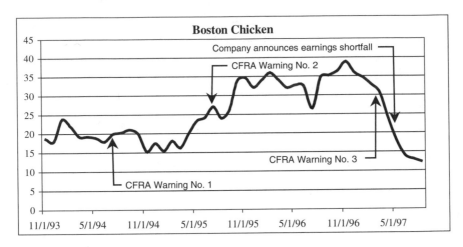

**Fig. 6-2**

Table 6-4. Income from Core Operations versus Other Income
Measures, 1995–1996

|          | Income from Core Operations | Pretax Income* | Net Income     | EPS    |
| -------- | --------------------------- | -------------- | -------------- | ------ |
| 1996     | ($14.7 million)             | $109.9 million | $67.0 million  | $1.01  |
| 1995     | $7.9 million                | $54.4 million  | $33.6 million  | $0.66  |
| % Change | (186.1%)                    | 102.0%         | 99.4%          | 53.0%  |

\* Excludes minority interest in subsidiary.

penses, and general and administrative expenses.) Table 6-5 gives
more details on the company's problems and its aggressive accounting policies.

**Watch for Income Boost from Gain on Stock Sale.** For Boston
Chicken, the second major factor causing a divergence between
income from core operations and net income was a series of one-
time gains recognized on the sale of stock in a subsidiary. Specifically, BOST's income received a boost in both the third and fourth
quarters of 1996 from one-time gains derived from the sale of
stock in the company's Einstein/Noah Bagel subsidiary. Such
gains amounted to $14.8 million and $23.3 million in the third and

fourth quarters, respectively, or a total of $38.1 million. As shown in Table 6-6, BOST's 1996 net income would have been approximately $26.2 million lower than the reported amount had such gains been excluded, and EPS would have been reduced by $0.39, to $0.62 from the reported $1.01.

**Watch for Netting One-Time Gains against One-Time Losses.** Sometimes companies use the occasion of a one-time gain to write off future operating expenses. (More on this trick in Chapter 10.) Both Boston Chicken and Waste Management (WMI) used one-time gains and simultaneously wrote off future-period expenses.

Table 6-5. Warning Signs: Boston Chicken

| Problem Indicated | Evidence | Shenanigan |
|---|---|---|
| Aggressive accounting: Included investment income as part of revenue | BOST included interest income in revenue. | No. 3 |
| Operational problems | The restaurant business was losing money. | — |
| Aggressive accounting: Failed to write down impaired assets | BOST failed to accrue bad debt reserves. | No. 4 |
| Control environment | There were many related-party transactions. | — |

Table 6-6. Adjustment of 1996 Reported Income, Based on Exclusion of Gain from Stock Sale

|  | Reported | Adjustment* | CFRA-Adjusted |
|---|---|---|---|
| Pretax income | $109.9 million | $38.1 million | $71.8 million |
| Net income | $67.0 million | $26.2 million | $40.8 million |
| EPS | $1.01 | $0.39 | $0.62 |

*For pretax income, adjustment is based on total gain of $38.1 million; for net income, adjustment is based on assumed effective tax rate of 39.1 percent; EPS is adjusted proportionally with net income.

BOST recorded nonrecurring charges of $38 million for asset write-offs and equipment purchases during 1996, the same year it reported a gain of $38 million from the sale of stock in a subsidiary. It deserves noting that the charges of $15 million in the third quarter and $23 million in the fourth quarter corresponded almost precisely to the portion of the gain reported in each of those periods. BOST's decision to record write-offs in the same period as the one-time stock gains resulted in a "smoothing" of the company's net income.

Similarly, in its 1995 financial statements, Waste Management used a $160 million gain that it realized on the exchange of its interest in a company known as ServiceMaster to offset $160 million in unrelated operating expenses and misstatements, most of which had been identified as misstatements in 1994 and earlier. WMI offset the misstatements and expenses against the gain and reported the result as Sundry Income. The amount netted represented 10 percent of 1995 pretax income before special charges. WMI made no disclosure of the netting.

During the 1996 audit, Arthur Andersen quantified misstatements in the company's financial statements equal to 7.2 percent of pretax income from continuing operations before special charges. The company also netted and misclassified gains and profits of approximately $85.1 million on the sales of two subsidiaries, which Arthur Andersen also identified as improper; if corrected in 1996, this would have further reduced pretax income from continuing operations before special charges by 5.9 percent.

## Technique No. 3: Reporting Investment Income or Gains as a Reduction in Operating Expenses

One-time gains or other nonoperating sources of income can be hidden as a reduction in operating expenses. Here's how it works.

- A company experiences a windfall gain from its pension assets, causing the reported pension expense to evaporate or, better yet, result in pension income.
- A company generates a windfall gain from selling an investment and includes the gain as a reduction in operating expenses.

Accounting Capsule

## Calculating Pension Expense (or Income)

| | |
|---|---|
| Service cost | Current-period obligations for benefits earned that period |
| Interest cost | An adjustment for the fact that estimated obligations are now one period closer |
| Actual return | Interest, dividends, rentals, and changes in market value of assets |
| Amortization of prior service costs | Costs of additional benefits given by the employer |
| Deferral/amortization of gains or losses | Adjustments made for variations between actual results and estimates |

### Windfall Gains from Pension Assets

One operating expense for many companies is pension expense. Under unusual circumstances, the gains that result from investing the pension assets will be larger than the pension expense, resulting in pension income. What circumstances would lead to this? A bull market may produce oversized gains for a company whose pension plan is overfunded, or management may change some of the accounting assumptions used in the calculation of the pension expense.

**Watch for Windfall Gain on Overfunded Pension Plans.**   It's like winning the lottery—twice. Because investment gains in recent years had resulted in an overfunded pension plan, during fiscal 1998 Lucent recorded *income* of $558 million from its pension plan, after netting the other related pension costs.

**Watch for Changes in Pension Accounting Assumptions.**   You can sometimes still win the lottery even if the bull market ends: simply change to more aggressive accounting assumptions in computing the pension expense. During the fiscal year ended September 1999,

Lucent obtained a boost to reported earnings from an increase in pension income—an increase that was solely due to the company's December 1998 pension plan accounting change.

During the December 1998 quarter, Lucent changed the way it calculated the value of its pension assets, which are used in determining periodic pension expense or income. Under its former method, LU had amortized realized and unrealized gains and losses over a five-year period as one component of pension expense/income. Under the new method, the company recorded an estimate of investment gains or losses each period based upon the plan's historical returns, with any difference between the estimated and actual values amortized over a five-year period.

Had the company not changed the way in which it accounted for its pension plan, earnings for fiscal 1999 would have been cut by $283 million, or $0.09 per share: to $1.13 from the reported $1.22. In addition, without this change, earnings growth for fiscal 1999 would have dropped to 31 percent from the reported 42 percent.

### Windfall Investment Gain Included as a Reduction in Operating Expenses

Investment gains should appear on the statement of operations separate and distinct from normal operating income. One trick for artificially boosting operating income is to use one-time gains to offset operating expenses. Computer giant IBM did just that when it failed to segregate a rather large ($3.7 billion) gain on selling a business to AT&T in 1999. That gain was virtually impossible to find in IBM's statement of operations: It appeared as a reduction in selling, general, and administrative expense (SG&A).

An IBM spokesman says that the company has been putting one-time gains and charges into SG&A since about 1994 and categorizes such items as "general" expenses (see Table 6-7).

## Technique No. 4: Creating Income by Reclassification of Balance Sheet Accounts

Generally, appreciation in an investment results in income only when the investment is sold at a gain. Under certain circum-

Table 6-7. IBM's One-Time Gains and Charges, 1994–1999

| Year ($ in thousands) | 1994 | 1995 | 1996 | 1997 | 1998 | 1999 (Sept. 30) |
|---|---|---|---|---|---|---|
| Operating income | 5,005 | 7,591 | 8,596 | 9,098 | 9,164 | 8,905 |
| SG&A | 15,916 | 16,766 | 16,854 | 16,634 | 16,662 | 10,284 |
| Gain in SG&A | 11 | 339 | 300 | 273 | 261 | 4,554 |
| Charges in SG&A | 0 | 0 | 0 | 0 | 0 | 2,488 |
| Gain as % of operating income | 0.2 | 4.5 | 3.5 | 3.0 | 2.8 | 51.1 |
| Charges as % of operating income | — | — | — | — | — | 27.9 |

stances, however, companies record income resulting from appreciation in value of investments that have not been sold. Generally, such treatment is reserved for companies with an active trading portfolio. Curiously, Apple Computer (AAPL) obtained a significant artificial boost to net income in the June 1998 quarter by electing to record the unrealized appreciation in value of an equity holding in an unusual manner. Specifically, AAPL classified its residual ownership in a publicly offered equity holding as "trading" securities rather than as "available for sale" securities, and consequently recognized a gain on the unrealized appreciation of that holding—in contrast with the usual approach taken by companies outside of the financial services sector.

By selecting the "trading" designation, AAPL was able to immediately mark the securities up to the higher market value and record an additional $16 million gain. In contrast, had the company used the "available for sale" designation, the entire gain would have been deferred until the eventual sale of those shares. If AAPL had chosen to record the residual holding as available for sale, as CFRA would advocate, the company's net income for the June quarter would have been reduced by $16 million, or $0.09 per share: to $0.56 from the reported $0.65.

Some companies received a boost to income when the FASB issued a new rule (SFAS No. 133) related to accounting for currency gains and losses. Amazon received a nice gift in the March 2001 quarter, recording a $46 million gain from "non-cash gains and losses" from foreign currency. Prior to 2001, these gains were included on the balance sheet.

## A Look Ahead

Until now, the shenanigans described have inflated profits by improperly recording revenue or one-time gains. More profits can also be created by fiddling with the reported expenses. Those tricks are discussed in Chapters 7 and 8.

# 7

# SHENANIGAN NO. 4: SHIFTING CURRENT EXPENSES TO A LATER OR EARLIER PERIOD

Failing to report all your expenses to the Internal Revenue Service makes no sense, since it results in your paying higher taxes. However, this trick works just fine if your goal is to impress your shareholders and bankers with higher profits. There are two versions of this trick: one that affects asset accounts (the focus of this chapter) and one that affects liability accounts (the focus of Chapter 8).

This chapter discusses five techniques that are used to boost profits by excluding expenses. Each technique achieves the goal of improperly recording a business cost as an asset rather than as an expense.

1. Capitalizing normal operating costs, particularly if the company recently changed from expensing it
2. Changing accounting policies and shifting current expenses to an earlier period

3. Amortizing costs too slowly
4. Failing to write down or write off impaired assets
5. Reducing asset reserves

Normal business costs fall into two groups: those that provide short-term benefits (e.g., rent, salaries, and advertising) and those that provide longer-term benefits (e.g., inventory and plant and equipment). Under accounting rules, those costs that provide short-term benefits must be charged immediately as expenses against earnings. Those costs that provide longer-term benefits, in contrast, should first be recorded as assets and then charged to expense at a later time, when the benefits are actually received. Sometimes these longer-term items suddenly become worthless and must be written off against income immediately.

*Guiding Principle: An enterprise should capitalize costs incurred that produce a future benefit, and expense those that produce no such benefit.*

## Technique No. 1: Capitalizing Normal Operating Costs, Particularly If Recently Changed from Expensing

The first technique involves capitalizing normal operating costs (those that produce short-term benefits) and shifting those costs to future periods. That is, the costs are improperly recorded as an asset (rather than as an expense), and the asset is then amortized over future periods. The costs that are most often improperly amortized are marketing and solicitation costs, landfill and interest costs, software development costs, store preopening costs, and repair and maintenance costs. Examples of improper amortization of each of these costs are given in Table 7-1.

### Marketing and Solicitation Costs

Most companies must spend money to advertise their products or services. Accounting guidelines normally require that companies immediately expense such costs as normal recurring short-term

Table 7-1. Examples of Improper Amortization

| Aggressive Capitalization | Industry | Companies |
| --- | --- | --- |
| Marketing and solicitation costs | Membership & subscription | Cendant/CUC, AOL, Excel Communications |
| Landfill costs and interest | Trash haulers | Chambers Development |
| Software and research and development costs | Software and other technology companies | Medaphis, Lucent |
| Store preopening costs | Retailers and restaurants | Lechters, Ryan's Famous Steak House |
| Repair and maintenance costs | Industrial | Rent Way |

operating costs. However, certain companies, particularly those that sells memberships to customers (e.g., health clubs and Internet access providers), have aggressively capitalized these costs and spread them over several periods. Three such companies are profiled here.

**AOL.**  AOL (discussed in Chapter 2) improperly capitalized marketing costs for the three years ended June 1996. Normally, these costs are recorded as an expense immediately and charged against net income. AOL, instead, recorded marketing costs as an asset on the balance sheet and amortized them over future periods. It called the costs associated with sending disks to potential customers *deferred membership acquisition costs* (DMAC). For fiscal years 1993, 1994, and 1995, AOL generally amortized DMAC on a straight-line basis over a 12-month period. Beginning July 1, 1995, the company increased that amortization period to 24 months.

By June 1996, the DMAC on AOL's balance sheet had ballooned to $314 million, representing 33 percent of total assets and 61 percent of shareholders' equity. Had these costs been properly expensed as incurred, AOL's 1995 reported pretax loss would have increased from $21 million to $98 million (including the write-off of DMAC that existed as of the end of fiscal year 1994), and AOL's 1996 reported pretax income of $62 million would have been transformed to a pretax loss of $175 million. On a quarterly basis, the effect of capitalizing DMAC was that AOL reported profits for six of the eight quarters in fiscal years 1995 and 1996, rather than reporting losses each period.

---

Accounting Capsule

## Advertising Costs

Normally, advertising expenses are charged against income immediately. According to the AICPA's Statement on Accounting Policy (SOP) 93–7, "the costs of advertising should be expensed either as incurred or the first time the advertising takes place." There is a narrow exception to this general rule: "An entity must operate in a sufficiently stable business environment that the historical evidence upon which it bases its recoverability analysis is relevant and reliable." A company that falls under this exception can capitalize these costs.

---

AOL contended that it was permitted to capitalize its marketing costs based on the exception in SOP 97–3. To do so, the company would have to show *persuasive evidence* that the advertising would result in future benefits *similar* to the effects of past direct-response advertising activities.

*SEC Disagrees and Sues AOL.* According to the SEC, AOL did not meet the essential requirements of SOP 93–7 because *the unstable business environment precluded reliable forecasts of future net revenues.* AOL was not operating in a stable environment; its business was characterized, during the relevant period, by these factors:

• AOL was operating in a nascent business sector characterized by rapid technological change.

- AOL's business model was evolving.
- Extraordinarily rapid growth in AOL's customer base was causing significant changes in its customer demographics.
- AOL's customer retention rates were unpredictable.
- AOL's product pricing was subject to potential change.
- AOL could not reliably predict the future costs of obtaining revenues.

**Cendant/CUC.**   In certain businesses, cash that is received and paid out is deferred on the balance sheet until the service has been provided to the customer. Thus, cash payments for normal operating expenses appear on the balance sheet as an asset, and cash received for services to be performed appears on the balance sheet as a liability.

Cendant/CUC (profiled in Chapter 1) sold memberships that enabled customers to receive discounts at restaurants and other business establishments. Since it was required to defer the revenue over the membership contract period, CUC also deferred the marketing and solicitation costs over the same period. As shown in Table 7-2, during the year ended January 1988, the total costs deferred (that is, capitalized) increased by 73.7 percent, to $45.4 million, while the revenue deferred increased only 21.2 percent, to $52.4 million. Net cash outflows for promotion increased by over $19 million, from $26.2 million to $45.4 million. At the same time, net cash inflows from customers grew by a shade more than $9 million, from $43.2 million to $52.4 million. By increasing the capitalized membership, solicitation, and prepaid commission costs faster than the deferred revenue, CUC successfully boosted its sagging earnings.

**Excel Communications.**   In the third illustration, Dallas-based Excel Communications, a provider of long-distance telephone service, decided to change its accounting from expensing to capitalizing marketing costs at a most propitious time—right before it registered with the SEC to become a public company.

Table 7-2. CUC's Capitalization of Membership Acquisition Costs

| ($ in thousands) | January 1988 | January 1987 |
| --- | --- | --- |
| Noncurrent assets: | | |
| Deferred membership charges, net | 22,078 | 13,112 |
| Prepaid solicitation costs | 17,089 | 4,915 |
| Prepaid commissions | 6,267 | 8,127 |
| Total capitalized | 45,434 | 26,154 |
| Deferred membership income | 52,384 | 43,205 |

---

**RED FLAG**

**Watch for Changes in Capitalization Policy Just Before the IPO**

---

Excel went public in May 1996. To ensure a successful initial public offering (IPO), the company needed to dress up its rather modest earnings. Not a problem. It decided to change its accounting related to sales commission. Until 1995, Excel had expensed these marketing costs immediately. Beginning in 1995, it capitalized and then amortized them over a 12-month period. The immediate impact on reported profits was enormous. In 1995, earnings almost tripled, to $44.4 million (or 46 cents) from $15.9 million (or 18 cents) a year earlier. The aggressive accounting inflated profits by $22.7 million (or 51 percent of the 1995 earnings). Stated differently, *simply by changing to a more aggressive accounting policy, Excel artificially boosted its profits by 105 percent.*

Had investors simply read the following footnote contained in Excel's SEC filing, they would have sold the stock short rather than buying it.

> The Company has adopted an accounting convention of amortizing capitalized subscriber acquisition costs to expense over a period of 12 months in order to better match those costs with the revenues from subscribers' long distance usage during the first 12 months of service to such subscribers. Marketing services costs, as reflected in the Company's Consolidated Financial

Statements, include the effect of the capitalization of the portion of commissions paid for the acquisition of new subscribers during a period, as well as the effect of the current period amortization of amounts capitalized in the current and prior periods. The net effect of capitalizing and amortizing a portion of commissions expense was a reduction in marketing services costs reflected in the Company's Consolidated Financial Statements of $3.6 million, $13.1 million, $51.4 million, and $27.6 million for the years ended December 31, 1993, 1994, and 1995, and for the three months ended March 31, 1996, respectively.

## Landfill and Interest Costs

Companies in the trash disposal business also seem to have a propensity to capitalize normal operating costs in order to inflate earnings.

**Watch for Capitalized Costs of Developing New Landfills.**   Chambers Development, one of the 1990s' early disasters, improperly capitalized certain expenses in its landfill asset account. These expenses included executive salaries (for time spent on the projects), public relations costs, travel and legal expenses, and interest costs (on money borrowed during the development period).

   In 1992, after having missed the problem for several years, the outside auditors forced management to restate earnings and expense these operating costs. Several months later, upon further reflection and examination, the auditors required further restatements. When the smoke cleared, the company had removed nearly $50 million in capitalized landfill development costs and interest costs from its 1991 balance sheet and charged this amount against income. Chambers Development originally reported income of $49.9 million. The first restatement to investors reported income of $1.5 million; the second restatement indicated a loss of $72.2 million.

## Software and Research and Development Costs

Another common operating cost that sometimes finds its way to the balance sheet is the cost of software that is either purchased or developed in-house. Early-stage research and development costs for software would typically be expensed. Later-stage costs (those incurred once a project reaches "technological feasibility") typically would be capitalized. Investors should be alert for companies that capitalize a disproportionately large amount of their software costs or companies that change their accounting policies and begin to capitalize costs.

**Watch for Disproportionately Large Amounts of Capitalized Software.**   In 1995, Medaphis (MEDA) capitalized roughly $33.5 million (or 52 percent of pretax earnings), up an astounding 423.4 percent from 1994. This trend continued during the first quarter of 1996; in that quarter, MEDA capitalized an additional $12.5 million (or 57.5 percent of pretax earnings).

**Watch for Companies that Begin to Capitalize Software Costs.**   Lucent also obtained a nice earnings boost as a result of its capitalization of internal-use software costs based on a recently adopted AICPA Statement of Position. Through September 1999, Lucent expensed all costs for internal-use software as incurred. However, during the December 1999 quarter, the company planned to adopt Statement of Position (SOP) 98-1, "Accounting for the Costs of Computer Software Developed or Obtained for Internal Use"; and based on that SOP, LU began capitalizing a portion of its internal-use software costs (see Table 7-3).

SOP 98-1, the adoption of which is mandatory, classifies selected costs associated with software used internally, software installations, and upgrades as costs that must be, may be, or may not be capitalized. Nevertheless, by capitalizing costs that in the past had been expensed as incurred, Lucent not only obtained a boost to earnings during each period, but also, as a result, received

Table 7-3. Lucent's Capitalized Software Costs and Year-over-Year Growth

| ($ millions, except %) | Year, 9/99 | Year, 9/98 | Year, 9/97 |
|---|---|---|---|
| Capitalized software balance | 470 | 298 | 293 |
| Annual growth | 57.7% | 1.7% | — |

a boost to its year-over-year earnings growth rate during each of the subsequent four quarters.

## Store Preopening Costs

Like research and development costs, most other normal operating costs should be expensed immediately. Occasionally, companies that are expanding their operations and opening new facilities or stores capitalize certain operating costs during the preopening period. Retailers and restaurant chains, for example, may capitalize training costs and other operating expenses related to opening a new facility. Capitalizing such costs is generally regarded as aggressive accounting. Consider two of the more egregious situations.

**Watch for Capitalizing Store Preopening Costs.**   During the early 1990s, retailer Lechter's, Inc. and restaurant operator Ryan's Family Steak Houses capitalized preopening costs. Lechter's capitalized these costs over a period of 24 months from the date operations commenced at the new store. Ryan's capitalized primarily employee costs and amortized them over five years, commencing when the restaurant opened.

## Repair and Maintenance Costs

While capitalizing software costs or store preopening costs could be acceptable under certain conditions, repair and maintenance expenses are clearly normal operating costs that should be charged against income.

One company that failed to understand this was Rent-Way (RWAY), one of the nation's largest rent-to-own stores. In fiscal 1999, RWAY artificially reduced some expenses to boost income in an unusual way: It began recording vehicle maintenance costs as assets that will be written off these costs over many years. Figure 7-1 shows the effect that revealing these practices had on Rent-Way's stock price. Table 7-4 gives more details on the company's aggressive accounting practices.

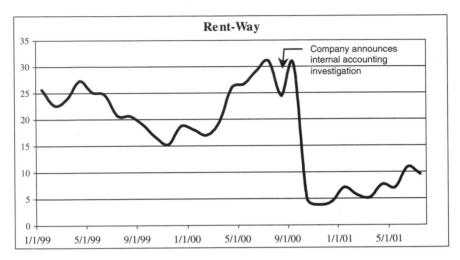

**Fig. 7-1. Rent-Way Stock Price, January 1999–September 2001**

Table 7-4. Warning Signs: Rent-Way

| Problem Indicated | Evidence | Shenanigan |
|---|---|---|
| **Aggressive accounting:** Capitalized normal operating costs Failed to write off impaired assets | • RWAY capitalized vehicle maintenance costs. • RWAY delayed writing off missing or discarded merchandise. • RWAY kept scrapped furniture on the balance sheet. | No. 4 |
| **Aggressive accounting:** Failed to record liabilities | • RWAY stopped recording accounts payable (and related expense) weeks before the close of a quarter. | No. 5 |

## Technique No. 2: Changing Accounting Policies and Shifting Current Expenses to an Earlier Period

The first technique discussed in this chapter helped companies get out of a messy situation by shifting operating costs to a future period. But that only defers the day of reckoning to a later period. Alas, Technique No. 2 provides a longer-term solution for a management that is intent on simply making those costs disappear forever. By shifting the costs to an earlier period (thus skipping the statement of income), the mission is accomplished.

## Snapple, Crackle, and Pop!

Beverage giant Snapple (SNAP) can give both AOL and Cendant/ CUC a lesson in accounting shenanigans related to accounting for marketing costs. It made marketing costs disappear by shifting certain future-period expenses to a prior quarter.

Here's how it was done. Back in 1994, Snapple discovered an interesting variation on shifting costs out of the current period in order to boost profits. Rather than doing it the old-fashioned way and shifting them to the future, SNAP shifted the costs to earlier periods. Here are the details.

On June 7, 1994 (three weeks before the quarter ended), Snapple announced an accounting change related to advertising costs. Rather than expensing the costs as incurred, it began using a variety of estimates related to unit sale costs for the year charged as expense based on these estimates. With the change, $1.6 million of current- and future-period expenses were shifted to the (already completed) first quarter. As a result, these expenses essentially disappeared from the books without any impact on the income statement. (Costs shifted to the first quarter are reflected on the balance sheet.)

---

**RED FLAG**

Snapple's announcement of the accounting change just weeks before the quarter ended was a sign to investors that a problem existed.

---

**What Ever Happened to Snapple?**   Two months after the accounting change became known, the company announced the business problems and the share price was cut in half, to $14 (see Fig. 7-2). Over the following months, the price was again cut in half, to $7. In November 1994, Quaker Oats (OAT) purchased Snapple for $1.8 billion, or $14 per share.

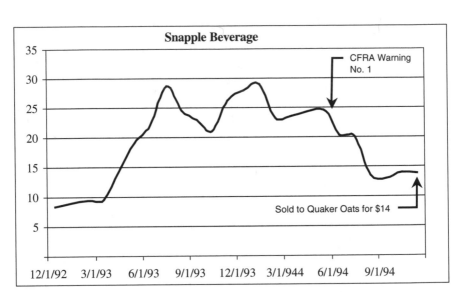

**Fig. 7-2**

After the acquisition, SNAP's business continued to struggle, causing major problems at OAT. OAT finally sold SNAP to Triarc for $300 million. This acquisition by OAT must be considered among the worst in recent years.

*Warning Signs at Snapple.* Several signs pointed to problems at Snapple. The most glaring red flag was a change in accounting policies three weeks before the quarter ended. Other warning signs included collapsing cash flow from operations, receivables growing much faster than sales, and inventory turnover slowing.

A more recent example of shifting current and future expenses to an earlier period, can be found with JDS Uniphase (JDSU). In July 2001, JDSU announced a $44.8 billion write-off related to goodwill on acquisitions that had been a bust. Curiously, JDSU pushed $38.7 billion into the March 2001 quarter. Thus, 86 percent of the write-off will have no adverse impact on current or future earnings. Indeed, the future earnings will be artificially inflated because the goodwill amortization has been completely eliminated as a result of a new accounting rule.

## Technique No. 3: Amortizing Costs Too Slowly

Expenditures that provide a company with longer-term benefits (e.g., inventory, plant and equipment, and goodwill) should be expensed over the same period in which the benefit is received. The technical term for allocating costs against the related revenue is *matching*. Companies can artificially inflate earnings by failing to allocate sufficient costs to the appropriate period through depreciating fixed assets too slowly; amortizing intangible assets or leasehold improvements over too long a period; changing to a longer period to depreciate or amortize an asset; and amortizing inventory, marketing, and software costs too slowly.

While GAAP encourage companies to write off costs quickly as benefits are received, managers have several motivations for writing off assets slowly. First, slow depreciation or amortization keeps assets on the balance sheet longer, resulting in a higher net worth; and second, with slow amortization, expenses are lower and profits higher.

### Question Companies That Depreciate Fixed Assets Too Slowly

By comparing depreciation policies with industry norms, investors can determine whether a company is writing off assets over an appropriate time span. Investors should be concerned when a company writes off fixed assets too slowly, especially in industries that are experiencing rapid technological advances. Companies that are slow to modernize will be stuck with outmoded equipment.

---

Accounting Capsule

## Depreciation of Plant Assets

A company purchases a building for $500,000 and records it as an asset. It also decides to depreciate the building over 25 years, resulting in an annual depreciation expense of $20,000 ($500,000/25 years).

| | | |
|---|---|---|
| *Increase:* | Depreciation Expense | $20,000 |
| *Decrease:* | Building | $20,000 |

At this point, the balance sheet shows a building with a book value of $480,000 ($500,000 − $20,000) and the statement of operation shows depreciation expense of $20,000.

Instead, the company might have chosen to depreciate the building over a longer period—say, 50 years—to slow down the amortization. The result would be an annual depreciation expense of $10,000 ($500,000/50 years):

| | | |
|---|---|---|
| *Increase:* | Depreciation Expense | $10,000 |
| *Decrease:* | Building | $10,000 |

### Be Alert for Overly Long Amortization Periods for Intangibles and Leasehold Improvements

As with depreciation, the longer a company amortizes its intangible assets or its leasehold improvements, the higher will be its earnings during the early years. One should be wary of companies that amortize intangible assets or leasehold improvements over too long a period.

Investors in Cineplex Odeon, the movie theater chain, should have questioned the company's policy of amortizing leasehold improvements, such as seats and carpeting, over an average of 27 years—an unrealistically rosy estimate of these assets' actual life. That overly aggressive accounting practice overstated Cineplex's "true" earnings. Had it amortized the leasehold improvements over a more conservative 15 years, as its competitor Carmike Cinemas did, its net income in 1988 would have been cut by 65 percent to only 54 cents per share.

### Watch for a Change to a Longer Depreciation or Amortization Period

A company that chooses an overly long depreciation or amortization period is guilty of using aggressive accounting. A more serious offense, however, is a company's changing to a longer period. This suggests that the company's business may be in trouble and that the company needs to change the accounting assumption to camouflage the deterioration. In some cases management may be justified in changing assumptions, but investors should be wary when changes appear to be designed to boost earnings.

General Motors lengthened the useful life on plant and equipment, reducing 1987 depreciation and amortization charges by $1.2 billion.

Newcourt Credit (later acquired by CIT, which was in turn acquired by Tyco) initially amortized goodwill from an acquisition over 20 years. Curiously, one quarter later, the company stretched out the amortization period to 35 years, thereby pushing expenses to later periods.

## Watch for Slow Amortization of Inventory Costs

In most industries, the process of writing off inventory is uncomplicated: When a sale takes place, inventory is transferred to the expense Cost of Goods Sold. In certain businesses, though, determining when to expense inventory and how much to expense is difficult.

In the film business, for example, the costs of making movies or TV programs are capitalized before their release. These costs are then matched (charged as expense) against revenue based on the receipt of revenue. Since revenue may be realized over several years, however, a film company must project the number of years of anticipated revenue flow. If it chooses too long a period, the inventory and profits will be overstated.

Consider, for example, a film that cost $20 million. If the company assumed that revenue would be received over two years, it would expense $10 million each year. If, instead, it assumed that revenues would come in over four years, it would expense $5 million each year. As a result, profits would be $5 million more each year. If the film is a bust, of course, the entire cost should be written off immediately.

Unfortunately, several filmmakers have chosen overly long amortization periods and have failed to write off losing films. Examples include Cannon Group and Orion Pictures.

**Cannon Group.**   The SEC charged that by overestimating its 1985 film revenue, Cannon was writing off its inventory (unamortized film costs) much too slowly. The result was that Cannon's assets were materially overstated, and its expenses for that year were understated.

**Orion Pictures.**   Orion Pictures also had difficulty estimating future revenue (and consequently amortized its film costs too slowly). Furthermore, it was slow in writing off the costs of failed films—in some cases waiting years before doing so. In 1985, for example, Orion posted a $32 million loss—half of it resulting from the write-off of 40 films released since 1982. Clearly, not all of these losses were from 1985; on the contrary, they represented the residual from Orion's fictitious reporting of profits in the prior years (see Table 7-5).

In an October 1991 *Wall Street Journal* article, Orion was criticized for continuing to capitalize film costs that should have been written off years earlier. In fact, as a result of either writing off films too slowly or failing to write off its "dogs," Orion's unamortized film costs grew so large that they exceeded the amount of total revenue that the company reported in fiscal 1990.

One of the more questionable estimates that Orion made was related to the projected revenue from its TV syndication rights to the *Cagney and Lacey* series. Orion was amortizing the costs slowly, assuming that revenues would continue for many years and would eventually total $100 million. Unfortunately, revenues topped out at $25 million—meaning that Orion had expensed its inventory costs far too slowly.

### Watch for Change to Longer Amortization of Marketing or Software Costs

As discussed earlier in this chapter, companies generally expense marketing and software costs immediately. Aggressive companies

Table 7-5. Orion: Inventory Versus Sales Growth

| ($ in millions) | 1991 | 1990 | 1989 |
|---|---|---|---|
| Revenue | $584 | $485 | $468 |
| Net income | −63 | 15 | 13 |
| Inventory/revenue | 766 | 666 | 467 |

capitalize such costs, but over a relatively short period. Very aggressive companies extend the amortization period beyond the original estimate.

AOL used a similar ploy to push marketing costs further into the future. Before a 1995 stock offering, AOL lengthened its already aggressive amortization period from 12 to 24 months. That change alone inflated profits by $48.1 million (to the reported $29.8 million, from a loss of $18.3 million).

Similarly, Medaphis artificially boosted its earnings by stretching out its original five-year amortization period to seven years beginning in 1995.

## Technique No. 4: Failing to Write Down or Write Off Impaired Assets

*Guiding Principle: When there is a sudden and substantial impairment in an asset's value, the asset should be written off immediately and in its entirety, rather than gradually.*

One of the more difficult and subjective decisions that management must make is gauging when an asset is "permanently impaired." (In practice, this is often a tough call.)

An asset is overvalued when its book value exceeds the amount that is expected to be realized through its use or sale. The amount of this overvaluation is a loss that has not been recognized. Certain assets, such as inventory and accounts receivable, will be overvalued if the related reserve account is understated. A failure to establish sufficient reserves or improperly releasing those reserves would understate expenses and inflate profits.

Not uncommonly, companies that announce big restructuring charges (Shenanigan No. 7) had earlier failed to write off impaired assets (Shenanigan No. 4).

### One Classic Example: Lockheed's Ill-Fated TriStar Program

Lockheed (which later merged with Martin Marietta to become Lockheed Martin) provides one of the best examples of the difficulty of knowing when to write off an impaired asset. During the

early 1970s, Lockheed had to decide whether to continue capitalizing start-up costs related to the development of a new aircraft,
the TriStar L-1011, or to write off those costs. The accounting
method used for the planes was the "program method": Each
plane in the program (300 were envisaged) was to be assigned a
presumed average cost, regardless of the actual production costs.
Thus, any costs in excess of the assigned costs that were incurred
on earlier planes would be deferred until the learning curve took
on a favorable slope, so that costs incurred on the later planes
would be less than the average (thereby permitting the absorption
of the previously deferred costs). In theory, this sounds fine—unless, of course, the incremental cost per plane always exceeds the
incremental revenue. Unfortunately for Lockheed, this was the
case.

By late 1975, the company had accumulated approximately $500
million in an asset account, and the ill-fated TriStar program
showed no signs of profitability. The handwriting was on the wall,
however, and Lockheed began writing off the half-billion-dollar
"blob." But it did so on an installment plan, at the rate of $50
million annually (even though the company continued to have
staggering losses on the TriStar program).

Lockheed continued to include the $500 million "development
cost" as an asset, net of its annual $50 million amortization, as the
losses mounted to almost $1 billion (see Table 7-6). Clearly, the
evidence indicated that the asset was impaired and thus should
have been written off in its entirety.

Table 7-6.  Results of
Lockheed's Tri-Star Program

| Losses (in millions) | |
| --- | --- |
| 1975 | $ 94 |
| 1976 | 125 |
| 1977 | 120 |
| 1978 | 119 |
| 1979 | 188 |
| 1980 | 199 |
| 1981 | 129 |
| Total | $974 |

Finally, by the end of 1981, Lockheed wrote off about $400 million after taxes (representing $730 million before taxes, which had previously been reported as an asset). By delaying its decision to write off the asset until 1981, Lockheed overstated its profits in the previous years.

## Watch for Bad Loans and Other Uncollectibles That Have Not Been Written Off

One example of a worthless asset that companies sometimes fail to write off is a loan receivable from a financially distressed client. GAAP require that such receivables be written down to their net realizable value (i.e., the amount the company expects to collect). The process of adjusting the receivables to their net realizable value requires the company to estimate the amount of defaults (or bad debts) and to record a reserve that reduces the net receivables by this amount. If a company wants to increase its profits, it may simply use a lower estimate of uncollectible receivables. That's precisely what has happened in the banking and casualty insurance industries during the last few years.

Banks must continually estimate what portion of their loans will ultimately go bad and, for such loans, must charge an expense while crediting a reserve. Similarly, property and casualty companies must estimate the amount that they will ultimately pay out on current insurance policies. These amounts are deducted from profits in the year in which the loan is made or the policy is written, not in the year in which a claim is paid out or a loan becomes worthless. When a loan is written off, the bank removes it from assets and deducts an equal amount from the reserve (a bookkeeping entry that does not affect the income statement).

Ideally, the total amount in the reserve should be enough to cover all loans on the books that the bank believes are in default or will be in default based on conditions that exist at the date of the financial statements. The additions to reserves that are charged against income each year should be just enough to keep the reserves at the appropriate level. When management fails to reserve a sufficient amount for losses, however, net income and receivables can be substantially overstated.

## Be Wary of Worthless Investments

Besides monitoring loans and other receivables to ensure that they are conservatively valued and that they remain so, investments in stocks, bonds, and real estate must be written down if their market value declines and that decline is "other than temporary." This principle is especially significant for certain types of companies, such as insurers, for whom investments represent a major portion of their assets. Sometimes insurance companies fail with little apparent warning. One reason for the lack of warning is that many insurers carry most of their investments at cost, rather than at their lower market value.

An example of an insurance company that failed to write down its investments was California-based First Executive Life Insurance Corporation, which listed $10 billion in assets at the end of 1990. Much of that, however, was in junk bonds, whose market value had plunged. In April 1991, regulators seized First Executive Life and its affiliates, stranding thousands of policyholders. It was the biggest insurance failure in American history.

# Technique No. 5: Reducing Asset Reserves

Companies must adjust certain assets to reflect customer defaults, inventory obsolescence, and other decreases in asset values. In doing so, they establish a variety of reserves (also called contra accounts) that must be adjusted in each period. (This is the same process used by banks and insurance companies that was discussed in the section on bad loans.) Failing to add a sufficient amount to these reserves or reducing them inappropriately creates artificial profits. The reserves typically relate to receivables, inventory, plant and equipment, goodwill, and deferred taxes (see Table 7-7).

## Watch for a Decrease in Receivable Reserves as Gross Receivables Increase

Companies must record receivables at the amount they expect to collect, called the *net realizable value*. To do this, a reserve (called

Table 7-7.

| Asset Type | Reserve Account |
| --- | --- |
| Receivables | Allowance for doubtful accounts |
| Inventory | Allowance for obsolescence |
| Plant & equipment | Accumulated depreciation |
| Goodwill | Accumulated amortization |
| Deferred taxes | Allowance for decline |

allowance for doubtful accounts) that reflects the expected defaults should be established and maintained. Normally, the reserve grows at the same rate as the gross receivables. Declining reserves when gross receivables are increasing signals an underreporting of Bad Debt Expense. That apparently occurred at HBO & Company (HBOC) before the McKesson acquisition. Its accounts receivable balance soared 60 percent in fiscal 1996, yet its allowance for doubtful accounts (ADA) declined by 1.1 percent. On a percentage basis (i.e., ADA as a percentage of gross receivables), ADA was slashed to 3.16 percent of receivables in 1996 from 5.01 percent in 1995. Had HBOC maintained its allowance at a constant 5.01 percent throughout the period, operating income would have been lowered by $3.6 million and earnings would have been reduced by roughly $2.1 million.

Similarly, Lucent (LU) obtained a boost to reported earnings for the six months ended March 1999 from a reduction in its allowance for doubtful accounts. The allowance declined by 11 percent during the period, even though receivables increased by 26 percent. Consequently, the allowance percentage dropped sharply, to 3.99 percent of receivables at March 1999 from 5.62 percent at September 1998. Had Lucent maintained a constant allowance percentage of 5.62 percent throughout the first six months of fiscal 1999, its September 1998 net income would have been reduced by roughly $94 million, or $0.03 per share.

International banking giant HSBC used a similar trick to boost profits. Its provision for bad debts decreased significantly: by HK$1,223 million, or 86.2 percent, to HK$196 million compared with the prior year. Two reasons were given: a substantial reduction in new provisions and a large increase in amounts released from the reserve. There was a net release of HK$3 million from general provisions, with provisions of HK$122 million made against loan growth for the year, and a release of HK$125 million from the additional general provision of HK$250 million made in 1997. In view of the slowdown in the U.S. economy and its possible implications for the Hong Kong economy, the balance of the additional provision of HK$125 million has been transferred to the general provisions for bad and doubtful debts.

## Watch for the Absence of Loan Reserves

A more extreme misstatement of income occurs when companies fail to make any bad debt provision at all. Boston Chicken (BOST) and its subsidiary established no reserve for loan losses from area developers, even though the outstanding loan balances at the end of 1996 had soared to $787.9 million. Had BOST established a modest 2 percent reserve for loan losses in 1996, operating income would have declined by $15.8 million and net earnings would have declined by $9.6 million.

## Watch for Reduction in Reserve for Inventory Obsolescence

The inventory shown on the balance sheet may be adjusted for either decreases in replacement value or the use of the LIFO (last in, first out) method. As with accounts receivables, a reserve account is used to reflect the downward adjustment to inventory. Typically, the reserve grows at the same rate as inventory. If the reserve fails to keep pace (or actually declines), this usually means that the company has released reserves to inflate earnings.

Consider the following illustration involving Lucent. Despite a large jump in inventory during the fiscal year ended September 1999, Lucent's reserve fell both in absolute dollars and as a percent of gross inventories. As shown in Table 7.8, inventory jumped 42 percent, to $5.87 billion from $4.124 billion, yet the inventory reserve declined from $845 million to $822 million. Had Lucent kept the reserve percentage unchanged at 20.5 percent, earnings for the September 1999 period would have been reduced by roughly $0.08 per share.

Table 7-8. Reserve for Inventory Obsolescence (RIO) versus Gross Inventory (INV)

| ($ millions, except %) | Q4, 9/99 | Q4, 9/98 | Q4, 9/97 | Q4, 9/96 |
|---|---|---|---|---|
| RIO | 822 | 845 | 880 | 815 |
| INV | 5,870 | 4,124 | 3,931 | 4,145 |
| RIO/INV | 14.0% | 20.5% | 22.4% | 19.7% |

## Watch for Reversal of Questionable Reserves

Failing to establish a sufficient reserve would be considered aggressive accounting. Reversing a bogus reserve will get the attention of the SEC.

Lucent obtained a boost to reported earnings during the September 1999 quarter by reversing a previously established restructuring reserve. Specifically, it reversed $54 million during the quarter, thus providing a boost to earnings of $36 million, net of tax.

In 1985, MiniScribe increased its reserve for excess inventory as a result of general decline in demand for its Winchester disk drives and severe competition. In 1986, this reserve was reduced by $2.1 million as a result of improvement in demand. (More on the MiniScribe fraud in Chapter 12.)

## Watch for Changes in Deferred Tax Valuation Reserves

A reserve related to Deferred Tax Assets is required if the company has tax benefits from the IRS but is uncertain whether these rebates will ever be realized. These benefits will be realized as a reduction in future taxes paid. However, if the company is unprofitable and likely to remain so, no taxes will be paid, and so no rebate will be received. If, however, the company becomes profitable (or expects to do so shortly), the reserve will be eliminated and the reported Income Tax Expense on the Statement of Operations will be reduced as well. The impact on earnings, of course, will be positive.

In 1994, Boston Chicken decided to eliminate its $3.8 million reserve for deferred taxes, producing a much-needed boost to its earnings.

## A Look Ahead

Chapter 8 describes another approach to boosting profits: failing to record all liabilities.

# 8

# SHENANIGAN NO. 5: FAILING TO RECORD OR IMPROPERLY REDUCING LIABILITIES

An executive was telling a new secretary what was expected of her. "I want you to be neat, organized, and courteous to all clients," he said. "Above all, I expect you not to gossip about me."

"Oh, yes, sir," replied the secretary. "I won't tell anybody anything. You have my total confidence." Then she leaned over the desk and whispered, "Just what is it you've done, sir, that you don't want others to know about?"

When it comes to recording liabilities, some companies share the "less said the better" attitude expressed in this anecdote. That philosophy results in a policy of disclosing as little as possible about pending lawsuits, long-term purchase commitments, and other potential obligations. In addition to those obligations that should appear on the balance sheet, companies may have many obligations that should be disclosed in the footnotes. Investors and lenders should read the financial statements, the accompanying footnotes, and the proxy statements to search for a company's total obligations. This chapter describes techniques for uncovering unreported or underreported liabilities.

1. Failing to record expenses and related liabilities when future obligations remain
2. Reducing liabilities by changing accounting assumptions
3. Releasing questionable reserves into income
4. Creating sham rebates
5. Recording revenue when cash is received, even though future obligations remain

There are two general approaches for underreporting expenses on the income statement. Chapter 7 discussed techniques that *inflate the assets*. Chapter 8 focuses on techniques that *deflate the liabilities*. Chapter 17, on Enron, shows that failure to detect unrecorded liabilities led to duped investors in the country's biggest ever bankruptcy.

**Guiding Principle:** *An enterprise has incurred a liability if it is obligated to make future sacrifices.*

---

Accounting Capsule

## Accruing Expenses

Suppose you have received something of value and you have received the invoice for it, but you have not yet paid for it. For example, suppose that on December 15 your attorney drafts a contract and remits an invoice. Here's the correct accounting entry:

---

| *Increase:* | Legal expense |
| *Increase:* | Accounts payable |

---

If you decide not to record this entry until after year-end, your profits will be inflated because legal expenses will be excluded.

---

## Technique No. 1: Failing to Record Expenses and Related Liabilities When Future Obligations Remain

The first technique boosts income by failing to record expenses and the related liabilities. Two companies that used this trick were Oxford Health Plan and Rent-Way.

### Oxford Health Plan (OHP)

In 1997, Oxford, a Delaware-based health maintenance organization (HMO), was having enormous problems with its newly installed computer system. It got so bad that OHP had no idea how much it was due in premium income and how much it owed to medical providers. As a result, OHP substantially understated its premium liabilities on the balance sheet.

After many complaints by the providers, the New York State Insurance Department began an investigation. By October 1997, it concluded the investigation; it imposed a $3 million fine, ordered a $50 million increase in reserves, and directed the company to terminate the employment of the CFO and other key personnel. That month, after the company announced a loss of $0.88 a share (rather than the previously estimated $0.47 gain), the value of Oxford's common stock dropped 62 percent (see Fig. 8-1). The following December, after Oxford announced an increase of $164 million in medical reserves and a loss for the quarter of $120 million, the stock dropped 15 percent.

**Warning Signs and Lessons from Oxford Health Plans.** Computer upgrades in September 1996 caused tremendous delays in generating premium bills, which severely restricted the company's ability to collect past premiums and negatively affected revenues and earnings.

The delays caused by the computer upgrade further created a backlog of unprocessed medical claims, which negatively affected the company's ability to determine medical liabilities and resulted in the company's underreserving to cover medical costs, which also inflated earnings.

Apparently, the underreporting of liabilities at OHP was unin-

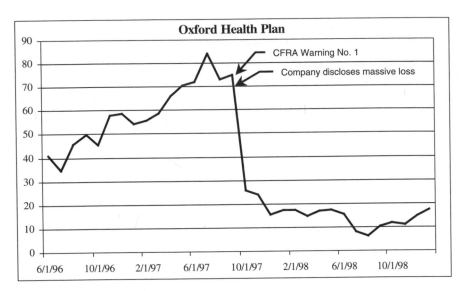

Fig. 8-1.  Oxford Health Plan Stock Price, June 1996–1998

tentional and the result of computer problems. In our next illustration, the misstatements were planned.

### Rent-Way

Several weeks before the close of its 1999 fiscal year, Rent-Way's accounting department stopped booking accounts payable and the related expenses. By doing this, Rent-Way artificially reduced expenses in fiscal 1999 by $28.3 million, and the following year the ploy cut expenses by $99 million. On October 30, 2000, Rent-Way disclosed accounting improprieties related to underreporting $127 million of expenses during the previous two years. The stock price plummeted 72 percent, to $6.50 from $23.44.

The scheme became known when the controller and chief accounting officer were away on vacation. The new chief financial officer discovered that Rent-Way's in-store inventory system indicated that there was less merchandise in the stores than in the accounting records.

Some liabilities require only footnote disclosure and have no impact on reported earnings. However, investors should pay close attention to any commitments and contingencies discussed in the footnotes or the management discussion and analysis section of the financial report. Sometimes unrecorded liabilities for commitments and contingencies are more serious than the liabilities reported on the balance sheet.

## Consider All Important Commitments and Contingencies

Clearly, existing obligations that have resulted from past transactions must be reported as liabilities, with a corresponding charge to an expense. Further, GAAP require that contingent liabilities be accrued in some circumstances. What about future commitments or contingencies that companies have? For instance, a company may have a long-term rental or purchase agreement. GAAP are less clear on these "future" liabilities, giving management greater flexibility. If these obligations are substantial and the company may be adversely affected by unfavorable terms in the agreements, a detailed footnote is the minimum required disclosure. When companies fail to provide all the details, investors and financial analysts must read between the lines to learn the full story.

Consider the case of Columbia Gas Systems. When Columbia released its first-quarter financial statements for 1991, most analysts were still bullish on the company and were recommending that clients buy it. Within weeks, Columbia dropped a bombshell, disclosing that it had a $1 billion gas supply problem and warning that it could be forced to file for bankruptcy. The market reacted quickly to this news: The stock price tumbled 40 percent—erasing $700 million in market capitalization in one day.

The company was criticized for having failed to highlight the significance of a future obligation to purchase a large amount of natural gas under a "take or pay' " contract. This contract obligated Columbia to purchase 200 billion cubic feet a year at above-market prices, for a total cost of about $125 million. As we later learned, after this contract was signed, gas prices plummeted, and Columbia's customers were opting for cheaper fuel. While Columbia had to live up to its commitments to producers, its utility customers were free to buy gas from the cheapest source.

## Question Whether Any Loss Contingencies Exist

Losses should be accrued for expected payments related to litigation, tax disputes, and so forth. GAAP require that companies accrue a loss when two conditions are both present: (1) There is a probable loss, and (2) the amount of the loss can be reasonably estimated.

---

Accounting Capsule

## Estimating a Loss Contingency

When both requirements for a contingent loss have been met, a loss should be accrued. For instance, assume that a company is about to lose in litigation and almost certainly will have to pay out $6,000. Since both conditions for accruing the loss are present, the following entry should be made:

| | | |
|---|---|---|
| *Increase:* | Loss from Litigation | $6,000 |
| *Increase:* | Estimated Liability | $6,000 |

Recording this transaction increases liabilities and reduces net income. Conversely, failing to record the transaction would overstate profits.

---

## Probe for a Troubled Company with Fixed Payments Coming Due

Many other companies have similar long-term commitments, particularly related to leases for facilities. These commitments can become a problem if business deteriorates and the company cuts back its operations. Such long-term commitments proved to be a major problem for computer vendor Businessland in early 1991. Its business declined significantly, and it still had to pay rent on dozens of facilities that it no longer occupied and for which it was unable to find tenants.

As companies downsize during the difficult economy in 2002, many will require less office space for their smaller number of employees. In analyzing such companies, remember to find out whether there are any long-term lease commitments that will continue. If there are, the cost of those commitments will be a drag on future periods' profits.

### Consider the Impact on Earnings of Unrecorded Stock Option Liabilities

Stock options granted to employees are one of the largest and most costly liabilities that are excluded from most companies' balance sheets. The enormous real economic impact of stock options on profits and cash flows is also hidden from investors. Much of this information, however, is contained in the accompanying footnotes.

During the decade of the 1990s, the granting of stock options became a popular tool for attracting and retaining employees. Even directors got into the act. Of 350 companies surveyed by William Mercer, a consultancy, 93 percent rewarded their directors with stock incentives; in 1992, only 63 percent did.

The dimensions of these unrecorded costs have only recently become known to investors. According to Bear, Stearns & Co. accounting analyst Pat McConnell, if options were fully expensed, the average earnings growth rate for companies in the Standard & Poor's 500 stock index would have been cut from 11 percent to 9 percent for the three years to mid-2000. Veteran short seller James Chanos of Kynikos Associates Ltd. calls the treatment of options "a national outrage . . . an ongoing shame."

These hidden expenses and inflated profits are more pronounced among technology companies. At Cisco, for example, expensing stock options would have reduced reported income by $1.1 billion, or 42 percent, in the year through July 2001. Furthermore, Cisco's three-year compounded earnings growth rate would have sunk to 33 percent from 41 percent.

Moreover, the actual cash costs that a company can incur to buy back shares to distribute to those who hold stock options is staggering. According to *The Economist*, between 1991 and 2000 Microsoft issued 1.6 billion shares as stock options and bought back 677 million shares to partly offset the equity dilution. The buyback cost was a whopping $16.2 billion. There is, however, a silver lining: Microsoft was able to claim a deduction on its tax return and received $12 billion in tax relief. Thus, for tax purposes Microsoft showed stock options as an enormous expense, yet it made no such revelation in the accounts it presented to shareholders. That's called winning the lottery—twice.

According to a study by Smithers and Company, if Microsoft had expensed its stock options, in 1998 it would have reported an almost unbelievable loss of $17.8 billion, rather than the profit of $4.5 billion that it did report. Smithers, which has crunched the numbers for America's biggest companies, found that if options had been properly accounted for when granted, the profits of large listed companies in 1998 would have been two-thirds lower.

Given the vast sums that managers make from stock options, it is a little surprising to find that companies who grant options do not appear to perform any better than those that do not. According to a study by the Harvard Business School, "Results indicate that no aspect of a company's pay-plan design predicts the company's performance." Instead, it suggested, "The primary reason for linking executive pay to performance may be to provide 'cover' for huge payouts to senior management."

In fact, it is possible to argue that stock options provide managers with an incentive that is diametrically opposed to the long-term interests of shareholders. The main reason is that stock options leave recipients free to buy or not to buy. If things go well, they will buy; if something goes wrong, they are free to pass, whereas shareholders may have to sell at a loss.

All the facts seem to suggest that stock options should be included in calculating profits. They are issued every year. The tax authorities treat them as tax-deductible expenses. According to the accounting rules, liabilities should be recorded in the year in which they are incurred. There is a widely accepted way of pricing options, first developed in 1973 by two economists, Fischer Black and Myron Scholes. And a financial institution that sold options would invariably record and hedge them at the time when they were written. Yet when the FASB tried a few years ago to change the rules so that options would be treated as an expense, it ran into fierce opposition from Silicon Valley.

## Technique No. 2: Reducing Liabilities by Changing Accounting Assumptions

This technique demonstrates some of the flexibility that management has in selecting accounting policies and estimates. Companies that provide pensions and other postretirement benefits to employees can change their assumptions in ways that reduce the recorded liability and related expense. Similarly, companies that lease equipment make a variety of estimates on such matters as residual value and interest rates that will have a bearing on the reported liability and expense. Airlines make estimates of unearned income related to frequent flyer points granted. Profits can be boosted (and liabilities reduced) by changing certain accounting or actuarial assumptions.

### Boosting Income by Changing Pension Assumptions

During a raging bull market, pension plans can become a fruitful source of extra earnings. Companies generally can't take money out of their pension funds, but by juggling several factors, including the actuarial present value of benefits, interest rates, and expected returns on assets, they can reduce or even eliminate the amount they have to pay into their plans in any given year and inflate profits. According to Gabrielle Napolitano, the accounting guru at Goldman, Sachs & Co., for example, IBM picked up $195 million (1.7 percent of pretax income) in 2000 when it raised the expected rate of investment return from 9.5 to 10 percent.

Similarly, Lucent obtained a boost to reported earnings in the December quarter as a result of a change in the manner in which it accounts for its pension and postretirement benefits plans. Lucent artificially boosted reported earnings by implicitly assuming an increase in the expected rate of return on plan assets.

Lucent recorded a pretax credit of $108 million during the December quarter, which reduced that period's pension and postretirement benefit expense; it recorded a one-time nonoperating pretax catch-up gain of $2.15 billion in the same December quarter to capture the adjustment for prior periods; and it will continue to record reduced pension and postretirement benefit expense in future periods. CFRA estimated that the December period boost constitutes an addition to LU's normal quarterly pension income of roughly $150 million.

## Boosting Income by Changing Lease Assumptions

Xerox (XRX) was having difficulty with its Mexican and South American leasing business. One assumption that lessors make when they compute revenue is the implicit interest rate. In South America's highly inflationary environment, lessors generally use a high assumed interest rate. Xerox changed to a lower assumed interest rate, thereby recording a much larger portion of revenue in the early years of a lease. (Chapter 14 discusses special challenges related to lease accounting issues.)

## Boosting Income by Changing Air Traffic Liability Assumptions

In 1993, Continental Airlines changed its estimate of unearned income, called "air traffic liability." This account represents the value of tickets sold for which air transportation has not yet been provided. The change increased revenue by $75 million.

# Technique No. 3: Releasing Questionable Reserves into Income

For companies, one of the benefits of taking special charges is that future-period operating income will be inflated because future costs will have already been written off through the charge. (This issue is covered in Chapter 10, "Shenanigan No. 7.") A second benefit of taking a special charge is that the liability created with the charge becomes a reserve that can be released into earnings in a later period. Technique No. 3, releasing questionable reserves into income, illustrates that the improved results after a restructuring charge sometimes prove to be illusory.

Various reserves appear on the balance sheet. Failing to maintain a sufficient amount of reserves or releasing reserves artificially inflates earnings. Chapter 7 discussed reserves related to assets.

Technique No. 3 of this chapter describes tricks related to liability reserves.

---

Accounting Capsule

## Release of Restructuring Reserve

Assume that the company announces a 1,000-person layoff with a severance package totaling $10 million.

| | | |
|---|---|---|
| *Increase* | Restructuring Expense | $10 million |
| *Increase* | Liability for Severance | $10 million |

Six months later, the layoffs have been completed, yet only 700 employees lost their jobs. The company eliminates the remaining liability and boosts income by reducing an expense:

| | | |
|---|---|---|
| *Decrease:* | Liability | $3 million |
| *Decrease:* | Expense | $3 million |

---

### Watch for the Release of Excess Reserves into Income

Sunbeam (SOC) was the master of this trick. When Al (Chainsaw Al) Dunlap became the new CEO, he ordered big restructuring charges. Later, the excess funds that had been placed in reserves were released into income. Until the fourth quarter of 1996, the reversals were fairly minimal: The company took into income only $500,000 in the first quarter, $4.5 million in the second, and $1.5 million in the third. However, with the year's final quarter a hopeless mess, Sunbeam opened the tap fully and poured $21.5 million from reserves into income. Shifting the reserves into income enabled SOC to disguise the calamitous erosion in the company's profit margins. It helped to cover up the deep discounts that Sunbeam had been giving to customers in order to stuff and load the retail channels. Had it not been for the reserve, the company's pretax margin would have collapsed in the quarter, falling to only 12.1 percent instead of the 18.5 percent reported. Instead of being up 26 percent to $388.1 million, Sunbeam's sales would have increased by only 7 percent.

Similarly, HBO & Co. (HBOC) set the stage for this shenanigan by recording a series of large special charges on a regularly recurring basis. It recorded a $95.3 million acquisition-related special charge during the December 1997 quarter. The charge included several items that *could* be considered normal, recurring operating expenses, such as a write-down of long-lived assets, product-related costs, and purchased R&D. In the June 1998 quarter, HBOC reversed $3.0 million of the reserve recorded in 1997 for product-related acquisition costs.

Medaphis (MEDA) used a different spin in its ploy to create and then release bogus reserves. In the first quarter of 1996, MEDA directed a subsidiary to reverse into income an accrual for vested employee bonuses of $1.4 million.

## Technique No. 4: Creating Sham Rebates

A less common ploy to artificially reduce expenses and inflate profits involves receiving sham rebates from suppliers. This trick needs the assistance of the supplier. Here's how it works.

Tell a supplier that you will agree to purchase $10 million of inventory over the next year. In exchange for this large order, you ask the supplier to pay a $1 million "rebate" upon signing the agreement. Then you record the rebate as a reduction of your expense (the cost of goods sold). The proper accounting would involve reducing the asset account Inventory, which will have no impact on profits during the current period. When the inventory is sold, of course, the cost of goods sold will be lower, and profits will rise.

In February 1999, the SEC sanctioned Sunrise Medical Inc. for a variety of accounting shenanigans initiated during fiscal years 1994 and 1995. One such scheme was to underreport expenses and inflate profits by receiving a bogus rebate from a supplier. Specifically, Sunrise contacted a supplier and worked out a deal to receive a $1 million rebate for purchases that had already been made during the fiscal year. What was in it for the supplier? Sunrise agreed to a price increase on purchases made in the next fiscal year to offset the rebate. A "side letter" was executed to seal this caper. Sunrise recorded the rebate as a decrease in 1995 expenses, without disclosing to investors or to the auditor that the supplier had tied the rebate to a price increase on future purchases.

## Technique No. 5: Recording Revenue When Cash Is Received, Even Though Future Obligations Remain

Companies use five main techniques to keep debt off the books and inflate profits. The first four deflate expenses, and the fifth inflates revenue.

Many businesses typically receive cash before they have actually earned it. Franchisers, for example, must often provide continuing services over several years, and airlines reward frequent flyers with free trips and other gifts. When companies such as franchisers or airlines fail to defer revenue and record a liability until it has been earned, profits are overstated, and the financial statements are misleading.

### Frequent Flyer Liability

Consider the accounting by airlines that offer frequent flyer points to passengers. A recent business trip to London earned me more than 10,000 frequent flyer points, roughly 25 percent of the 40,000 total needed for a free flight. In return for my purchase of an airline ticket, the airline received $800, but a portion of that amount should be deferred as a liability.

---

Accounting Capsule

## Recording Airline Revenue

| Correct Entry | | |
|---|---|---|
| *Increase:* | Cash | $800 |
| *Increase:* | Unearned revenue | $200 |
| *Increase:* | Revenue | $600 |
| Incorrect Entry | | |
| *Increase:* | Cash | $800 |
| *Increase:* | Revenue | $800 |

---

As the recording of airline revenue illustrates, deciding what portion of the cash received is earned and what represents a future obligation can be problematic. Although GAAP offer general guidance, interpretation of the specific facts is left to management. Unfortunately, management often has a bias toward understating liabilities or hiding them from investors and lenders. While the meaning and interpretations of revenue and liability appear clear and unambiguous in theory, many companies have difficulty separating the two in practice. For instance, when a company receives payment from a customer, the following question must be asked to determine whether to record that payment as revenue or as a liability: "Was this payment received in exchange for services that *we have already provided*, for which *we have no additional responsibilities*, and for which *the benefits (and risks) of ownership have already passed* to the buyer?" In short: "Has the payment *been earned?*" If the answer is yes, then revenue should be recorded; otherwise, a liability must be recorded.

### Ascertain That Cash Received Has Been Earned

Just as a liability should be set up for businesses that earn revenue over time (such as airlines and franchisers), a liability should be recorded if the "risks or benefits" have not passed to the buyer. As discussed in Chapter 4, when important contingencies (such as uncollectibility or possible returns and/or cancellations) still exist, no revenue should be recorded. Rather, a liability must be shown on the balance sheet. Thus, if a company records revenue while such contingencies still exist, revenue and profits have been overstated and liabilities understated.

## A Look Ahead

Shenanigans No. 1 through No. 5 all padded profits. The final two Shenanigans, No. 6 and No. 7, intentionally *understate current profits:* No. 6 by deflating revenue, and No. 7 by inflating expenses.

What are the motives?

The objective of underreporting profits is to benefit a later period in which the needs will be greater. Here are scenarios in which this strategy may be attractive.

- A very healthy company creates a reserve for a rainy day.
- A company that is about to be acquired intentionally holds back revenue until after the merger to benefit the acquirer.
- An acquisitive company tries to write off the costs from the acquisition (i.e., merger costs, in-process R&D) to relieve future periods of these expenses.
- A sick company tries to write off enormous asset costs (e.g., inventory or plant and equipment) to relieve future periods of these expenses.
- A healthy company accelerates future expenses into the current period.

Chapter 9 addresses techniques related to the first two scenarios; Chapter 10 considers the other three.

# 9

# SHENANIGAN NO. 6: SHIFTING CURRENT REVENUE TO A LATER PERIOD

The objective of Shenanigan No. 6 is to deflate current profits and shift them to a later period when the need for them is greater. Here are scenarios in which this strategy may be attractive.

- A very healthy company creates a reserve for a rainy day.
- A company that is about to be acquired intentionally holds back revenue until after the merger to benefit the acquirer.

There are two major techniques for doing this:

1. Creating reserves and releasing them into income in a later period
2. Improperly holding back revenue just before an acquisition closes

**Guiding Principle:** *Revenue should be recorded in the period in which it is earned. If service is provided in the current period, it is improper to report the revenue in a later period.*

## Technique No. 1: Creating Reserves and Releasing Them into Income in a Later Period

When business is booming and earnings are far exceeding Wall Street estimates, companies may be tempted to not report all their revenue, but instead to save some for a rainy day. Shifting profits from an already strong quarter to a future weaker one also helps companies "smooth" earnings.

Consider the Florida-based chemical company W. R. Grace. In the early 1990s, Grace's health care subsidiary experienced a significant and unanticipated increase in revenue as a result of changes in Medicare reimbursements. Senior management of that division deferred some of the unanticipated income by increasing or establishing reserves. The excess reserves ballooned to more than $50 million by the end of 1992. By creating and releasing some of these reserves during the 1991–1995 period, the health care subsidiary reported steady earnings growth of from 23 to 37 percent. The actual growth rates ranged from minus 8 percent to plus 61 percent.

When W. R. Grace sold this subsidiary in 1995, it released the entire excess reserve into income, labeling it a "change in accounting estimate."

### The Punishment

In December 1998, the SEC sued W. R. Grace, alleging that the company had diverted up to $20 million of 1991 and 1992 earnings into reserves. The suit charged that Grace had shifted the money back into income in later, weaker years.

### Warning Signs and Lessons from W. R. Grace

**Use of Excess Reserves.** At various times, former Grace senior management decided to release some of the company's excess reserves in order to increase Grace's earnings. For example, former Grace senior management directed NMC senior management to decrease its excess reserves in order to report an additional $1.5 million in income for the fourth quarter of 1994 because Grace

Table 9-1. Warning Signs: W. R. Grace

| Problem Indicated | Evidence | Shenanigan |
|---|---|---|
| **Aggressive Accounting:** Created reserves and released them into income in a later period | • Grace had its health care unit create bogus reserves. | No. 6 |
| **Aggressive Accounting:** Released questionable reserves into income | • Grace released some of the reserves when they were needed and then released the remainder when the unit was sold. | No. 5 |

needed the additional income for its consolidated results of operations (See Table 9-1).

**Reversal of the Excess Reserves.** In the second quarter of 1995, Grace's board of directors decided to dispose of the health care unit through a spin-off transaction. As a result, the group was reported as a discontinued operation on Grace's financial statements as of June 30, 1995 (see Fig. 9-1).

## Watch for Evidence of Postdating Shipping Documents

A few decades earlier, catsup king H. J. Heinz did not simply set up a reserve; it went much further to trick its shareholders. Some observers have speculated that Heinz employees were driven to their actions by the company's management incentive plan (MIP), which awarded bonuses largely on the basis of the net profit after tax (NPAT)—but only up to a certain level for each year. Once that level was achieved, there was no incentive to show any additional profit that year. Rather, there was an incentive to begin building up an "inventory of profit" for the next year. By holding back income (or prepaying expenses) in good years, when the NPAT goal had already been surpassed, managers were creating a "reserve" that could be tapped in bad years.

Public disclosure of its fraudulent financial statements was a

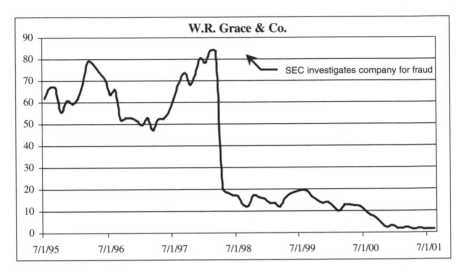

**Fig. 9-1.   Effect of Investigation on W. R. Grace Stock Price.**

serious, but only a temporary, setback for shareholders in Heinz. With new management and a renewed commitment to the integrity of the company's financial reporting, its stock price increased over 1,400 percent during the 1980s.

While Microsoft has received no challenge from SEC regulators, its enormous reserve buildup deserves some scrutiny.

During the last decade, Microsoft (MSFT) came to dominate not only software companies, but also the technology industry as a whole. Indeed, the company became so dominant that the U.S. Department of Justice sued it for using its monopoly illegally, to the detriment of American consumers.

Very healthy companies often have the ability to create accounting reserves that can shift current revenue to a later period when business growth might be slower. MSFT has had little difficulty exceeding Wall Street earnings' expectation and thus has had the opportunity to defer revenue to later periods.

## Warning Signs and Lessons from Microsoft

In the September 1999 quarter, Microsoft's cash flow from operation showed surprising weakness. A detailed examination of the company's deferred revenue growth, shown on the balance sheet,

Table 9-2. Microsoft's Unearned Revenue and Revenue, Quarterly Trend

| ($ millions, except %) | Q1, 9/99 | Q4, 6/99 | Q3, 3/99 | Q2, 12/98 | Q1, 9/98 | Q4, 6/98 | Q3, 3/98 |
|---|---|---|---|---|---|---|---|
| Beginning balance | 4,239 | 4,195 | 3,552 | 3,133 | 2,888 | 2,463 | 2,038 |
| Additions | 1,253 | 1,738 | 1,768 | 1,361 | 1,010 | 1,129 | 885 |
| Usage | (1,363) | (1,694) | (1,125) | (942) | (765) | (704) | (460) |
| Ending balance | 4,129 | 4,239 | 4,195 | 3,552 | 3,133 | 2,888 | 2,463 |
| Net addition (subtraction) | *(110)* | 44 | 643 | 419 | 245 | 425 | 425 |
| % change sequentially | *(2.6%)* | *1.0%* | 18.1% | 13.4% | 8.5% | 17.3% | 20.9% |

Table 9-3. Warning Signs: Microsoft

| Problem Indicated | Evidence | Shenanigan |
|---|---|---|
| **Operational problems** | • Sequential sales declined 6.6 percent in September 1999.<br>• Cash flow from operations lagged behind net income. | — |
| **Aggressive accounting:** Created reserves and released them into income in a later period | • MSFT's deferred revenue ballooned to over $4 billion, then declined. | No. 6 |

told an interesting story. Until the June 1999 quarter, Microsoft had apparently continued to add large amounts to its reserves, deferring billions in revenue to later periods (see Table 9-2). In the June 1999 quarter, the reserve grew by only a modest $44 million. In the September quarter, Microsoft released $110 million from the reserve. See Table 9-2 for a summary of Microsoft's aggressive accounting, and Fig. 9-2 for the effect on the stock price.

### Smoothing Income

Both W. R. Grace and Microsoft hoped to smooth out the often-unpredictable peaks and valleys in their businesses. Smoothing of income is not an uncommon strategy for management to engage in, as Wall Street rewards solid and predictable profit growth.

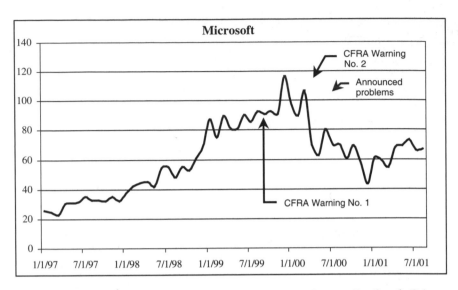

**Fig. 9-2.  Effect of Microsoft's Aggressive Accounting on Its Stock Price**

However, the use of reserves to shift income to a later period can be as serious an income manipulation ploy as front-end loading of revenue. In each case, the effect is to intentionally mislead investors and creditors. When revenue is front-end loaded, future years' income is recorded in the current year; conversely, with income smoothing, the current year's income is shifted to a future period. One result of income smoothing could be that companies that have been profitable for several years would defer part of each year's income by setting up a reserve. Then, when earnings begin to slump, they would be able to tap into the reserves and continue to report consistently high profit over the years.

While income smoothing (i.e., using reserves) arguably is not as egregious as shenanigans that overstate profits, investors, lenders, and auditors should be equally vigilant in searching for it. Consider the following case. A company has two outstanding years in a row. Expecting a slowdown in business, it sets up a reserve in year 2. In year 3, sales and cash flows decline steeply. The company taps into its reserve, and the financial statements show a healthy profit. Investors and others have been duped and will later be shocked when the company announces plant closings and a severe cash crunch. Had the company reported earnings more accurately, of course, the plant closings and cash crunch might have been equally unavoidable; but the investors (who are, after all, the *owners* of the company) would have had some advance warning. Another possible scenario, though, is more optimistic: An early warning system allows major investors the time to investigate problems and to work with management to correct them.

---

Accounting Capsule

## Creating a Reserve

Assume that a company made a cash sale for $900. The correct entry would be:

| | | |
|---|---|---|
| *Increase:* | Cash | $900 |
| *Increase:* | Sales Revenue | $900 |

This transaction increases both assets and revenue. An accounting trick that a company uses when it wants to defer some sales revenue until later is to record a liability initially and to wait until the following year to transfer the liability to revenue. This trick, also known as "setting up reserves," shifts income from a year in which a company may have a large profit to a later year in which profits are expected to be weaker.

The journal entries to set up and later tap a reserve are as follows.

| | | |
|---|---|---|
| For this year, | | |
| *Increase:* | Cash | $600 |
| *Increase:* | Deferred Revenue | $600 |
| For next year, | | |
| *Decrease:* | Deferred Revenue or Operating Expense | $200 |
| *Increase:* | Sales Revenue | $200 |

The result is that this year's sales revenue is recorded as having been earned in a later period.

---

# Technique No. 2: Improperly Holding Back Revenue Just Before an Acquisition Closes

### How to Make a New Friend

Imagine that you recently signed an agreement to sell your business, with the closing in two months. You also receive instructions to refrain from booking any more revenue until the merger is consummated. Somewhat baffled, you comply and record no more revenue. In so doing, you have made a friend for life, as the two months of revenue you held back will be released by the acquiring company.

**Be Alert for Companies Holding Back Revenue Just Before an Acquisition.**  In the second quarter of 1996, Medaphis acquired an information technology provider and consulting firm based in Texas. Before the completion of the acquisition, Medaphis directed the Texas firm to make entries that improperly reduced its income for the first quarter of 1996 by $2.5 million by *decreasing revenues and increasing reserves.* In June 1996, Medaphis instructed the Texas firm, now a wholly owned subsidiary, to reverse this $2.5 million reserve into income. The improper reversal of the Texas firm's reserve into income materially inflated Medaphis's consolidated earnings in the second quarter of 1996.

After the initial instruction from Medaphis to establish the $2.5 million reserve, the accounting staff at the Texas firm began preparing two sets of financial statements, one for internal use and a second set for reporting to Medaphis. The financial statements included in this second set of books became part of Medaphis's consolidated financial statements, which were filed with the Securities and Exchange Commission and reported to shareholders.

Software giant Computer Associates International (CA) benefited when Platinum Technologies (PLAT) apparently held back a substantial portion of profits just before merging by deferring certain revenue for recognition in a future period. During the March quarter of 1999, PLAT's revenue plunged to its lowest level in seven quarters, falling by more than $144 million sequentially and by more than $23 million from the year-ago period (see Table 9-4). PLAT attributed the sharp decline to delays beyond the end of

Table 9-4. PLAT Revenue ($ millions), Quarterly Trend

| Q1, 3/99 | Q4, 12/98 | Q3, 9/98 | Q2, 6/98 | Q1, 3/98 | Q4, 12/97 | Q3, 9/97 | Q2, 6/97 |
|---|---|---|---|---|---|---|---|
| 170.1 | 314.7 | 250.3 | 217.4 | 193.4 | 242.7 | 190.8 | 164.2 |

the quarter in the closing of customer contracts as a result of the proposed acquisition of the company by CA. As a result, CA probably obtained an artificial boost to future revenue (as the contracts signed subsequent to the March period were reported by the combined company).

## A Look Ahead

Chapter 10 describes other techniques to inflate tomorrow's profits—taking large one-time charges today.

# 10

# SHENANIGAN No. 7: SHIFTING FUTURE EXPENSES TO THE CURRENT PERIOD AS A SPECIAL CHARGE

*The sun'll come out tomorrow, bet your bottom dollar that tomorrow there'll be sun!*
*Annie*, Broadway show

When companies face troubled times because of business slowdowns and other setbacks, their managers frequently take certain (bookkeeping) steps to ensure that the sun will come out tomorrow. They may shift future-period expenses into the current dismal period as a special charge, thereby relieving tomorrow's earnings of those burdens. Chapter 10 discusses three techniques for accomplishing that goal and guaranteeing that the sun will come out tomorrow:

1. Improperly inflating the amount included in a special charge
2. Improperly writing off in-process R&D costs from an acquisition
3. Accelerating discretionary expenses into the current period

*Guiding Principle:* Expenses should be charged
against income in the period in which the benefit is
received.

## Technique No. 1: Improperly Inflating the Amount Included in a Special Charge

Special charges offer a wonderful opportunity to artificially boost future operating profits. Simply announce a large special charge, inflating the amount to include future operating expenses. Profits in future periods will be higher, since those periods' expenses were included in the earlier period's charge. Pretty sneaky—but it works! And few questions are asked about what's included in the special charge.

Suppose you are a new CEO who has come aboard to help turn around a company with big problems. Such executives typically receive rich stock option incentive packages to improve company performance. What can you do to guarantee that performance improves?

During your first few weeks on the job, announce some bold initiatives to clean up the mess left by your predecessor. Include in your announcement reorganizations, downsizing, and writing off overvalued assets from the balance sheet. The larger the amount, the better. Oh, and remember to report this big write-off as a "special charge." If you do that, investors will look the other way and ignore the charge in valuing the company's stock today. When tomorrow comes, you will report much improved profits, since many of tomorrow's costs had already been written off as part of the special charge.

### The Saga of Chainsaw Al Dunlap

That's how Sunbeam's Al Dunlap managed to look so smart—at least for a while. When Dunlap arrived in July 1996, Sunbeam was a struggling company. Dunlap had a reputation as a turnaround artist.

During the 18 months in which he headed the Scott Paper Company, Dunlap drove up the stock price by 225 percent, increasing the company's market value by $6.3 billion. The company was then sold to Kimberly-Clark for $9.4 billion, with Dunlap pocketing $100 million as a going-away present. During his short stay at Scott, Dunlap fired 11,000 employees, slashed expenditures on plant improvements and research, and then sold the company to a major rival. Wall Street cheered as Scott became the sixth company sold or dismembered by Dunlap since 1983.

The day Sunbeam announced that Dunlap would be the new CEO, the share price jumped 60 percent, the largest one-day jump in the company's history (see Fig. 10-1). A Wall Street analyst was so excited by the hiring of Dunlap that he said, "This is like the Lakers signing Shaquille O'Neal."

By 1997, the apparent turnaround had begun to impress investors. The stock, which had been $12.50 the day before Dunlap's hiring was announced, peaked at $45 in early 1998. Dunlap was given a new contract, doubling his base salary to $2 million per year.

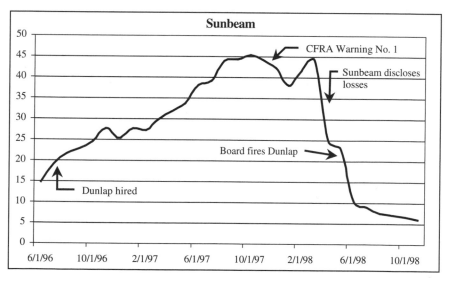

**Fig. 10-1.   Sunbeam Stock Price, 1996–1998**

Then the truth became known. On April 3, 1998, the stock plunged 25 percent to $34.63 when the company disclosed a loss for the quarter. Two months later, negative statements in the press about the company's sales practices prompted Sunbeam's board to begin an internal investigation. This resulted in the termination of Al Dunlap and the CFO and extensive restatement of earnings from the fourth quarter of 1996 through the first quarter of 1998. The restatement wiped out half the reported 1997 profits. The company subsequently filed for protection under Chapter 11 of the U.S. Bankruptcy Code.

In a May 2001 enforcement release, the SEC charged that from the last quarter of 1996 until June 1998, SOC had created the illusion of a successful restructuring to "inflate its stock price and thus improve its value as an acquisition target." The commission found that management had created $35 million in improper restructuring reserves and other "cookie jar" reserves, which were released into income the following year.

## Warning Signs and Lessons from Sunbeam

Signs of aggressive accounting practices became evident shortly after Dunlap took over, with excessive write-offs and reserves being taken late in 1996 (see Table 10-1). Other warning signs in-

Table 10-1. Warning Signs: Sunbeam

| Problem Indicated | Evidence | Shenanigan |
|---|---|---|
| **Aggressive accounting:** Improperly inflated the amount included in a special charge | • SOC created $35 million in reserves with a special charge. • SOC created a litigation reserve. | No. 7 |
| **Aggressive accounting:** Released questionable reserves into income | • SOC inflated 1997 profits by releasing bogus reserves. | No. 5 |
| **Aggressive accounting:** Recorded bogus revenue | • Company recorded bill and hold sales in 1997. | No. 2 |

cluded reserves being released into income, receivables growing much faster than sales, cash flow from operations plummeting, and gross margins growing faster than seemed possible in this type of business.

**Watch for Excessive Charges Shortly After a New Chief Executive Arrives.** During the December 1996 quarter, SOC recorded a special charge of $337.6 million for restructuring and another $12 million charge for a media advertising campaign and "one-time expenditures for market research." According to the SEC lawsuit, the 1996 restructuring charge was inflated by at least $35 million, and Sunbeam also improperly created a $12 million litigation reserve.

**Watch for Declines in Reserves.** Having taken excessive charges and created bogus reserves, Sunbeam was able to release those reserves into income.

**Watch for Receivables Growing Much Faster than Sales.** One warning sign on Sunbeam's balance sheet was the rapid rise in receivables relative to sales. Receivables jumped 59 percent, whereas sales increased only 16 percent (see Table 10-2).

**Remain Alert for Plummeting Cash Flow from Operations (CFFO).** Even more troubling was the fact that Sunbeam was bleeding cash while reporting a spectacular increase in operating income. Run-

Table 10-2. Sunbeam's Operational Performance

| ($ in millions) | 9 months 9/97 | 9 months 9/96 | % Change |
|---|---|---|---|
| Revenue | 830.1 | 715.4 | 16% |
| Gross profit | 231.1 | 124.1 | 86% |
| Operating income | 132.6 | 4.0 | 3215% |
| Receivables | 309.1 | 194.6 | 59% |
| Inventory | 290.9 | 330.2 | 12% |
| CFFO | −60.8 | −18.8 | |

ning a $60 million cash flow deficit with reported operating income of $132 million defies credibility.

**Watch for Gross Margins Growing at an Unrealistic Pace.** The sudden improvement in gross margins also stretched the limits of believability. Rarely do gross margins increase by 1,000 basis points in one year. Sunbeam's jumped from 17.3 percent to 27.8 percent.

While most special charges pertain to severance payments and plant closings, companies sometimes write off inventory, intangible assets, or even accounts receivable.

### More Common During Tough Times

You don't have to be a new CEO to understand the joy of magically making future-period costs disappear. The slowing economy and weak stock market in 2001 resulted in numerous special charges that will lead to inflated earnings in future periods. It's pretty easy to play this game. In April 2001, Cisco announced two enormous special charges (see Table 10-3). The first one, of up to $1.2 billion, is for the cost of laying off workers, closing buildings, and erasing goodwill from its balance sheet. The other is to write off $2.5 billion of excess inventory, primarily raw materials that Cisco says have zero value. Will Cisco sell the inventory or use it in products later? When asked this question, a Cisco spokesperson

Table 10-3. Cisco's April 28, 2001, Special Charge

|  | ($ in millions) |
| --- | --- |
| In-process R&D | $109 |
| Payroll tax on stock option exercises | 10 |
| Amortization of goodwill and other acquisition-related charges | 346 |
| Restructuring costs and other special charges | 1,170 |
| Excess inventory charge | 2,249 |
| Total (pretax effect) | **$3,884** |

said that the inventory is worthless and "we have no plans to use it, period." However, the spokesperson also indicated that the items that had been written off might be used and sold in the future if there was a pickup in demand. If Cisco were to sell items of inventory that had been written off, it would boost income because cost of goods sold on a product written off would be zero.

Like Cisco, Toys 'R' Us accumulated excess inventory that the company had failed to sell. In February 1996, TOY announced its decision to take a $395 million (pretax) charge to cover the cost of "strategically repositioning" the merchandise assortment that was offered at the stores, as well as closing twenty-five stores and consolidating three distribution centers. CFRA warned that TOY might have bundled into the charge normal operating costs that would otherwise have been included as normal operating expenses in future periods. The portion of the charge that was related to repositioning of inventory amounted to $184 million. The company explained that the inventory was removed from the stores and sold at lower prices through alternative distribution channels. Normally, the inventory would be written down to the net realizable value and the difference charged as an operating expense.

**Watch for Large Goodwill Write-offs.**    During the difficult economy of 2001, some companies wrote off the cost of previous acquisitions. In July 2001, JDS Uniphase (JDSU) wrote off an almost incomprehensible $44.8 billion from acquisitions, almost all of which was goodwill. However, JDSU found a way to keep most of the write-off from ever hitting its earnings. *It allocated $38.7 billion (86 percent) of the write-off to the previous quarter* (Shenanigan No. 4, Technique No. 2, Changing accounting policies and shifting current expenses to an earlier period).

**Be Alert for Unusual Write-offs — Accounts Receivable.**    Special charges for layoffs and inventory write-offs have become fairly routine. Charges for accounts receivables write-offs are infrequent and should be viewed with skepticism.

An accounts receivable charge suggests that the related revenue recorded may be bogus. In June 2000, Appnet (later acquired by Commerce One) announced strong sales for the quarter. It also announced an accounts receivable restructuring charge. What happened? The company recorded revenue during the period, but it never collected the money once the customers declared bankruptcy.

Appnet decided that it was proper to keep the revenue on its books, knowing full well it would never collect. Strange! This is the equivalent of me billing a dead man for services and counting that as revenue!

### Remove Nasty Future Hit to Earnings

Taking a one-time charge helped AOL out of a messy situation in 1996. It was facing the prospect of amortizing close to $400 million of deferred marketing costs over the next two years. Earnings would have collapsed, along with the company's stock price. AOL had a big problem and needed a clever solution. And it found one. On October 29, 1996, AOL announced that as of September 30, 1996, it would write off the entire $385 million of deferred marketing acquisition costs. AOL stated that the write-off was necessary to reflect changes in its evolving business model, including reduced reliance on subscribers' fees as the company developed other revenue sources.

## Technique No. 2: Improperly Writing Off In-Process R&D Costs from an Acquisition

The first technique comes in handy for a newly appointed CEO or for a company that is hitting the skids. The big write-off games also work great for acquisitive companies. It's real easy to do: Just write off as much of the purchase price as possible and convince your auditor that you are just trying to be "conservative."

### Writing Off In-Process R&D Costs from an Acquisition

Lucent made numerous acquisitions and wrote off much of the acquisition cost, calling it "acquired in-process R&D." Of the $4.2 billion paid for ten recent acquisitions, the company wrote off $2.4 billion (58 percent of the cumulative purchase price) as in-process R&D. These write-offs will have the effect of reducing operating expenses in the current and future periods and thereby boosting reported operating and net income.

The game of writing off huge amounts of the acquisition price reached epic proportions during the late 1990s. Sometimes it got to an absurd level. Consider General Instrument and Compaq Computer.

**General Instrument Corporation (GIC).** In September 1995, upon acquiring Next Level Communications, GIC *wrote off more than 100 percent of the purchase price.* Specifically, GIC paid $93 million and wrote off as "purchased research and development" $140 million— 150 percent of the purchase price.

**Compaq (CPQ).** Compaq's June 1998 acquisition of the struggling Digital Equipment Corporation created many challenges— one of which was stretching the limits of acceptable accounting.

Generally, under a "purchase" acquisition, the acquirer will be saddled with goodwill that must be amortized against future-period earnings (until 2002, when new rules become effective). CPQ figured out how to inflate future-period earnings by creating "negative" goodwill. If goodwill will adversely affect future-period earnings with an "amortization expense," the company reasoned, then it should follow that "negative goodwill" should boost future-period earnings with a "negative amortization expense"—income.

Let's look at CPQ's accounting. CPQ paid $9.1 billion for DEC and allocated $13.2 billion for tangible and intangible assets (over liabilities). This exceeded the purchase price by $4.1 billion. CPQ also assigned a whopping $5.7 billion to "purchased in-process R&D." Because of the large portion of the acquisition cost that was written off, the $9.1 billion paid was considerably below the tangible and intangible net assets acquired. The $4.1 billion shortfall is the "negative goodwill."

Under accounting guidelines, negative goodwill should be allocated among the noncurrent assets (of the acquired company), reducing their value. Accordingly, CPQ reduced the value of the long-term assets by $4.1 billion. By writing down the value of such long-term assets, future-period income is boosted (because of the lower depreciation or amortization expense).

Several other merger-related charges in recent years proved to be controversial, as well. Consider U.S. Robotics's charge just before being acquired by 3Com and Walt Disney's acquisition of ABC.

**U.S. Robotics (USRX).** USRX provided 3Com (COMS) with a wonderful welcoming gift just before the two parties closed on a merger. Specifically, the $426 million "merger-related" charge taken during August 1997 would lift COMS operating income for a number of future periods. Of the total charge, $92 million related to the write-off of fixed assets, goodwill, and purchased technology. Naturally, writing off these assets will reduce future-period depreciation and amortization expense and increase net income. COMS also wrote off $121 million related to eliminating duplicate products and for the return of discontinued products in the distribution channel.

**The Walt Disney Company (DIS).** Disney created a $2.5 billion reserve to cushion losses connected with its 1995 acquisition of ABC. In a report published in *Barron's*, accounting professor Abraham Briloff asserted that the reserve masked Disney's costs and expenses from its $19 billion purchase of Capital Cities/ABC Inc. in early 1996. Briloff argued that without it, Disney's 25 percent earnings increase in the fiscal year ended September 30, 1997, would have been sliced 10 percent. Briloff also argued that Disney has largely exhausted the reserve and that it might now run into difficulties in keeping up profits.

## Taking a Big Acquisition-Related Charge Could Be a Sign of Real Problems

Sometimes big charges related to acquisitions are real and represent a new obligation for the acquiring company. That was the case when CUC acquired Ideon.

Not only did CUC inherit a company with operational problems, but it acquired numerous litigation liabilities. Ideon was involved in thirteen lawsuits, in the vast majority of which it was the defendant. Twelve of the lawsuits involved Peter Halmos, Ideon's former chairman, executive management consultant, and co-founder. As a result of this substantial litigation, CUC took a $125 million charge upon acquiring Ideon to reserve for related liabilities.

### A New Twist to One-Time Write-offs: Offering Stock Warrants

New-economy companies have learned to use their stock and stock warrants in a variety of clever ways. Priceline.com (PCLN) took a charge for the value of stock warrants given to participating airlines in lieu of future-period cash payments to the airlines. Here's the deal. To secure a business relationship with airline and hotel partners, PCLN must pay those partners. If a partner accepts stock warrants in lieu of cash, future-period income will be inflated because PCLN writes off the entire amount immediately as a special charge. Specifically, PCLN recorded "one-time" charges in the amount of $88 million during the September 2000 quarter and expects to record additional charges in excess of $1.1 billion in the fourth quarter for warrants to purchase 20 million shares of PCLN common stock issued to airlines participating in PCLN's airline ticket service.

CFRA believes that such costs may be more appropriately classified as ongoing expenses over the life of the respective agreements than as "one-time" items, since they appear to represent the normal cost of doing business with such partners. Thus, PCLN is ridding itself of what could be considered normal operating costs in future periods by recording those costs as one-time expenses (during periods in which the company is already incurring significant losses).

## Technique No. 3: Accelerating Discretionary Expenses into the Current Period

If a company has already met its income projections for the current period, it may attempt to shift next year's expenses into that period. Heinz, in addition to improperly shifting income, was found guilty of prepaying expenses to boost the next year's profit. One of its subsidiaries engaged in other ploys as well, such as misstating its cost of sales, improperly soliciting bills from vendors for advertising, and expensing invoices for services that had not yet been received.

## Be Alert for Prepayment of Operating Expenses

In one of the more ingenious moves in recent years, a senior executive at a large New York–based company ordered his subordinates to do whatever they could to incur expenses by the end of the year. Profits were going to be robust no matter what he told them, so it would be wise to save a little for an encore the following year. One middle manager bought $12 million worth of postage metering, an item that could be deducted immediately even though the benefits would endure through millions and millions of letters (at today's postal rate, over 35 million letters).

## Be Concerned When the Depreciation or Amortization Period Decreases

In Chapter 7, we illustrated how a company could boost its profits simply by depreciating or amortizing certain assets over a longer period of time. Conversely, if the objective is to defer some of the current year's profits until the future (i.e., to shift expenses into the current period), a company might depreciate fixed assets and amortize intangibles and leasehold improvements over a shorter period of time.

## Watch for Accelerating of Depreciation Expense by Changing Accounting Estimates

IBM implemented an accounting change for the depreciable lives of personal computers. Under a new asset management strategy being implemented by the company, PCs will be replaced, on average, every three years rather than every five years. The company currently, on average, depreciates PCs used internally over five years. This change in depreciable lives better reflects the expected useful life of PCs within IBM. As a result, the company recorded an after-tax charge of approximately $241 million.

## A Look Back . . . and Ahead

Chapters 4 through 10 identified seven categories of financial shenanigans and thirty techniques. Since companies that perpetrate
these tricks try to hide that fact, detecting early warnings is essential.

Chapter 11 discusses databases that can be used to screen for
financial shenanigans. Chapter 12 illustrates techniques for analyzing financial reports, focusing on signs of accounting abnor-
malities.

# PART THREE
# TECHNIQUES FOR DETECTING SHENANIGANS

# 11
# DATABASE SEARCHES

There are a variety of commercial databases that allow you to screen for signs of operational deterioration and evidence of financial shenanigans. Some products focus more on the numbers (quantitative) found on the financial reports; others allow you to probe the narrative (qualitative) in the footnotes, management discussion and analysis, and press releases. Even if you use none of these services, you can screen your own portfolio using the techniques described in this chapter.

## Quantitative Screening

The commercial database that is most widely used for quantitative screening is Compustat, a product sold by McGraw-Hill's Standard & Poor's division. A derivative of this product that bundles other databases as well is sold by Factset Corporation. If you have access to such products, consider running screens to identify the companies with:

- The steepest decline in cash flow from operations (CFFO) relative to net income
- The greatest year-over-year sales growth, followed by declining or negative sequential growth
- The greatest growth in receivables relative to sales
- The largest bulge in inventory relative to sales and to cost of sales

- The biggest or smallest deterioration in gross margins
- Big increases in "soft" assets
- Big increases in deferred revenue

The following examples show how these screens would have alerted investors to some serious accounting and operational problems at companies that later suffered big share price declines. Q0 represents the most recent quarter; Q-1 represents one quarter earlier.

## Operating Cash Flows Lagging Behind Net Income (See Table 11-1)

Table 11-1. CFFO versus Net Income (Excluding Nonrecurring Charges)

| ($ in millions) | Q0 | Q-1 | Q-2 | Q-3 | Q-4 |
|---|---|---|---|---|---|
| Oxford Health Plan | −121.4 | −57.4 | −27.3 | 114.0 | 97.1 |
| Rite-Aid | −158.7 | −99.8 | 82.6 | 206.2 | 2.9 |

## Sequential Sales Declining (see Table 11-2)

Table 11-2. Sequential Sales Growth Slowing

| (Percentage) | Year-over-Year | Q0 | Q-1 | Q-2 | Q-3 | Q-4 |
|---|---|---|---|---|---|---|
| Microsoft | 28.4% | −6.6% | 18.8% | −1.7% | 17.8% | 5.0% |
| Cambridge Technology Partners | 50.3% | 2.9% | 8.1% | 13.5% | 19.0% | — |

## Receivables Growing Faster or Slower Than Sales (See Table 11-3)

Days' sales outstanding (DSO) is a commonly used measure of bloated receivables. The calculation of DSOs is a two-step process. First take the sales and divide by the average accounts receivable balance for the year, giving you the number of times receivables turn over in a year. Then take 365 days and divide by the number of turns to get the DSOs.

Table 11-3. Accounts Receivable Growing Substantially Faster (or Slower) than Sales

| (Days' Sales Outstanding) | Q0 | Q-1 | Q-2 | Q-3 | Q-4 |
|---|---|---|---|---|---|
| Sabratek | 168 | 106 | 104 | 119 | 121 |
| Cambridge Technology Partners | 73 | 104 | 91 | 89 | 81 |
| Wireless Facilities | 45 | 54 | 32 | 21 | 10 |

## Inventory Rising Faster than Cost of Sales (See Table 11-4)

Days' sales in inventory (DSI) is a commonly used measure of bloated inventories. The calculation of DSIs is also a two-step process. First take the cost of goods sold and divide by the average inventory balance for the year, giving you the number of times inventory turns over in a year. Then take 365 days and divide by the number of turns to get the DSIs.

Table 11-4. Bulge in Inventory Relative to Cost of Goods Sold (DSI)

| (Days' Sales in Inventory) | Q0 | Q-1 | Q-2 | Q-3 | Q-4 |
|---|---|---|---|---|---|
| Sabratek | 407 | 282 | 239 | 273 | 241 |

## Gross Margins Turning Sharply Higher or Lower (See Table 11-5)

Table 11-5. Gross Margins Rising or Declining Rapidly

| (Percentage) | Q0 | Q-1 | Q-2 | Q-3 | Q-4 |
|---|---|---|---|---|---|
| Sunbeam | 29.4% | 30.7% | 25.9% | 20.9% | 19.1% |
| Compaq | 21.5% | 22.7% | 23.5% | 23.9% | 23.6% |

## Big Jump in Soft Assets (See Table 11-6)

Soft assets include prepaid expenses, other current assets, and other assets.

Table 11-6. Big Jump in Soft Assets

| ($ in millions) | Q0 | Q-1 | Q-2 | Q-3 | Q-4 |
|---|---|---|---|---|---|
| Cambridge Technology Partners (prepaid expenses) | 16.7 | 14.2 | 2.0 | 3.8 | 3.3 |
| Baan (prepaid expenses and other assets) | 146.7 | 72.3 | 52.8 | 41.8 | 35.9 |

## Big Decline in Deferred Revenue (See Table 11-7)

Table 11-7. Change in Deferred Revenue

| ($ in millions) | Q0 | Q 1 | Q 2 | Q 3 | Q 4 |
|---|---|---|---|---|---|
| Microsoft | −110.0 | 44.0 | 643.0 | 419.0 | 245.0 |
| Microstrategy | 11.3 | 15.2 | 12.3 | 11.4 | 10.0 |
| Wireless Facilities | 3.4 | 9.5 | 11.1 | 5.2 | 2.0 |

# Qualitative Screening

Reading financial statements takes quite a bit of time, and most people wouldn't consider it a fun activity. Therefore, investors should use products that allow them to screen financial reports and press releases for terms, account titles, etc., that provide early signs of problems. The low-cost choices can be found on the Web at *http://www.10kwizard.com* or *http://www.edgar-online.com*. A more comprehensive and expensive alternative is using the Lexis/Nexis service.

Here are some of the more valuable things to search for using these qualitative screening databases. Try these phrases in searches.

• Change in accounting estimate or principle
• Offering customers financing or extended credit terms

- Changes in accounting policies
- Changes in account classification
- Change in auditors
- Extended payment terms
- Percentage of completion
- Unbilled receivables
- Bill and hold
- More liberal credit terms
- Insider stock sales
- Decline in backlog
- Layaway sales
- Nonmonetary transactions
- Related-party transactions

## Using the Screens in Tandem

The use of both quantitative and qualitative screens may provide additional insights that are not found when either type of screen is used exclusively. For example, in the Compustat screens, Cambridge Technology Partners (CATP) exhibited two curious (and apparently unrelated) issues: Prepaid expenses jumped (see Table 11-8), and receivables (as measured in DSOs) declined dramatically (see Table 11-9). Using the Lexis/Nexis database for qualitative screens, we searched for and found reference to a *change in account classification*. Now, with both the quantitative and qualitative data, we were able to determine that CATP had "solved" its problem of expanding DSOs by reclassifying almost $13 million of receivables as "prepaid expenses."

Table 11-8. Quarterly Prepaid Expense Balance ($ in millions)

| Q1, 3/97 | Q4, 12/96 | Q3, 9/96 | Q2, 6/96 | Q1, 3/96 |
|----------|-----------|----------|----------|----------|
| 16.7     | 14.2      | 2.0      | 3.8      | 3.3      |

Table 11-9. DSO Improvement

| 12/96 | 9/96 | 6/96 | 3/96 | 12/95 |
|-------|------|------|------|-------|
| 73    | 104  | 91   | 89   | 81    |

## A Look Ahead

Chapter 12 provides a detailed case study analyzing the Mini-Scribe Corporation. The techniques used are vertical and horizontal analyses of common-size financial reports, studying the footnotes, and comparing cash flow from operations with net income.

# 12

# Analyzing Financial Reports

Chapter 11 focused on screening across many companies for characteristics that indicate operating or accounting problems. Now we are ready to drill down to the analysis of a specific company. Chapter 12 discusses various techniques for analyzing and interpreting a company's financial reports. Here are the three major steps:

1. Create and analyze the common-size balance sheet and statement of operations.
2. Carefully read the footnotes and other qualitative information.
3. Compare cash flow from operations and net income.

## The Fraud at MiniScribe

In early 1987, MiniScribe Corporation, a fast-growing manufacturer of disk drives, filed with the SEC documents for a large debt offering. The company had just completed a very stunning turnaround from its dismal results in 1985. MiniScribe successfully floated the offering, and its future looked rosy. But a black cloud was hanging over the company, although the truth would not become known until two years later: MiniScribe had "cooked its books." According to a report issued by the Independent Evalu-

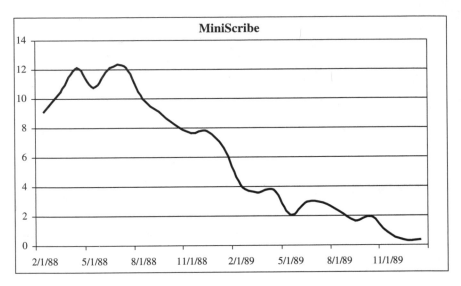

**Fig. 12-1**

ation Committee of its board, MiniScribe had falsified inventory and sales figures, using a series of bizarre methods ranging from altering the numbers in the auditors' report to delivering shipments of bricks to distributors and reporting $4.3 million worth of "disk-drive sales." The effect on the stock price when this became known is shown in Fig. 12-1.

Using only the published financial reports of MiniScribe and basic analytical techniques, let's compile a list of warning signs. To begin analyzing the balance sheet and income statement, first use a technique known as common-size analysis.

---

Accounting Capsule

## Common-Size Analysis

Common-size analysis is a technique that enables analysts to determine the component makeup of a company's balance sheet and income statement in relation to a critical component (total assets or total sales). When this technique is used in conjunction with a balance sheet, all balance sheet items will be represented as a percentage of total assets. When it is used in conjunction with the income statement, all items will be represented as a percentage of net sales or revenues. This type of analysis can give important clues concerning a company's financial health and profitability. Common-size analysis can either be vertical or horizontal.

In vertical analysis for a given year, all balance sheet items are expressed as a percentage of total assets and all income statement items as a percentage of net sales. This technique enables analysts to quickly spot structural changes in the balance sheet or income statement over a period of time. For example, if inventory represented 20 percent of total assets in Year 1 and jumped to 28 percent in Year 2, an analyst could quickly spot that change using vertical analysis. Generally, the percentages remain fairly stable over time.

Horizontal analysis develops trends in balance sheet or income statement percentages over time. A particular year is designated the base year and percentage changes in subsequent years are computed. Generally, the percentage change in sales would also be reflected in the percentage change in expense accounts and in working capital accounts on the balance sheet.

---

## Create a Common-Size Balance Sheet and Income Statement

Let's look at the balance sheet and income statement and see what warning signs were flashing after the company released its 10-K in March 1987. The middle column (%Δ) of numbers will be used for the horizontal analysis, and the two right-hand columns (% of assets and % of sales) will be used for the vertical analysis. Notice, for example, that inventories grew 100.46 percent (from $22.5 million to $45.1 million) and now represent 32.95 percent of assets ($45.1 divided by $136.88), up from 27.49 percent ($22.5 divided by $81.87).

The common-size balance sheet (and the related pie charts in Figs. 12-2 and 12-3) for 1985 and 1986 reveals several incredible and troubling changes: a shrinkage in cash and equivalents from 28.4 percent of assets to 11.9 percent, a jump in accounts receivable from 19.6 percent of assets to 29 percent; and bloated inventory that rises from 27.5 percent of assets to 32.9 percent. Such large structural changes on a balance sheet are rare and should raise suspicions.

The common-size statement of operations (see Table 12-2) includes information that will be helpful in doing vertical and horizontal analysis.

Table 12-1. Consolidated Balance Sheet — MiniScribe Corporation and Subsidiaries

| ($ in thousands) | 1986 | 1985 | Horizontal % | Vertical % of Assets 1986 | Vertical % of Assets 1985 |
|---|---|---|---|---|---|
| **ASSETS** | | | | | |
| Current assets | | | | | |
| Cash and cash equivalents | 16,329 | 23,244 | −29.75% | **11.93%** | **28.39%** |
| Accounts receivable, less allowance for doubtful accounts of $736 and $752 | 39,766 | 16,041 | **147.90%** | **29.05%** | **19.59%** |
| Inventories | 45,106 | 22,501 | **100.46%** | **32.95%** | **27.49%** |
| Other current assets | 936 | 239 | **291.63%** | 0.68% | 0.29% |
| Total current assets | 102,137 | 62,025 | 64.67% | 74.62% | 75.76% |
| Property and equipment, net | 33,606 | 19,588 | 71.56% | 24.55% | 23.93% |
| Other assets | 1,13 | 253 | **348.22%** | 0.83% | 0.31% |
| Total assets | 136,877 | 81,866 | 67.20% | 100.00% | 100.00% |
| **LIABILITIES & EQUITY** | | | | | |
| Accounts payable | 37,160 | 12,228 | **203.89%** | **27.15%** | **14.94%** |
| Current portion of long-term debt | 946 | 1,74 | −45.69% | 0.69% | 2.13% |
| Accrued compensation and related expenses | 2,82 | 1,74 | 61.51% | 2.06% | 2.13% |
| Accrued warranty expense | 1,37 | 2,08 | −34.04% | 1.00% | 2.54% |
| Other current liabilities | 4,38 | 3,27 | 33.96% | 3.20% | 4.00% |
| Total current liabilities | 46,686 | 21,073 | 121.54% | 34.11% | 25.74% |
| Long-term debt | 23,877 | 20,771 | 14.95% | 17.44% | 25.37% |
| Preferred stock, $1.00 par value | 118 | 133 | −11.28% | 0.09% | 0.16% |
| Common stock, $0.01 par value | 226 | 193 | 17.10% | 0.17% | 0.24% |
| Common stock warrants | 7 | 15 | −53.33% | 0.01% | 0.02% |

Table 12-1. (*Continued*)

| ($ in thousands) | 1986 | 1985 | Horizontal % | Vertical % of Assets 1986 | Vertical % of Assets 1985 |
|---|---|---|---|---|---|
| Capital contributed in excess of par value of pre- ferred and com- mon stock | 65,348 | 62,021 | 5.36% | 47.74% | 75.76% |
| Notes receivable from officers col- lateralized by common stock | — | (260) | — | −0.19% | — |
| Treasury stock, at cost, 2,000 shares | (16) | — | — | −0.01% | — |
| Retained earnings (accumulated deficit) | 631 | (22,080) | −102.86% | 0.46% | −26.97% |
| Total stockholders' equity | 66,314 | 40,022 | 65.69% | 48.45% | 48.89% |
| Total liabilities and equity | 136,877 | 81,866 | 67.2% | 100% | 100% |

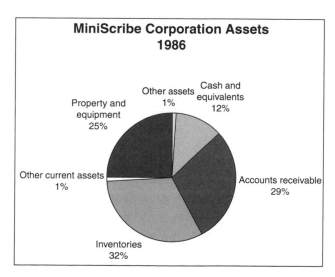

Fig. 12-2

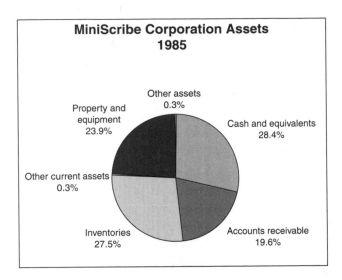

**Fig. 12-3**

**Warning Signs (WS) Found Using Vertical Analysis.**   Vertical analysis allows analysts to quickly spot structural changes among balance sheet and statement of operation accounts. The pie charts help to highlight important changes from 1985 to 1986.

**WS No. 1:** *Receivables represent a much larger percentage of total assets.* Receivables jumped from 19.6 percent of assets to 29.0 percent of assets from 1985 to 1986.

**WS No. 2:** *Inventories represent a much larger percentage of total assets.* Inventories jumped from 27.5 percent of assets to 32.9 percent from 1985 to 1986.

**WS No. 3:** *Cash and equivalents represent a much smaller percentage of total assets.* Cash and equivalents plummeted from 28.4 percent of assets to 11.9 percent from 1985 to 1986.

**WS No. 4:** *Gross margins expanded by an astounding amount.* From 1985 to 1986, gross margins jumped from 2.20 percent to 25.38 percent (a tenfold improvement). Gross margins tend to remain fairly stable over time. An increase of this magnitude should have raised the highest concerns.

**WS No. 5:** *There was a big improvement in selling expense relative to sales.* Selling, general, and administrative expenses as a per-

Table 12-2. Consolidated Statement of Operations — MiniScribe
Corporation and Subsidiaries

| ($ in thousands, except per share data) | 1986 | 1985 | Horizontal % | Vertical % of Sales 1986 | Vertical % of Sales 1985 |
|---|---|---|---|---|---|
| Net sales | 184,861 | 113,951 | **62.23%** | 100.00% | 100.00% |
| Cost of sales | 137,936 | 111,445 | 23.77% | 74.62% | 97.80% |
| Gross profit (margins) | 46,925 | 2,500 | 1772.51% | **25.38%** | **2.20%** |
| Selling, general, and administrative expenses | 14,459 | 12,217 | 18.35% | 7.82% | 10.72% |
| Research and development | 8,550 | 4,200 | 103.50% | 4.63% | 3.69% |
| Total operating expenses | 23,014 | 16,421 | 40.15% | 12.45% | 14.41% |
| Income (loss) from operations | 23,911 | (13,915) | −271.84% | 12.93% | −12.21% |
| Other income | 1,290 | 708 | 82.34% | 0.70% | 0.62% |
| Other expenses | (2,142) | (3,174) | −32.51% | −1.16% | −2.79% |
| Income (loss) before income taxes and extraordinary credit | 23,060 | (16,381) | −240.77% | 12.47% | −14.38% |
| Provision for income taxes | 2,770 | 392 | 608.93% | 1.50% | 0.34% |
| Income (loss) before extraordinary credit | 20,281 | (16,773) | −220.91% | 10.97% | −14.72% |
| Extraordinary credit— reduction of income taxes from utilization of tax loss carryforward | 2,430 | | | 1.31% | 0.00% |
| Net income | 22,711 | (16,773) | −235.40% | 12.29% | −14.72% |
| **Income (loss) per share** | | | | | |
| Income (loss) before extraordinary credit | $0.50 | ($0.88) | −163.64% | | |
| Extraordinary credit | $0.00 | | | | |
| Net income (loss) | $0.60 | ($0.88) | −171.59% | | |
| Common and common equivalent shares used in computing per share amounts | 35,982 | 19,026 | 89.12% | | |

centage of sales declined from 10.72 percent to 7.82 percent. Such a big improvement may result from capitalizing normal operating costs (Shenanigan No. 4).

**Warning Signs (WS) Found Using Horizontal Analysis.**  Horizontal analysis highlights growth in sales relative to growth in key asset and expense accounts.

**WS No. 6:** *Receivables were growing faster than sales.* Sales grew 62 percent, yet accounts receivable shot up 148 percent.

**WS No. 7:** *Inventory was growing faster than sales.* Inventory shot up 100 percent. Moreover, the work-in-process and finished goods inventory grew by 153 percent. The big increase in inventories relative to sales may be evidence of a failure to write down obsolete inventory (Shenanigan No. 4).

**WS No. 8:** *Inventory was growing faster than cost of sales.* Other evidence of an inventory problem can be found by comparing inventory growth to the growth in cost of sales. Inventory grew 100 percent, while cost of sales grew 24 percent.

**WS No. 9:** *There was a big decline in the cash balance.* Cash and equivalents declined 29.75 percent while sales jumped 62 percent. Increased sales should translate into increasing cash and equivalents.

**WS No. 10:** *Other current assets and other assets were growing much faster than sales.* Another sign of capitalizing operating costs (Shenanigan No. 4) can be fast growth in "soft assets" like other current assets and other assets. These accounts spiked up (292 percent and 348 percent, respectively) in 1986.

**WS No. 11:** *Accounts payable grew much faster than inventory.* Accounts payable jumped 203.89 percent (a rate twice as fast as inventory growth), a perplexing fact. Perhaps the accounts payable include certain other items. An interview with management often sheds light on such issues.

**WS No. 12:** *Selling, general, and administrative expense (SG&A) grew much more slowly than sales.* Although sales grew 62 percent, SG&A advanced only 18 percent. Major improvements in SG&A and cost of goods sold relative to sales could be evidence of capitalizing operating costs (Shenanigan No. 4) or of improperly inflating revenue (Shenanigan No. 1 or No. 2).

**Warning Signs (WS) Found in Footnotes to the Financial Reports.** The footnotes sometimes indicate problems that are not found in the numbers. We found several warning signs in MiniScribe's footnotes. Where pertinent, we include the precise language from the footnote.

**WS No. 13** *MiniScribe released various inventory reserves into income.*

In 1985, MiniScribe increased its reserve for excess inventory as a result of general decline in the demand for micro-winchester drives and severe price competition. In 1986, this reserve was reduced by $2.1 million as a result of a general improvement in demand and the ability of the Company to sell the inventory at higher prices than had been anticipated (Shenanigan No. 4, Technique No. 5).

**WS No. 14** *MiniScribe released accounts receivable reserves into income:* Despite the fact that gross receivables increased 141 percent (from $16.79 million to $40.50 million), MiniScribe lowered its reserve for bad debts. Had the company increased the bad debt expense and reserve in line with the growth in receivables, the reserve would have increased to $1.81 million from the reported $0.736 million (Shenanigan No. 4, Technique No. 5).

**WS No. 15** *MiniScribe released plant and equipment reserves into income.*

In 1985, the Company established a reserve of $1.3 million to provide for excess manufacturing capacity, predominantly leasehold improvements and manufacturing equipment. In 1986, this reserve was reduced as the Company began to fully utilize its manufacturing capacity (Shenanigan No. 4, Technique No. 5).

**WS No. 16** *MiniScribe was in violation of a lending covenant.*

At December 28, 1986, the Company was in violation of one of the financial ratio covenants of the revolving credit facility. Subsequent to December 28, 1986, the Company was in violation of certain covenants related to the timely submission of certain financial information to the banking group. The banking group has waived these violations without requiring any modifications to the terms and conditions of the agreement.

**WS No. 17** *MiniScribe was under SEC investigation.*

On January 14, 1987, the Company was advised that it is the subject of an informal inquiry by the Securities and Exchange Commission. The Company has no reason to believe that the outcome of the inquiry will have a materially adverse effect upon the financial condition of the Company.

Little did MiniScribe know how "material" the results would be.

**WS No. 18** *There were related-party transactions.*

A director of the Company is also a director of Xidex Corporation, from which the Company formerly purchased substantially all of its thin film media and some of its oxide media. During 1986 and 1985, the Company's purchases from Xidex totaled approximately $12.2 million and $3.2 million, respectively. Purchases from Xidex prior to 1985 were not significant. Additionally, the Company's Chairman of the Board and Chief Executive Officer is Chairman of the Board of Silicon General, Inc., from which the Company purchases certain microchips. During 1986 and 1985, the Company's purchases from Silicon General totaled approximately $1.7 million and $1.2 million, respectively. Purchases from Silicon General prior to 1985 were not significant.

**WS No. 19** *The company made loans to its officers.*

Also, during 1984, the Company issued shares of Common Stock subject to stock restriction agreements to certain officers of the Company in exchange for noninterest or interest-bearing notes. The notes from each officer were collateralized by the related shares. Payment terms ranged from one to four years and shares vested during that time period.

**WS No. 20** *The company was facing pending litigation.*

In October 1986, Rodime, Inc. and Rodime PLC (Rodime) filed a complaint in the United States District court for the District of Colorado initially charging MiniScribe with infringement of United States Patent No. 4,568,988. In February 1987, Rodime amended the complaint and added an additional patent (United States patent No. 4,368,383) accused to be infringed by MiniScribe.

Litigation arising from the accounting fraud would later doom the company.

**WS No. 21** *Long-term debt increased, yet interest expense decreased.*

Interest expense for the years ended December 28, 1986, December 29, 1985, and December 30, 1984, which is included in other expenses in the consolidated statements of operations, was approximately $2,142,000, $3,010,000, and $948,000, respectively. The decrease in interest expense might be a sign that interest was being capitalized (Shenanigan No. 4).

**Warning Signs (WS) Found in the Statement of Cash Flows.** Although in 1987 companies were not required to prepare a statement of cash flows, cash flow from operations (CFFO) could have been derived from MiniScribe's statement of changes in financial position.

**WS No. 22** *CFFO materially lagged behind net income.*

Ominously, CFFO lagged behind net income by over $14 million in 1986 (see Table 12-3).

Table 12-3. CFFO vs. Net Income

| ($ in thousands) | Fiscal 1986 | Fiscal 1985 |
|---|---|---|
| CFFO | 8,543 | (21,654) |
| Net income | 22,711 | (16,773) |
| CFFO—net income | (14,168) | (4,881) |

## Analysis of the Statement of Cash Flows

Since the issuance of SFAS No. 95 by the FASB in 1987, companies have been required to include a statement of cash flows along with the balance sheet and statement of operations. We will use as an illustration the statement of cash flows that Oxford Health Plans filed shortly before the stock price imploded in October 1997 (see Table 12-4).

### Analysis of Oxford Health Plans

**Compare Cash Flow from Operations and Net Income.** Oxford Health Plans' June 1997 statement of cash flows provided a screaming warning sign of a problem. Let's compare the CFFO and net income during the first six months of 1996 with those for 1997. In 1996, Oxford's business generated positive cash flow of $139.19 million, exceeding net income by $98.2 million. The performance in 1997 was horrible; Oxford had a net cash outflow of $107.25 million, although net income jumped to $71.55 million. As a result, CFFO − net income plummeted by $277.02 million, from positive $98.21 to negative $178.81, from 1996 to 1997 (see Table 12-5, page 198).

Interestingly, until the December 1996 quarter, Oxford's CFFO comfortably exceeded net income. In fact, from September 1994 until that quarter, CFFO had never fallen below the reported net income (see Fig. 12-4, page 198). Then, in December 1996, OHP reported the first of three successive quarters in which CFFO lagged behind net income. By the June 1997 quarter, the deficit had reached $121.41 million (net income $37.18 million, CFFO negative $84.23 million). No one should have been surprised when the share price imploded in October 1997, *sinking 42 points in one day.*

### Analysis of Rite Aid Corporation

Another horrific accounting fraud of the late 1990s, that of drug chain Rite Aid Corporation, could have been detected through an examination of the statement of cash flows and the ominous recent trend in the numbers found there. (The effect of the discovery of

Table 12-4. Oxford Health Plans, Inc. and Subsidiaries Consolidated Statements of Cash Flows Increase (Decrease) in Cash and Cash Equivalents Six Months Ended June 30, 1997 and 1996 (in Thousands)

|  | 1997 | 1996 |
|---|---|---|
| **Cash flows from operating activities:** | | |
| Net earnings | **$ 71,554** | **40,975** |
| Adjustments to reconcile net earnings to net cash | | |
| Depreciation and amortization | 27,491 | 20,124 |
| Deferred income taxes | 3,865 | 180 |
| Realized gain on sale of investments | (7,477) | (2,655) |
| Equity in net loss of affiliate | 1,020 | 2,050 |
| Other, net | 240 | 240 |
| Changes in assets and liabilities: | | |
| Premiums receivable | (106,702) | (26,941) |
| Other receivables | 7,020 | (3,351) |
| Prepaid expenses and other current assets | 738 | (1,056) |
| Medical costs payable | (92,122) | 126,975 |
| Trade accounts payable and accrued expenses | 20,235 | 9,553 |
| Income taxes payable | 17,500 | 14,772 |
| Unearned premiums | (46,572) | (41,277) |
| Other, net | (4,041) | (402) |
| **Net cash provided (used) by operating activities** | **(107,251)** | **139,187** |
| **Cash flows from investing activities:** | | |
| Capital expenditures | (42,730) | (29,896) |
| Purchases of available-for-sale securities | (304,867) | (446,373) |
| Sales and maturities of available-for-sale securities | 416,415 | 166,399 |
| Investments in unconsolidated affiliates | (20,564) | (6,305) |
| Other, net | 394 | 115 |
| **Net cash provided (used) by investing activities** | **48,648** | **(316,060)** |
| **Cash flows from financing activities:** | | |
| Proceeds from issuance of common stock | — | 220,541 |
| Proceeds from exercise of stock options | 10,252 | 6,243 |
| **Net cash provided by financing activities** | **10,252** | **226,784** |
| Net increase (decrease) in cash and cash equivalents | **(48,351)** | **49,911** |
| Cash and cash equivalents at beginning of period | 72,160 | 58,450 |
| Cash and cash equivalents at end of period | **$ 23,809** | **108,361** |

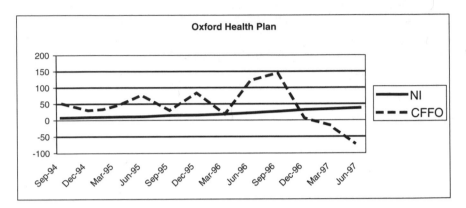

**Fig. 12-4. Oxford Health Plan CFFO and NI, September 1994–June 1997**

Table 12-5. Oxford Health Comparison of CFFO
and Net Income

|  | June 1997 | June 1996 |
| --- | --- | --- |
| CFFO | −107,251 | 139,187 |
| Net income | 71, 554 | 40,975 |
| CFFO—net income | −178,805 | 98,212 |

this fraud on the stock price can be seen in Fig. 12-5.) Despite reporting solid year-over-year net income growth during the May and August periods in 1998, the company's strong operating cash flow surpluses from 1997 were transformed into deficits during 1998 (see Fig. 12-6). As shown in Table 12-6, CFFO plunged to *negative* $77.5 million in the August quarter from *positive* $63.5 million in the year-earlier period, and to negative $9.0 million from $151.6 million for the May quarter. As a result, CFFO trailed net income by more than $150 million for the quarter and by over $250 million for the six months ended August 1998 (see Table 12-7). In contrast, CFFO had *exceeded* net income during the corresponding prior-year periods.

## Other Warning Signs on the Statement of Cash Flows

In addition to enabling an evaluation of the CFFO relative to net income, the statement of cash flows contains valuable informa-

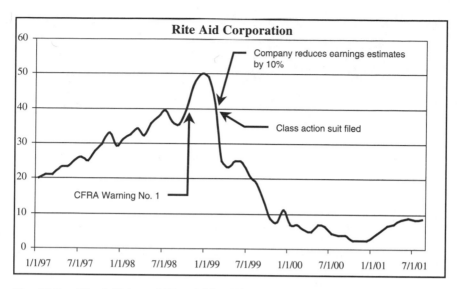

Fig. 12-5.   Stock Price of Rite Aid, 1997–2001

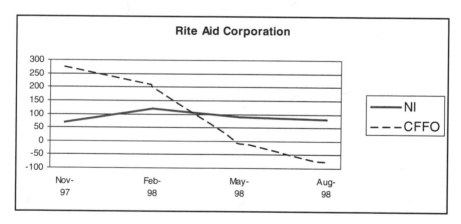

Fig. 12-6.   Onset of Rite Aid Deficits During 1998

tion concerning the sources and uses of cash. Among the warning signs to watch for are cash flow generated mainly from sale of assets, additional borrowing, and selling stock. In contrast, an attractive profile would include sufficient CFFO to cover capital expenditures and debt repayment, and perhaps to retire some of the company's outstanding (treasury) stock. Ideally, a company with such a profile can use CFFO to fund its future growth without

Table 12-6. Cash Flows from Operations (CFFO) versus Net Income (NI), Year-over-Year Comparison

| ($ in millions) | Q2, 8/98* | Q2, 8/97 | Q1, 5/98 | Q1, 5/97 | Q4, 2/98 | Q4, 2/97 | Q3, 11/97 | Q3, 11/96 |
|---|---|---|---|---|---|---|---|---|
| CFFO | (77.5) | 63.5 | (9.0) | 151.6 | 202.3 | 103.9 | 274.1 | 9.6 |
| NI | 81.2 | 60.6 | 90.8 | 68.2 | 119.7 | 55.2 | 67.9 | 37.4 |
| CFFO − NI | (158.7) | 2.9 | (99.8) | 83.4 | 82.6 | 48.7 | 206.2 | (27.8) |

*Adjusted to exclude effect of $289.7 million ($173.8 million after tax) nonrecurring charge. Excludes extraordinary loss of $45.2 million.

Table 12-7. CFFO versus NI, 6-Month and 12-Month Cumulative Results

| ($ in millions, except %) | 6 Months, 8/98 | 6 Months, 6/97 | 12 Months, 8/98* | 12 Months, 8/97 |
|---|---|---|---|---|
| CFFO | (86.5) | 215.1 | 389.9 | 328.6 |
| NI | 172.0 | 128.8 | 359.6 | 221.4 |
| CFFO − NI | (258.5) | 86.3 | 30.3 | 107.2 |

*Adjusted to exclude effect of $289.7 million ($173.8 million after tax) nonrecurring charge.

taking on additional debt or diluting its earnings per share (EPS) with additional stock offerings.

## A Look Ahead

While the financial reports of MiniScribe, Oxford Health Plans, and Rite Aid provided investors with many warning signs, the list of warning signs found there is far from complete. The Appendix to Chapter 12 following provides detailed checklists of warning signs. Chapters 13 and 14 discuss special areas of concern: acquisition accounting tricks and revenue recognition problems.

## Appendix. Comprehensive Checklist of Warning Signs

Balance Sheet and Statement of Operations

| Warning Sign | Problem Indicated or Shenanigan Used |
|---|---|
| 1. Cash and equivalents decline relative to total assets | Liquidity issues; may need to borrow |
| 2. Receivables grow substantially faster than sales | Perhaps aggressive revenue recognition—recording revenue too soon or granting extended credit terms to customers |
| 3. Receivables grow substantially slower than sales | Receivables may have been reclassified as another asset category |
| 4. Bad debt reserves decline relative to gross receivables | Underreserving and inflating operating income |
| 5. Unbilled receivables grow faster than sales or billed receivables | A greater portion of revenue may be coming from sales under the percentage-of-completion method |
| 6. Inventory grows substantially faster than sales, cost of sales, or accounts payable | Inventory may be obsolete, requiring a write-off; company may have failed to charge the cost of sales on some sales |
| 7. Inventory reserves decline relative to inventory | Underreserving and inflating operating income |
| 8. Prepaid expenses shoot up relative to total assets | Perhaps improperly capitalizing certain operating expenses |
| 9. Other assets rise relative to total assets | Perhaps improperly capitalizing certain operating expenses |
| 10. Gross plant and equipment increases sharply relative to total assets | Perhaps capitalizing maintenance and repair expense |
| 11. Gross plant and equipment declines sharply relative to total assets | Failing to invest in new plant and equipment |

Balance Sheet and Statement of Operations (*Continued*)

| Warning Sign | Problem Indicated or Shenanigan Used |
| --- | --- |
| 12. Accumulated depreciation declines as gross plant and equipment rises | Failing to take sufficient depreciation charge—inflating operating income |
| 13. Goodwill rises sharply relative to total assets | Perhaps tangible assets were reclassified to goodwill to avoid expensing them in future periods |
| 14. Accumulated amortization declines as goodwill rises | Failing to take sufficient amortization charge—inflating operating income |
| 15. Growth in accounts payable substantially exceeds revenue growth | Failed to pay off current debts for inventory and supplies—will require larger cash outflow in future period |
| 16. Accrued expenses decline relative to total assets | Perhaps company released reserves—inflating operating income |
| 17. Deferred revenue declines while revenue increases | Either new business is slowing or company released some reserves to inflate revenue |
| 18. Cost of goods sold grows rapidly relative to sales | Pricing pressure results in lower gross margins |
| 19. Cost of goods sold declines relative to sales | Company may have failed to transfer the entire cost of the product from inventory |
| 20. Cost of goods sold fluctuates widely from quarter to quarter relative to sales | Unstable gross margin could indicate accounting irregularities |
| 21. Operating expenses decline sharply relative to sales | Perhaps improperly capitalizing certain operating expenses |
| 22. Operating expenses rise significantly relative to sales | Company may have become less efficient, spending more for each unit sold |
| 23. Major portion of pretax income comes from one-time gains | Core business may be weakening |

## Balance Sheet and Statement of Operations (*Continued*)

| Warning Sign | Problem Indicated or Shenanigan Used |
|---|---|
| 24. Interest expense rises materially relative to long-term debt | Higher cash outflow expected |
| 25. Interest expense declines materially relative to long-term debt | Perhaps improperly capitalizing certain operating expenses |
| 26. Amortization of software costs grows more slowly than capitalized costs | Perhaps improperly capitalizing certain operating expenses |

## Statement of Cash Flows

| Warning Sign | Problem Indicated or Shenanigan Used |
|---|---|
| 1. CFFO materially lags behind net income | Quality of earnings may be suspect or expenditures for working capital may have been too high |
| 2. Company fails to disclose details of cash flow from operations | Company may be trying to hide the source of the operating cash problem |
| 3. Cash inflows come primarily from asset sales, borrowing, or equity offerings | Signs of weakness, especially if cash comes exclusively from asset sales, borrowing, or equity offerings |

## Narrative: Footnotes, Management Discussion, Proxy, Auditor's Letter

| Warning Sign | Problem Indicated or Shenanigan Used |
|---|---|
| 1. Change in accounting principle | Attempt to hide an operating problem |
| 2. Change in accounting estimate | Attempt to hide an operating problem |
| 3. Change in accounting classification | Attempt to hide an operating problem |
| 4. Change in auditor | Sign of risky client |
| 5. Change in CFO or outside counsel | Sign of risky client |
| 6. Investigation by the SEC | Could lead to accounting restatements |

Narrative: Footnotes, Management Discussion, Proxy, Auditor's
Letter (*Continued*)

| Warning Sign | Problem Indicated or Shenanigan Used |
|---|---|
| 7. Long-term commitments/contingencies | Potentially large drain on cash reserves |
| 8. Current or potential litigation | Potentially large drain on cash reserves |
| 9. Liberal accounting policies | Financial reports may inflate profits |
| 10. Misguided management incentives | May lead to some financial shenanigans to boost profits, bonuses, and share price |
| 11. Weak control environment | Creates easy opportunities to perpetrate financial shenanigans |
| 12. Auditor's concern | Sign of risky client |
| 13. Promotional management | May be more likely to use financial shenanigans than more modest executives |
| 14. Use of percentage of completion accounting | Revenue may be inflated |
| 15. Use of bill and hold accounting | Revenue may be inflated |
| 16. Overreliance on a few customers | Potential business problem if one of them leaves |
| 17. Financial problems at key customer | Business can be hurt if a key customer files for bankruptcy |
| 18. Seller finances customer | Revenue may be inflated and business may be much weaker than you realized |
| 19. Customer has right of return | Revenue may have been recorded too soon |
| 20. Barter transaction | Revenue may have been inflated |
| 21. Seller gives customer stock warrants | Revenue may have been inflated |
| 22. Capitalized interest or software | Operating income may be inflated |
| 23. Unrecorded liabilities, such as stock options | Future cash obligations may be greater than expected and operating income may be inflated |

## Narrative: Footnotes, Management Discussion, Proxy, Auditor's Letter (*Continued*)

| Warning Sign | Problem Indicated or Shenanigan Used |
|---|---|
| 24. Noncompliance with debt covenant | Bank may call loan, causing a substantial cash crunch |
| 25. Absence of unaffiliated directors on board | Weak control environment may create opportunities for management to perpetrate financial shenanigans |
| 26. Prepayment of future periods' operating expenses | Leads to inflated operating income in future periods |

## Checklist 1: Possible Signs of Misleading Financial Statements

| Choosing accounting policies | Too liberal |
|---|---|
| Changing accounting policies | Unjustified |
| Deferring expenses | Profits are overstated |
| Income smoothing | Profits are understated |
| Recognizing revenue too soon | Profits are overstated |
| Underaccruing expenses | Profits are overstated |
| Changing discretionary costs | Manipulating profits |
| Low quality controls | Risk of shenanigans |
| Changing auditor | Risk of shenanigans |
| Taking a "big bath" | Future profits are boosted |

# PART FOUR
# PROBLEM AREAS

# 13
# ACQUISITION ACCOUNTING TRICKS

Investors generally pay a premium for fast-growing companies. To turbocharge their growth, companies may acquire other companies. That strategy is fraught with risks for investors. This chapter identifies tricks used in connection with acquisitions that camouflage the underlying health of the acquiring company.

1. Rolling up unprofitable companies
2. Shifting losses to a stub period
3. Taking big write-offs before and after acquisitions
4. Releasing reserves created through big write-offs
5. Changing the allocation of the purchase price after an acquisition
6. Recording revenue related to the acquiring company
7. Labeling pooling as immaterial
8. Giving stock or warrants as an inducement for future purchase commitments

What do Cendant, McKessonHBOC, and many of the largest financial debacles of the last decade have in common? First, they used aggressive acquisition strategies to augment slowing sales. Then they used some acquisition accounting tricks to further camouflage the continued deterioration in the business. This chapter describes eight such tricks used in conjunction with acquisitions.

## Rolling Up Unprofitable Companies

Historically, acquisitions provided a vehicle that enabled companies to quickly expand into new markets or sell new products. The alternative, of course, was to rely solely on internal (or organic) growth. Hence, companies evaluated a "make-or-buy" decision. Let's call such acquisitions *strategic*.

A new type of acquisition strategy arose during the 1990s: the roll-up. Unlike companies making strategic acquisitions, companies using this strategy attempted to purchase hundreds of small companies within an industry (generally paying for them with stock) to create a large national chain of companies within that industry. The roll-up strategy touched such diverse industries as medical practices, accounting firms, office supply companies, and funeral homes. Notable roll-ups included Republic Industries (auto dealerships), Service Corporation of America (funeral homes), Sysco (food service companies), and Waste Management (garbage).

The acknowledged "king of roll-ups" was Washington, D.C.-based Jonathan Ledecky. He apparently also had many of the skills of a magician. Specifically, he would take small, weak, unprofitable companies, combine them, and immediately make the combined company profitable—at least for a short time, while the price of the stock shot up. Let's see how these investments panned out for other investors and see the magical formula for instant profit.

In four years, he reportedly had gone from financing his first venture with $250,000 on his credit cards to amassing a personal fortune worth $200 million. He hatched the idea of rolling his single-contract stationer with five others, selling stock to the public, and becoming a major player in the office supplies business. Thus U.S. Office Products (USOP) was born, and it was fed by rolling up 220 smaller outfits. In late 1997, USOP was a star, with surging sales and earnings. Its shares had more than quadrupled since its going public two and a half years earlier. The following year, sales slowed and the company reported a loss. The stock dropped to $5.375, half its February 1995 offering price.

That, in a nutshell, is the fate of most roll-ups. Despite the eventual collapse of USOP, Ledecky started several other roll-ups funded by Consolidation Capital, a $500 million blind pool from investors. These included a florist chain, USA Floral, an equipment financing company, UniCapital, and a heating and ventilation company, Building One Services. All met the same fate as USOP. Early investors (mainly Ledecky) made a lot of money, while later investors got wiped out as each company spiraled downward into bankruptcy.

By the end of the 1990s, investors had finally learned their lesson about the risk of roll-ups. Borrowing up to the hilt to roll up small, unprofitable companies was no problem during the go-go 1990s. Making those companies profitable is the trick. No one has found the magic formula for consistently making money using the roll-up game. Roll-ups often succumb to the weight of the high-cost debt used to acquire companies. And, other than the creator of the roll-up, who always seems to cash out early, investors generally suffer enormous losses.

In Chapters 9 and 10, we discussed two tricks to boost future periods' profits: shifting current revenue to a later period (Shenanigan No. 6) and shifting future expenses to the current period as a special charge (Shenanigan No. 7). Those tricks come in real handy for a company that is attempting to show higher earnings after the merger. The following acquisition accounting tricks produce that desired result.

## Shifting Losses to Stub Period

When companies with different year-ends merge, one of the companies may create a "stub period" to account for the month(s) before the acquisition. Assume, for example, the target company has an October year-end and the acquisition will close the following January 1. The target will report to investors results for the two-month stub period.

Watch for big losses buried in the stub period. Revenue may have been held back or expenses accelerated. Consider the pecu-

Table 13-1. Sales, USRX

| Two Months, 5/97 | Q2, 3/97 | Q1, 12/96 | Q4, 9/96 | Q3, 6/96 |
|---|---|---|---|---|
| 15.2 | 690.2 | 645.4 | 611.4 | 546.8 |

liar results included in the two-month stub period of U.S. Robotics (USRX) just before it merged into 3Com (COMS).

USRX reported a minuscule $15.2 million of revenue for the stub period (approximately $7.6 million per month), a tiny fraction of the company's recent sales level (see Table 13-1). During the March 1997 quarter, in contrast, USRX recorded $690.2 million, (or approximately $230 million per month).

It appears that COMS may have included in its August 1997 quarter revenue that USRX deferred during the stub period. Specifically, it appears that COMS may have taken advantage of the different reporting year ends of the two companies and *deferred revenue* from the two-month "stub period" of April–May 1997 to the August quarter.

If you can use the stub period to hold back revenue (Shenanigan No. 2, Technique No. 5), why not also use this period to accelerate future-period expenses as a one-time charge? USRX already thought of that trick. Specifically, the $426 million "merger-related" charge taken during the 1997 third quarter would lift COMS's operating income for a number of future periods. Of the total charge, $92 million was related to the write-off of fixed assets, goodwill, and purchased technology. Naturally, by writing off these assets, the company reduced future-period depreciation and amortization expense and thus increased net income. COMS also wrote off $121 million related to eliminating duplicate products and for the return of discontinued products in the distribution channel.

## Taking Big Write-offs Before and After Acquisitions

The big write-off by U.S. Robotics during the stub period can hardly be considered unusual. More common, however, are charges taken by the acquiring company after the acquisition closes.

Consider the retail chain PetsMart (PETM). On several separate occasions, PETM apparently used merger-related write-offs to "clear the deck" of normal operating expenses that would otherwise have been charged against future-period income. Curiously, PETM's general and administrative expense dropped sharply after these write-offs, suggesting that PETM bundled some of these costs into the merger charge.

## Releasing Reserves Created through Big Write-offs

Two benefits result from taking a big write-off at the time of an acquisition. The first, of course, is shifting future operating costs to the current period and labeling them "one-time." The second benefit may not be quite as obvious: A reserve created at the time the charge is recorded would be then available to inflate future earnings.

Remember our Chapter 1 Cendant/CUC Whopper? Back in July 1996, CUC acquired software maker Davidson for $1.0 billion and wrote off almost the entire amount. The reserve created through the charge gave CUC the opportunity to create future-period income simply by releasing the charge (Shenanigan No. 5, Technique No. 3).

## Changing the Allocation of the Purchase Price After an Acquisition

At the time of a purchase acquisition, the acquirer will allocate the purchase price to the identifiable assets and record those assets at their fair market value. The costs not allocated in this way will be recorded as goodwill. Sometimes companies, at a date after the acquisition, change this allocation, shifting more of the purchase price to goodwill. Since goodwill is no longer amortized under the new accounting rules companies have an incentive to reallocate more of the purchase price to goodwill.

Consider how craft store chain Michaels Store (MIKE) benefited by reallocating the cost of an acquisition. In July 1994, MIKE acquired a rival, Leewards. In conjunction with the acquisition, MIKE wrote down the assets associated with approximately

20 Leewards stores that it planned to close. At the same time, MIKE increased its goodwill account in amounts equal to the purchased assets that were deemed worthless—thus creating a dubious value for this asset. Moreover, by writing down certain asset categories (e.g., the inventory at stores that it planned to close), MIKE essentially will be writing off worthless assets over 40 years as it amortizes the goodwill.

Six months after the acquisition closed, MIKE increased its goodwill account by approximately $17 million. The adjustment was attributed to reserves established for litigation, settled leases, and other corporate uses, as well as an additional write-down of acquired inventory. Once again, this meant that MIKE would be keeping worthless inventory on the balance sheet and inflating profits. With the new accounting rules, this trick will become more common.

### New Accounting Rules

In 2001, the FASB voted to eliminate pooling of interest, so all future acquisitions must follow the purchase accounting rules. In addition, goodwill derived from a purchase will no longer be automatically subject to systematic amortization each period. Instead, goodwill amortization will be required only if the assets acquired have become impaired.

The new amortization rules are likely to lead to new accounting tricks that attempt to allocate much of the acquisition price to goodwill. And, of course, the plan will be not to amortize any of it, but rather to claim that no impairment has taken place. This trick will allow companies to keep most of the cost of an acquisition on the balance sheet, rather than charging those costs against income.

## Recording Revenue Related to the Acquiring Company

As discussed in Chapters 4 and 5 on revenue recognition, revenue should be recorded when the seller provides the service or delivers the product to a customer. Some companies have found a peculiar way to record revenue using an accounting acquisition trick: Buy an asset (or a business) and have the seller give you a rebate, then label that rebate as revenue. That's right—*you record revenue as the buyer, not as the seller, of an asset.*

FPA Medical (FPAM) figured out a way to *record revenue upon purchasing a group of medical practices* from Foundation Health Corporation. In December 1996, FPAM reported that it had paid $197 million for these facilities. As part of the acquisition, FPAM agreed to guarantee that Foundation patients would receive continued and uninterrupted access for the next 30 years. In exchange, Foundation (the seller) agreed to pay FPAM $55 million in rebates over 2 years. As FPAM received the payments each year, it recorded them as sales revenue. The rebate from seller to buyer should be an adjustment to the purchase price, not revenue. FPAM paid $197 million and received a $55 million rebate over 2 years, resulting in a net acquisition cost totaling $142 million. The impact that FPAM's aggressive accounting had on its December 1996 sales, operating income, and net income is shown in Table 13-2.

## Labeling Pooling as Immaterial

When companies use the pooling-of-interest method to account for acquisitions, prior-period financial reports generally are adjusted to reflect "pro forma" results so that current-period results will not appear inflated and misleading because of the later acquisition. There is one exception, however: companies are permitted to not restate prior periods if the pooling is deemed to be immaterial. Consider the decision of the business service company Maximus (MMS) to avoid restatements after an acquisition.

Table 13-2. FPA Medical, Adjusted Revenue, and Operating Income

| ($ in millions) | December 1996, reported | Adjustment to exclude rebate | December 1996, adjusted |
|---|---|---|---|
| Revenue | $151.0 | 10.0 | 141.0 |
| Operating income | $10.0 | 10.0 | 0 |
| Net income | 4.2 | 5.9 | −1.7 |

Table 13-3. Revenue Growth for Consulting Group, December
Quarter — Combined Company (CFRA-Adjusted) versus MMS
(Reported)

| ($ in millions, except %) | Q1, 12/98 | Increase | Q1, 12/97 | Growth |
|---|---|---|---|---|
| Reported | 31.4 | 11.5 | 19.9 | 57.8% |
| Less: Contribution from Poolings | 10.0 | 10.0 | 0 | NM |
| CFRA-Adjusted | 21.4 | 1.5 | 19.9 | 7.5% |

In 1998, MMS made several acquisitions, accounting for each
under the pooling-of-interest method. In each case, management
deemed the effect on earnings to be immaterial, requiring no restatement of prior years' financial statements. As Table 13-3 illustrates, the pooled entities contributed $10.0 million of the $11.5
million increase in the company's Consulting Group division. Ab-
sent those pooled entities, year-over-year Consulting Group revenue growth for the December 1998 quarter would have been cut
to 7.5 percent from the reported 57.8 percent.

MMS's decision not to restate prior years' financial statements
for poolings deemed immaterial resulted in an overstatement of
the consulting segment's year-over-year revenue growth in the
December 1998 quarter. As shown in Table 13-3, 87 percent ($10.0
million of the $11.5 million) of the revenue increase was derived
from revenues from the acquired companies.

## Giving Stock or Warrants as an Inducement for Future Purchase Commitments

During the 1990s, companies became more clever at using their
stock in a variety of transactions. In earlier chapters, we spoke of
employees receiving stock options in lieu of cash compensation,
resulting in misleadingly low reported expenses on the financial
statements. We also pointed out how Priceline.com used stock
warrants to entice certain airlines to sign on with the program.
The stock warrants avoided the payment of cash and expense recognition.

Fast-growing telecom giant Broadcomm (BRCM) found an interesting way to use its stock to lock in future revenue when making acquisitions. Before Broadcomm closed on an acquisition, the target company would ask its customers to sign agreements for future purchases. The target company gave the customer stock (or warrants) as an inducement for agreeing to the future purchase. After the target company was acquired by Broadcomm, the customer would receive shares in Broadcomm's stock. Thus, BRCM essentially used its stock as an inducement for the customer to sign a commitment for future orders. In reality, the fair market value of BRCM's stock represents a sales discount and should reduce its sales revenue recognized. Consider this simple illustration. If BRCM grants the customer stock warrants with a fair market value of $250 in return for a $1,000 purchase commitment, BRCM should record net sales of $750:

| | |
|---|---|
| Purchase price | $1,000 |
| Value of warrants | −250 |
| Net sale | $ 750 |

However, BRCM, using an acquisition accounting trick, recorded the sale at the gross amount ($1,000) and included the $250 as part of goodwill, amortizable over 40 years. And with the newly adopted accounting rules, goodwill need not be amortized at all. In effect, the value of the stock warrants granted may never be recorded as an expense.

## A Look Ahead

Chapter 14 discusses some trouble spots related to revenue recognition, such as long-term contracts, installment sales, consignment sales, and capital leases.

# 14
# REVENUE
# RECOGNITION

Accounting tricks related to revenue recognition historically have been the most lethal to investors. Whether a company is recording revenue too soon, inflating the actual amount of revenue, or simply fabricating a revenue generating transaction, investors should be vigilant for signs of such tricks. Certain transactions create particularly tempting opportunities for management to inflate revenue. Chapter 14 discusses four such areas of concern:

1. Revenue from long-term construction contracts
2. Consignment sales
3. Installment sales
4. Revenue from leasing assets

## Revenue from Long-Term Construction Contracts

Typically, companies record revenue after delivery of the product. That approach seems logical if the product will be delivered in a few days or weeks. But what about an aerospace company that has a contract to delivery jets over a 10-year period? Special accounting rules exist for such long-term contracts.

In 1990, for example, United Airlines agreed to purchase sixty-four airplanes from Boeing: thirty Boeing 747s to be delivered from 1994 through 2004, and thirty-four of the newly developed 777s to be delivered between 1995 and 2000.

How might Boeing account for the revenue on this contract? It has two choices: It can wait until the end of the contract to record revenue and profits (the *completed-contract* approach), or it can record a part of the revenue and profits each year based on the amount completed [the *percentage of completion* method (also called the *percentage method*)].

The percentage method is appropriate if the company seems likely to complete the contract, no important uncertainties exist, and accurate interim measures of the completion rate can be obtained. If important uncertainties exist and/or if reliable estimates cannot be obtained, however, the more conservative completed-contract approach should be used—with revenue and profits recorded only at the end of the five years.

## Weigh Uncertainties for Companies Using the Percentage Method.

A decision to use the percentage method may be well intentioned but still have undesirable consequences. Consider how world events might cause the financial statements of certain defense companies that are using the percentage method to be misleading. For example, in September 1991, President George Bush announced that the United States would begin eliminating nuclear armaments and scaling back the development of related weapon systems. As a result, the revenues of many defense companies that use the percentage method were overstated (since revenue whose receipt was anticipated upon the completion of contracts could no longer be counted upon).

Let's consider Boeing's $22 billion contract with United Airlines. Assume that the estimated costs are $12.0 billion. Costs incurred during the first three years are $1.2 billion, $1.4 billion, and $1.0 billion. Billings to United Airlines during the first three years are $0.6 billion, $0.8 billion, and $2.0 billion. Collections from United Airlines each year are $0.5 billion, $0.7 billion, $1.5 billion.

Using the percentage approach, the company would record 10 percent of the revenue (and profits) during Year 1, since 10

Table 14-1.

| Contract price | $22.0 billion |
|---|---|
| Estimated costs | $12.0 billion |
| Estimated profit | $10.0 billion |
| Percent completed: | |
| Year 1 | 10% |
| Year 2 | 14% |
| Year 3 | 12% |

Table 14-2.

| | | |
|---|---|---|
| **Year 1** | | |
| Construction-in-process (CIP) inventory | $1,200,000,000 | |
| Cash, payables, etc. | | $1,200,000,000 |
| Accounts receivable | $ 600,000,000 | |
| Billings on contracts | | $ 600,000,000 |
| Cash | $ 500,000,000 | |
| Accounts receivable | | $ 500,000,000 |
| **Impact on Balance Sheet** | | |
| Accounts receivable | $ 100,000,000 | |
| CIP Inventory | $1,200,000,000 | |
| Billing on contracts | $ 600,000,000 | |
| CIP in excess of billing | $ 600,000,000 | |
| **Impact on Income Statement** | | |
| Revenue | $2,200,000,000 | |
| Cost of sales | $1,200,000,000 | |
| Gross profit | $1,000,000,000 | |

percent of the $12.0 billion estimated costs were incurred (see Table 14-1).

The actual entries on Boeing's books are shown in Table 14-2.

Although the production has just begun and delivery will not occur for several years, Boeing would report revenue of $2.2 billion and gross profit of $1.0 billion. The CIP in excess of billing (also called "unbilled revenue" or "unbilled receivables") would total $0.6 billion.

---

**RED FLAG**

When unbilled receivables grow faster than billed receivables or sales, the use of the POC method may either be inappropriate or is being applied too aggressively.

---

## Consider the Risks of Companies Using the Percentage Method.

First, the percentage method relies on estimates of future costs and future events; it can therefore be manipulated by distorting cost estimates or stage-of-completion records. Second, changes in estimates may be motivated more by a desire to control reported profits than by new information.

But what happens if the company either fails to complete the project or fails to complete it within the required time or under the agreed-upon conditions? As we saw with the defense contractor illustration, the reported revenue and profit will be substantially overstated. For that reason, the percentage of completion method is considered an aggressive accounting practice that can overstate earnings.

The *completed contract method (CCM)* is a rarely used alternative method for recording revenue on long-term contracts. For example, in the Boeing illustration, no revenue would be recorded until the contract is completed. If applied properly, this method is considerably more conservative than the POC. However, opportunities for shenanigans also exist under the CCM when it is used improperly.

Consider the unusual accounting of Caribiner International (CWC), a firm providing conference-planning services. CWC's decision to use the completed contract method was unusual, since its typical service contracts were completed in several months, rather than running for years, and POC is generally more attractive for long-term contracts.

The typical client who wished CWC to make all the arrangements for a future sales conference would receive a bill for one-third of the amount due upon signing the contract, a bill for another third at midpoint, and a bill for the final third when the conference had run. The revenue recognition options available to CWC would be POC (booking revenue based on costs incurred, regardless of billing or collection), record revenue at the time of each of the three billings, or CCM (recording no revenue until the contract is complete).

Surprisingly, CWC opted for the rarely used CCM. Even though it had been working on a contract for months and had billed and collected two-thirds of the total, CWC elected to record zero revenue until completion.

The company defers all revenues and expenses until the completion of the project, with future revenues (generated as a result of customer billing) recorded in a "deferred income" liability account, and future expenses (generated when an expense is incurred) in a "deferred charges" asset account. CWC allocates a portion of the deferred income (corresponding to the anticipated gross profit on the contract) to a *long-term* deferred income account, and the remainder to a current account of the same name. Upon completion of the project, all deferred income relating to the contract is transferred to a revenue account, and all associated deferred charges are expensed.

As shown in Table 14-3, CWC not only deferred recording revenue on cash received (DIC and DIL), but also deferred recognizing expenses on cash paid out (DC, PD, and OA). Notice how the

Table 14-3. Caribiner Selected Balance Sheet Accounts

| ($ in millions) | September 1997 | June 1997 | March 1997 | December 1996 |
|---|---|---|---|---|
| **Assets** | | | | |
| Deferred charges (DC) | 10.2 | 11.2 | 13.5 | 9.6 |
| Prepaid expenses (PD) | 9.1 | 11.0 | 6.2 | 4.0 |
| Other assets (OA) | 3.6 | 3.3 | 2.2 | 0.4 |
| Total: DC + PD + OA | 22.9 | 25.5 | 21.9 | 14.0 |
| **Liabilities** | | | | |
| Deferred income—current (DIC) | 12.2 | 18.1 | 21.7 | 15.8 |
| Deferred income—long-term (DIL) | 5.6 | 7.3 | 8.9 | 6.2 |
| Total: DIC + DIL | **17.8** | 25.4 | 30.6 | **22.0** |

asset balance related to *cash outflows increased* from $14.0 million to $22.9 million, while the liability balance related to *cash inflows decreased* from $22.0 million to $17.8 million. Since the amount of expenses deferred to future periods exceeded the amount of revenue deferred, the company actually reported higher income by using the completed-contract method.

The presence of a sharp drop in both revenue and deferred income (which constitutes a potential major source of future revenues) for CWC's service segment may indicate a slowdown in the company's business—a concern that is exacerbated somewhat by the drop in deferred income relative to deferred charges. Service revenues fell sharply during the September quarter alone, while deferred income has dropped significantly over the past two quarters.

### Consignment Sales

With consignment sales, the seller (consignor) ships the product to a dealer (consignee), yet still retains title to the merchandise. Thus, the inventory remains on the consignor's books and no sales revenue should be recorded. When the dealer sells the goods to a customer and gets paid, it earns commission revenue. The consignor then records a sale and transfers the cost of the merchandise from inventory to cost of goods sold. If, instead, the dealer is unable to sell the product, it is returned to the consignor—and, of course, no revenue is recorded.

Assume that Walt Disney sells its animated movies to Wal-Mart on a consignment basis. Disney ships 800 tapes for sale at $60 each and pays $1,000 in transportation costs. The tapes cost Disney $20 each, and Wal-Mart earns a commission of 25 percent on each tape sold. During the year, Wal-Mart sells 500 tapes. At the end of the year, Wal-Mart remits the sales proceeds, less the commissions, to Disney.

---

**RED FLAG**

Watch for companies that record revenue when they ship goods to consignee in a consignment sale. This is a sign of Shenanigan No. 1, recording revenue too soon.

---

Table 14-4.

| | | |
|---|---|---|
| Inventory on consignment | 16,000 | |
|    Inventory | | 16,000 |
| (Segregate inventory on consignment from the rest of inventory) | | |
| Inventory on consignment | 1,000 | |
|    Cash | | 1,000 |
| (Include transportation costs in inventory) | | |
| NO ENTRY AT TIME OF SALE TO CUSTOMER | | |
| Cash | 14,400 | |
| Commission Expense | 3,600 | |
|    Consignment Sale | | 18,000 |
| (Record sale at end of year, when notified by consignee and proceeds are received) | | |
| Cost of consignment sales | 11,000 | |
| Inventory on consignment sales | | 11,000 |
| (Record cost of consignment sales on 500 units—5/8 of total) | | |

## Installment Sales

Most sales can be recorded after the product is shipped and the customer indicates satisfaction. An exception occurs, however, when significant uncertainty exists concerning the customer's ability to pay. In such cases, the more conservative installment method for recognizing revenue would be appropriate. Under the installment method, gross profit (sales less cost of goods sold) arising from a sale is deferred and recognized as cash collections take place.

Assume that Computer Super Store sells a $2,000 computer to a customer with poor credit and uses the installment method. The customer pays $200 down and has three equal installments of $600. Computer Super Store paid $1,200 for the computer.

In a regular (noninstallment) sale, the entire $800 gross profit would be reflected immediately. (The gross margin is 40 percent: $800 divided by $2,000.) Under the installment approach, the gross profit will be deferred until the cash is collected.

Clearly, the installment method is more conservative than recording the entire amount immediately, as would usually be done. The installment method may be appropriate when the customer may lack the wherewithal to pay, as discussed under Shenanigan No. 1, Technique No. 3.

Table 14-5 gives the accounting entries.

Table 14-5.

| | | |
|---|---|---|
| Cash | 200 | |
| Installment Receivables | 1,800 | |
|    Installment Sales | | 2,000 |
| (Record sale and down payment) | | |
| Cost of Installment Sale | 1,200 | |
|    Inventory | | 1,200 |
| (Record inventory transferred to cost of sales) | | |
| Cash | 600 | |
|    Installment Receivables | | 600 |
| (Record payment of first installment) | | |
| Installment Sales | 2,000 | |
|    Cost of Installment Sales | | 1,200 |
|    Deferred Gross Profit | | 800 |
| (Close sales and cost of sales to deferred gross<br>   profit) | | |
| Deferred Gross Profit | 320 | |
|    Realized Gross Profit | | 320 |
| (Record profit on 40 percent of cash collected—$800) | | |

## Revenue from Leasing Assets

Lessors can materially inflate their reported income by using aggressive accounting practices. Two tricks to watch for are changing from using operating leases to using capital leases, and changing the assumptions of the capital lease, including the discount rate and the residual value of the lease. First, here's some background information.

### Carefully Distinguish between a Lease and a Disguised Sale

The accounting for a lease and that for a sale with deferred payments differ markedly. A lessor records rental income as cash is received each month. In contrast, the seller of a product who receives monthly installments from the customer records the present value of the total amount immediately. Naturally, companies prefer the sales approach over the more conservative lease approach.

---

Accounting Capsule

A lease is an agreement that transfers the right to use property, plant, or equipment from the owner to a renter for a specified period of time. The owner is referred to as the *lessor* and the renter as the *lessee*. The lease specifies the terms under which the lessee has the right to use the property and the amount to be paid to the lessor in exchange for that right.

**Types of Leases:**
A *capital* (or *sales-type*) *lease*, which is sometimes referred to as a disguised sale, transfers all the risks and rewards of ownership in the leased asset to the lessee. Otherwise the lease is classified as an *operating lease*. For example, a landlord who receives monthly rent from tenants would record revenue as an operating lease. In contrast, a retailer who leases a PC over a 4-year period and offers the customer a bargain purchase option would account for revenue as a capital lease.

**Criteria for Capitalization of Leases:**
The lessee is required to capitalize a lease if any one of the following criteria is met at the inception of the lease:
• Ownership is transferred at the end of the lease term.
• The lease includes a bargain purchase option.
• The lease term represents 75 percent or more of the economic life of the asset.
• The present value of future lease payments is at least 90 percent of the asset's market value.

The lessor is required to capitalize a lease if the lease meets one of the criteria for the lessee, as listed above, and *both* of the following criteria:
• There are no uncertainties about the amount of unreimbursable costs to be incurred by the lessor in connection with the lease agreement.
• Collectibility of the minimum lease payments is reasonably certain.

## Accounting for Operating Leases

The accounting for an operating lease is straightforward, since there is no transfer of ownership. The asset remains on the lessor's books, and the lease is accounted for the same way rent is accounted for on the financial statements. When an asset is leased, the lessor sets up a lease revenue account to record and account for payments received from the lessee, while the lessee sets up a lease expense account to record and account for lease payments.

## Accounting for Capital Leases

At first glance, the accounting for capital leases appears straight-forward: The lessee records the leased asset on its books at the present value of the future lease payments. Because it has re-corded the asset on its books, the lessee must depreciate that asset over the life of the lease. The lessor, conversely, removes the asset from its books and records a receivable for the asset, also at the present value of the future lease payments.

## Opportunities for Financial Shenanigans

**Changing from an Operating Lease to a Capital Lease.** A company will generally record substantially more income in the first year of a sales-type lease than in the first year of an operating lease, since the present value of the future lease payments is recorded as revenue in the initial year under a sales-type lease, whereas just one period's rent is recorded under an operating lease. For ex-ample, Pyxis Corporation (now a division of Cardinal Health, Inc.) originally accounted for leases under the operating method. How-ever, before going public, the company selected the sales-type method to record its lease revenue. This approach enabled Pyxis (see Chapter 4) to front-end load revenue, and thereby to improve its apparent profitability over what it would otherwise have re-ported using operating leases.

**Change in Capital Lease Assumptions.** Another area in which a company is able to improve its profitability using capital leases is the determination of lease assumptions: the discount rate, which is the interest rate used to determine the present value of the lease, and the residual value of the leased item. The discount rate de-termines the amount of revenue and expenses related to the lease. The lessor will benefit from using a lower discount rate. Under a sales-type lease, a lower discount rate would result in a higher present value for the lease payments, thus enabling the lessor to report higher sales in the first year. Similarly, a higher residual value for a sales-type lease would result in lower cost of goods sold and would therefore increase the amount of profit recorded, in addition to generating higher interest income. The net effect of using a higher residual value is higher net income over the lease period. The overall effect of using a lower discount rate and a higher residual value is to inflate revenue or shift it to the first year of the lease.

Here's an illustration showing how to boost profits by lowering the assumed interest rate and raising the assumed residual value.

Assume that the lessor uses an 8.67 percent discount rate rather than a 9 percent rate and changes the residual value from $22,500 to $45,500. The total revenue reported over the lease term would remain $339,625; however, net income is higher in the first year and lower in subsequent years (see Table 14-6.)

## Financial Statement Impact of Operating and Capital Leases

Whether a lease is classified as a capital lease or an operating lease has several significant effects on a company's financial statements. Some of the differences between the two methods provide benefits to the company, while others do not. The following example is used to illustrate the differences between operating and capital leases and the effect on the company's balance sheet, income statement, and cash flow statement.

**Income Statement Effect.** At the inception of a capital lease, the lessor records revenue in an amount equal to the discounted present value of all anticipated future cash inflows (i.e., lease payments). Subsequently, on a pro rata basis for the duration of the lease, the lessor recognizes the residual portion of such cash inflows as nonoperating income. In contrast, for an operating lease, revenue is recognized on a pro rata basis throughout the lease term based on the full nominal value of the periodic lease payments that the lessor receives. This results in a higher net income in the earlier years under a sales-type lease; however, total income recognized over the lease term is identical under both methods (see Table 14-7).

**Balance Sheet Effect.** In connection with the recognition of revenue from a sales-type lease, a company records a receivable on

Table 14-6. Comparison of Income Statement Effect of Using an 8.67% versus 9% Discount Rate, and Higher Residual Value

| NI* | DR* = 9% | DR = 8.67% | Difference | RV*= $22,500 | RV= $45,500 | Difference |
|---|---|---|---|---|---|---|
| Year 1 | $136,425 | $141,894 | $5,469 | $136,425 | $143,309 | $ 6,884 |
| Year 2 | 35,678 | 34,844 | (834) | 35,678 | 36,298 | 620 |
| Year 3 | 33,039 | 32,230 | (809) | 33,039 | 33,715 | 676 |
| Year 4 | 30,163 | 29,389 | (774) | 30,163 | 30,899 | 736 |
| Years 5–10 | 104,320 | 101,268 | (3,052) | 104,320 | 110,356 | 6,036 |
| Total NI | $339,625 | $339,625 | $–0– | $339,625 | $354,576 | $14,952 |

*NI = Net Income; DR = Discount Rate; RV = Residual Value

Table 14-7. Comparison of Income Statement Effect of Capital Lease versus Operating Lease

| Net Income | Sales-Type Lease | Operating Lease | Difference |
|---|---|---|---|
| Year 1 | $ 136,425 | $ 33,963 | $ 102,462 |
| Year 2 | 35,678 | 33,963 | 1,715 |
| Year 3 | 33,039 | 33,963 | (924) |
| Year 4 | 30,163 | 33,963 | (3,800) |
| Years 5–10 | 104,320 | 203,773 | (99,453) |
| Total | $ 339,625 | $ 339,625 | –0– |

its balance sheet, "net investment in sales-type leases" (also called "sales-type lease receivables"), to reflect the total future minimum lease payments, less unearned income (the factor that reduces the amount recorded for the lease payments from nominal value to present value) and an allowance for uncollectible lease payments. The company simultaneously removes the leased asset from its balance sheet. With an operating lease, however, the leased asset remains on the company's balance sheet throughout the lease term.

**Cash Flow Effect.**  Total cash flow is not affected by the method used to account for a lease. However, the effect on operating and investing cash flows depends on whether the lease receivable is reported as an operating or an investing activity. In practice, most companies classify capital leases as an operating activity. If this is done, operating and investing cash flows are identical under operating and sales-type leases because there is no difference in the tax benefit related to the lease, as tax regulations generally recognize only operating leases. However, when the lease investment is reported as an investing activity, cash flow from the lease will move from the operating activity to the investing activity section.

# A Look Ahead

The final section of the book tracks the history of shenanigans during the last century (Chapter 15) and the history of attempts to eliminate them before investors were hurt (Chapter 16). There is also a profile of the biggest accounting fraud ever (Chapter 17).

# PART FIVE
# LOOKING BACK . . .
# LOOKING FORWARD

# 15

# HISTORY OF
# FINANCIAL
# SHENANIGANS

*That which hath been is that which will be,*
*And that which hath been done is that which*
*shall be done;*
*And there is nothing new under the sun.*
             KING SOLOMON, *Ecclesiastes*

As it was for Solomon, so it still is with " 'get rich quick" schemes
and financial shenanigans. Chapter 15 reviews some of the major
scams of the twentieth century.

## Pre-World War II Scams

The first half of the twentieth century witnessed numerous instances of financial shenanigans in corporate annual reports, leading to grossly overvalued stock prices and contributing to the collapse of the stock market between 1929 and 1932. For example,
the price of International Power, Inc.'s stock dropped 78 points in
a single day when it was reported that the company had "cooked
its books."

In addition to companies that issued misleading corporate financial reports, swindlers and con artists (such as Charles Ponzi, Ivar Kreuger, and Philip Musica) caused investors and bondholders to suffer great losses. One such scam occurred just after World War I, when many unsuspecting souls were reportedly swindled out of nearly $400 million in fraudulent liberty bonds.

A decade later, the infamous Charles ("Get Rich Quick") Ponzi, perhaps the best-known con artist in history, duped investors with promises of incredibly high returns. Ponzi, of course, used the money he received from late-coming investors to pay high returns to early investors—a technique known ever since as a Ponzi scheme. Ponzi had reportedly raised at least $15 million before *The Boston Globe* exposed his scheme. He was later sentenced to 10 years in prison for larceny and mail fraud.

A later and far larger financial scam was perpetrated by international financier Ivar Kreuger. He often switched companies' assets and liabilities or created fictitious assets when the existing ones weren't enough. After an extensive investigation, authorities found that Kreuger had bilked shareholders and moneylenders out of $500 million.

The late 1920s and 1930s witnessed the rise and fall of Philip Musica, alias Frank Donald Coster. A fugitive who was a convicted and twice-jailed swindler, Musica used fraudulent means and profits from the illegal sale of alcohol to purchase the McKesson & Robbins drug company, which subsequently named him its president. For years thereafter, he successfully hoodwinked banks, embezzled millions of dollars from the company, and fraudulently misrepresented its financial reports. One way in which he misrepresented those reports was by listing nonexistent inventory (generally accepted auditing standards at that time did not require that the taking of inventory be observed). The auditors eventually caught on to the scheme in 1937, when they discovered that $10 million of inventory and $9 million of accounts receivable (out of assets of $87 million) at McKesson & Robbins were fictitious. Musica shot himself on December 16, 1938.

## More Recent Shenanigans

During the second half of the twentieth century, the frequency of financial chicanery and the size of the schemes increased dramatically. Among the more notable scams during the 1960s, 1970s, and 1980s were the Great Salad Oil Swindle, Equity Funding Corporation, Wedtech Corporation, and Lincoln Savings & Loan (part of the savings and loan debacle of the 1980s).

### The Great Salad Oil Swindle

In 1963 it was reported that Anthony (Tino) De Angelis of Allied Crude Vegetable Oil Refining Corporation had devised an ingenious way of overstating the company's inventory of salad oil: He filled many of the company's vats with water, adding only a layer of oil on top. Underground pipes connected the vats, so that the layer of oil could be shifted across the vats as needed during the inventory observation procedure.

For the better part of a decade, financiers loaned De Angelis hundreds of millions of dollars to bankroll his worldwide salad oil deals. He had a vast storage center for salad oil in Bayonne, New Jersey, and each time he got a loan, he pledged part of his salad oil stock as collateral. (He didn't ship the salad oil to the financiers, but merely gave them papers stating that the oil was their property until the loan was repaid.)

Finally, in November 1963, De Angelis's salad oil company collapsed when the auditors discovered that the salad oil tanks were almost empty. De Angelis had sold his financiers $175 million of phantom salad oil—and the money was gone.

### Equity Funding Corporation—Wall Street's Watergate

One of the most massive and sensational financial frauds perpetrated by a major company occurred at Equity Funding Corporation of America during the 1960s and 1970s. (In fact, the story was subsequently made into a movie.) Equity Funding, a financial services institution, began operations in 1960 with $10,000. By 1973, the company purported to manage assets of $1 billion. Its record growth during the previous decade had exceeded that of all major diversified financial companies in the United States.

In April 1973, this "growth" was exposed as a fiction. After adjustments, the reported net worth at year-end 1972 of $143.4

million was restated to a *negative* $42.1 million. Equity Funding's stock, which had traded as high as $80 a share, became worthless, and the company filed for bankruptcy. Shockingly, according to court records, the company had engaged in "fictitious entries in certain receivable and income accounts" *as early as 1965*. Out of 99,000 policies representing $3.5 billion in insurance on the books, 56,000 policies representing $2 billion were fictitious. Equity Funding had faked assets of more than $100 million; it had counterfeited bonds and forged death certificates.

In November 1973, twenty-two people—twenty of them former employees of Equity Funding, the other two its auditors—were indicted on 105 counts of fraud and conspiracy. Stanley Goldblum, the company's co-founder and former president, was sentenced to 8 years in federal prison for his part in the fraud.

### Welbilt Electronic Die Corporation (Wedtech)

The 1980s were a period of rapidly rising stock prices, fueled in part by governmental deregulation—coupled with outrageous financial shenanigans. One of the most widely reported cases of financial improprieties occurred at Wedtech Corporation in the South Bronx in New York City.

Wedtech, a machine shop, was founded in 1965. Using a variety of fraudulent means, including bribing government officials, lying on government proposals and contracts, and misrepresenting its financial performance, the company caused investors to lose tens of millions of dollars.

One vehicle for its fraudulent financial reports was the inappropriate use of the percentage of completion method for recording revenue. (See Chapter 14 for more on this shenanigan.) Wedtech improperly accelerated its contract receipts, falsified invoices, reported revenue on contracts that was never received, paid bribes to government officials, and claimed falsely that the company was controlled by a Hispanic (thereby qualifying it for favored status in receiving government contracts).

Not only were charges of bribery and fraud brought against Wedtech officials, but lawsuits seeking $105 million in damages were filed against the company's auditors, charging that they knew about the fraud, corporate waste, and inaccurate financial reporting.

### Lincoln Savings & Loan

While all the previous financial frauds are noteworthy and troublesome, for sheer size and the number of people affected, nothing compares to the financial shenanigans committed in the savings and loan (S&L) industry during the 1980s. Estimates of the cost to taxpayers to bail out the industry run as high as $500 billion— or $2,000 for every man, woman, and child in the United States. That sum is greater than the combined inflation-adjusted cost of the Marshall Plan (which rebuilt Europe after World War II) and the bailouts of Chrysler Corporation, Continental Bank, and New York City.

While numerous S&Ls were simply guilty of poor judgment, questionable business practices, and creative accounting, many (including American Diversified of Costa Mesa, California Mesa and Vernon Savings of Vernon, Texas) perpetuated massive frauds. No S&L failure, however, stirred more interest and outrage than that of Lincoln Savings & Loan, which not only was expected to cost American taxpayers a record $2.5 billion but also allegedly involved the use of members of Congress (the "Keating Five") to influence banking regulators.

Charles Keating, who ran Lincoln Savings, used government-insured deposits to speculate on a massive and perhaps unprecedented scale. For example, he wagered $100 million of such deposits in a risk-arbitrage fund owned and operated by convicted shenanigan grandmaster Ivan Boesky. He also bought bonds from Eastern Airlines at a little more than par shortly before Eastern filed for bankruptcy. In fact, in its 1988 examination of Lincoln, the FDIC found that 77 percent of Lincoln's bonds were "junk bonds."

Moreover, Lincoln's parent, American Continental Corporation (ACC), gave new meaning to the term *nepotism* by including among its top eight officers not only Keating but also his son, his daughter, and his son-in-law. Some held top positions, receiving half a million dollars or more in salary at ages 24 to 28 (with his son pulling down a cool $900,000). In fact, from 1985 to 1988,

Keating and members of his family received $34 million in salary and sales of ACC stock.

After ACC filed for bankruptcy in April 1989, federal investigators hired Kenneth Leventhal & Co., a leading real estate accounting firm, to examine Lincoln's real estate investments and loans. On every one of the fifteen deals that it reviewed, Leventhal concluded that a profit should never have been recorded. In each deal, Leventhal said, Lincoln entered into some form of related transaction that had the effect of either nullifying the deal or making its contribution to Lincoln's income far less than reported.

Later that same month, the federal government seized control of Lincoln, claiming that it was being operated in an unsafe and unsound manner. Keating and his family were accused of looting the bank of $1.1 billion. Most of the family is being sued by 23,000 people who say that they were conned out of $250 million worth of uninsured bonds.

Curiously, Keating refused to be an officer or a director of Lincoln. When asked why by a representative of the Federal Home Loan Bank of Seattle, he reportedly said that he "did not want to go to jail." (Unfortunately for him, in April 1992, a judge sentenced him to a 10-year prison term.)


## MiniScribe Corporation

In early 1987, disk drive manufacturer MiniScribe was preparing for a debt offering that was needed to expand its growth and replenish its dwindling cash supplies. The auditors signed off on the financial reports, and the offering was a huge success. That was a decision that the auditors at Coopers & Lybrand (now part of PricewaterhouseCoopers) would regret. The reported profits were completely bogus, and the auditors had been duped. One trick the company used to fool the auditors who were counting the inventory was to fill the boxes with bricks. Since the auditors failed to open these boxes, they had no idea.

Two years later the company was unable to continue hiding the truth, and the fraud became known. Investors and creditors sued the company, its directors and officers, and the auditors for over $1 billion. When the lawsuits were finally settled out of court, the auditors paid more than $100 million.

## Shenanigans During the 1990s

During the 1990s, the pace of accounting scams continued unabated. Some of these (such as BCCI and Maxwell Communications) had global repercussions, while others have rocked and embarrassed local communities (such as Microstrategy of Vienna, Virginia).

### Bank of Commerce and Credit International (BCCI)

When it was founded almost 20 years ago, BCCI was proclaimed as the Bank of the Third World, extending services to Arab oil sheiks and hard-working Muslim immigrants in Europe. But eventually BCCI's open-arms approach attracted drug smugglers and embezzling dictators, who used the bank to launder millions in illegal profits. By the late 1980s and early 1990s, it had become the bank of choice for the underworld and such nefarious characters as terrorist Abu Nidal and dictator Manuel Noriega.

In July 1991, regulators from eight countries shut down BCCI (now often referred to as the Bank of Crooks and Criminals, International). In the 1991 indictment, New York District Attorney Robert Morganthau described BCCI as "the largest bank fraud in world financial history." An estimated *$20 billion* had been stolen, lost, or swindled.

### Maxwell Communications

Although it was no match for BCCI in sheer size, the massive fraud allegedly perpetrated by billionaire Robert Maxwell, head of Maxwell Communications, was equally daring. The story began unraveling shortly after Maxwell's body was found floating off the Canary Islands on November 5, 1991. In the days and weeks that followed, investigators found that Maxwell had engaged in a massive fraud to stave off the imminent collapse of his corporate empire, which included the publishing giant Macmillan, Inc., and such newspapers as the *New York Daily News* and the London-based *Daily Mirror*.

Overwhelmed by debt, Maxwell had allegedly resorted to one of history's great financial frauds, looting over $1.4 billion from Maxwell Communications, including $800 million from the employees' pension plan. Investigators also found some accounting gimmicks used by Mr. Maxwell, such as artificially inflating earnings through bogus real estate sales to other firms under his control. (See Chapter 6 for more on this shenanigan.)

## Cendant Corporation

When the hard-driving and acquisitive Henry Silverman of HFS bought CUC in 1997, Wall Street toasted the announcement. The celebration proved to be premature. Shortly after the merger, the auditors at HFS were perplexed when CUC's senior management refused to release some information. When they finally got a look, Silverman and his team couldn't believe what they had bought—a company that had "cooked its books." When the painful announcement was made to investors, the share price collapsed. Not only was the fraud massive, but it had been hidden for more than a decade.

The cost to the auditor to settle the resulting lawsuit was $335 million, and the company paid billions to defrauded shareholders.

## Microstrategy

In early 2000, one of the country's wealthiest entrepreneurs was 34-year-old Microstrategy founder and CEO Michael Saylor. But he was more than that. He was a media darling, exalted for his business success and flamboyant lifestyle. As a perk for his employees, they all went on a cruise to celebrate the company's achievements.

But there was just one small problem: The company was hemorrhaging, and the auditors at PricewaterhouseCoopers failed to notice it. Naturally, investors were buying the stock at the nosebleed price of $333 based on bogus financial results.

On March 20, 2000, the share price collapsed, dropping to $86, when the company announced that the financial reports would be restated to show a mammoth loss. One year later the stock price fell to $3 and the media has moved on to new darlings. Oh, and the companywide cruise has been discontinued.

## A Look Ahead

Chapter 16 discusses those leading the battle to combat financial shenanigans.

# 16

# LEADING THE BATTLE TO COMBAT SHENANIGANS

Although financial shenanigans have plagued investors for years, many good people have led the battle to clean up the mess. This chapter discusses the role and contribution of those who are leading the battle on behalf of investors:

- Rule makers
- Corporate executives and internal auditors
- Outside directors
- Independent auditors
- Regulators
- Educators
- Watchdog organizations and independent commissions
- Financial analysts
- Financial media
- Lawyers representing the investors

## Rule Makers

Improving financial reporting and eliminating financial shenanigans begins with the organizations that establish the rules. Ideally,

senior management would have little flexibility to choose accounting policies that result in misleading financial reports. On the international scene, a number of countries have their own rule makers. Most, however, follow the lead of either the Financial
Accounting Standards Board (FASB) or the International Accounting Standards Board (IASB).

## FASB

Established in 1973, the FASB has as its mission to establish and
improve standards of financial accounting and reporting. Because
its decisions are based on general acceptance, not fiat, critics have
sometimes made it difficult for the FASB to effectively carry out
its mission, especially when it issues rules that are perceived as
hurting corporate profits. The best recent example involves the
FASB's proposal that issuers of stock options be required to include as an expense the market value of the stock given out to
employees and others. Corporate America, particularly the technology industry, protested. The FASB withdrew the proposal and
issued a watered-down version that gave companies a choice as
to whether to include this cost as an expense, mandating only
some footnote disclosure of the earnings hit from the options. Almost no one chose to expense the options (*http://www.fasb.org*).

## IASB

Effective April 1, 2001, the International Accounting Standards
Board (IASB) took over from its predecessor body, the International Accounting Standards Committee, the responsibility for setting international accounting standards, designated International
Financial Reporting Standards. The European Commission presented legislation to require the use of IASC standards for all listed
companies no later than 2005 (*http://www.iasc.org.uk/cmt/0001.asp*).

## Corporate Executives and Internal Auditors

While the FASB should establish clear standards on financial accounting and reporting, senior management must take the position that these standards must be followed. Senior managements

that instead push to "make the numbers" at all costs represent the most serious threat to investors. The compensation structure should not encourage making the numbers at all costs.

Aiding senior management in establishing and enforcing financial and operational controls are internal auditors. Companies should maintain an effective internal audit function staffed with adequate personnel. Besides reviewing the financial aspects of the company, the internal auditors should consider the implications of their nonfinancial audit findings for the financial reporting function. The internal auditors should work with and report directly to the audit committee of the board to ensure their independence.

Corporate executives are responsible for following all legal and accounting guidelines in fairly reporting their companies' results to stakeholders. If they are found to have intentionally distorted the results, they can be charged with fraud.

### Corporate Executives

The chief financial officer is typically the person responsible for financial reporting to the shareholders and the government. The finance team also includes controllers, treasurers, and staff accountants. Several fine associations exist to help corporate executives carry out their responsibilities. The leading professional association for corporate financial executives is Financial Executives International (FEI) (*http://www.fei.org*).

### Internal Auditors

These professionals actually audit the senior financial executives. They typically report to the outside members of the board of directors, not to senior management. The professional association supporting internal auditors is the Institute for Internal Auditors (*http://www.theiia.org*).

## Outside Members of the Board of Directors

The independent (nonexecutive) members of a company's board of directors play an important oversight role. An effective board, and particularly the audit committee, should ensure that the company has fully complied with both the letter and the spirit of the FASB and SEC guidelines. The audit committees should take an active role in reviewing and evaluating management and should serve as an independent link to the external auditor. It should also increase its oversight of quarterly financial reports, approving these reports before their public release.

### The National Association of Corporate Directors (NACD)

Based in Washington, D.C., the NACD plays an important role in training board members. It runs seminars around the country and publishes monographs illustrating the best practices for outside board members (*http://www.nacdonline.org*).

## Independent Auditors

One positive result from the 1929 stock market crash was the requirement that companies undergo an annual financial audit. Independent auditors must be properly trained and vigilant to ensure companies' complete compliance with the rules. Most public companies are audited by one of the Big Five (Arthur Andersen, Deloitte & Touche, Ernst & Young, KPMG, and Pricewaterhouse-Coopers).

Auditors have recently come under scrutiny because of their failures to warn investors before certain financial debacles. The U.S. Congress and the SEC have held hearings, trying to find ways to improve auditors' effectiveness. The suggestions range from strengthening the auditors' independence to requiring quarterly reviews. Clearly, auditors need better training in the warning signs of financial shenanigans.

The leading professional organization supporting independent auditors is the American Institute of Certified Public Accountants (AICPA). The AICPA administers the CPA examination, promulgates auditing standards, and (very rarely) sanctions members for improper or unethical conduct (*http://www.aicpa.org/index.htm*).

# Regulators

The government and several stock exchanges have established an enforcement mechanism to protect investors from financial shenanigans. The leading regulators are the U.S. Securities and Exchange Commission, the National Association of Securities Dealers, and the New York Stock Exchange.

## U.S. Securities and Exchange Commission (SEC)

After the stock market crash of 1929, the federal government established the SEC to standardize and oversee the financial information presented to stockholders. The SEC today has broad powers to regulate more than 12,000 companies and their auditors. Enforcement actions against public companies and accountants are meant to serve as a deterrent. Unfortunately, the punishments are often inconsequential and late in coming. AOL, for example, was fined $3.5 million in 2000 for improper accounting practices during the period 1994 through 1996.

Regulators must rigorously review corporate filings to monitor compliance with the rules and must quickly punish any deviant behavior on the part of either the SEC registrant company or the auditing firms.

The SEC should seek explicit statutory authority to bar or suspend corporate officers and directors involved in fraudulent financial reporting from future service in that capacity.

A sign of the SEC Enforcement Division's commitment to improving financial reporting and rooting out fraud was the spring 2000 announcement of the formation of a Financial Fraud Task Force as a separate group within the Division of Enforcement. This group is designed to allow swift, aggressive investigation of suspected frauds.

The SEC also regulates outside auditors and can bring legal action for failure to perform an audit in accordance with the existing standards. One area of particular concern involves questionable independence of the auditor. In February 2001, the commission toughened its rules regarding independence and mandated proxy disclosure of fees received from clients for nonaudit (consulting) services (*http://www.sec.gov*).

## National Association of Securities Dealers (NASD)

A subsidiary of the NASD, NASD Regulation, is charged with regulating the securities industry and the Nasdaq stock market. The NASD was created in 1938 by the Maloney Act amendments to the Securities Exchange Act of 1934. NASD Regulation's jurisdiction extends to over 5,500 firms and over 683,000 securities industry professionals. NASD Regulation accomplishes this oversight through the registration, education, testing, and examination of member firms and their employees, and through the creation and enforcement of rules. Its Web site is *http://www.nasdr.com*.

## New York Stock Exchange (NYSE)

Every transaction made at the NYSE is under continuous surveillance during the trading day. Stock Watch, a computer system that searches for unusual trading patterns, alerts NYSE regulatory personnel to possible insider trading abuses or other prohibited trading practices. The Exchange's other regulatory activities include the supervision of member firms to enforce compliance with financial and operational requirements, periodic checks on brokers' sales practices, and the continuous monitoring of specialist operations.

The Division of Enforcement acts as the prosecutorial arm of the NYSE. Since 1817, there has been a provision in the NYSE constitution permitting the NYSE to take action for any violation of Exchange rules. The Securities and Exchange Act of 1934 mandates that every national securities exchange discipline violations of the act and of exchange rules by its members and member organizations. (*http://www.nyse.com*).

## Educators

In recent years, academic institutions have made important contributions in researching topics related to "quality of earnings." The American Accounting Association announced a special edition of its journal, *Issues in Accounting Education*, on quality of earnings. Several excellent sources of educational material are found on the Web.

### Social Science Electronic Publishing, Inc. (SSRN)

This organization provides research papers by leading academics (*http://papers.ssrn.com*).

### Rutgers Accounting Web (RAW)

This Web site provides links to some of the most important accounting and financial reporting web sites (*http://accounting. rutgers.edu/*).

## Watchdogs and Independent Commissions

Several watchdog organizations and independent commissions monitor the behavior of various parties involved in financial reporting and corporate governance and suggest areas for improvement. Two leading (for-profit) organizations that are helping to protect investors are the Investor Responsibility Research Center (IRRC) and the Center for Financial Research & Analysis (CFRA). The most important independent commissions are the National Commission on Fraudulent Financial Reporting (Treadway Commission) and the Blue Ribbon Committee on Improving the Effectiveness of Corporate Audit Committees (Whitehead Commission).

### Investor Responsibility Research Center (IRRC)

For over 25 years, the IRRC has been a source of impartial information on corporate governance and social responsibility issues affecting investors and corporations worldwide. It offers guidance and advice on proxy voting, enabling clients to make informed, considered decisions that reflect their investment philosophies. Unlike many other corporate research providers, IRRC does not advocate on any side of the issues it covers (*http://www.irrc.org/*).

## Center for Financial Research & Analysis (CFRA)

CFRA publishes independent quality of earnings reports on public companies for institutional investors. Its database contains reports on over 1,500 public companies based in North America and Europe. CFRA remains completely independent, making no recommendations and taking no position in companies it covers (*http:// www.cfraonline.com*).

## National Commission on Fraudulent Financial Reporting (Treadway Commission)

In 1985, the commission undertook a comprehensive study of the financial reporting system in the United States in response to a request that it "identify causal factors that can lead to fraudulent financial reporting and steps to reduce its incidence." Two years later, the commission issued many useful recommendations including the following:

- Management should set the proper tone at the top, demonstrating an understanding of the factors that may cause financial statements to be fraudulently misstated.
- The company should maintain internal controls that are adequate to prevent and detect fraudulent reporting.
- Each company should develop and enforce written codes of corporate conduct. This should foster a strong ethical climate and open channels of communication to help protect against fraudulent reporting. Additionally, the audit committee of the board should review compliance with the code annually, including compliance by top management.
- Auditors should have more responsibility for the detection of fraudulent financial reporting during an audit.
- Auditors should be required to review quarterly financial statements before the statements are released to the public.
- Accounting firms should recognize and control the organizational and individual pressures that potentially reduce audit quality.

## Blue Ribbon Committee on Improving the Effectiveness of Corporate Audit Committees (Whitehead Commission)

In 1998, the SEC, the NASD, and the NYSE commissioned this group to study and make recommendations to strengthen the audit committee function. John Whitehead (former co-chair of Goldman Sachs) and Ira Millstein (senior partner at Weil, Gotshal & Manges) chaired the committee.

Here are some of their recommendations:

- The board must perform active and independent oversight. Board membership is no longer just a reward for "making it" in corporate America; being a director today requires the appropriate attitude and capabilities, and it demands time and attention.
- A proper and well-functioning system exists when the three main groups responsible for financial reporting—the full board including the audit committee, financial management including the internal auditors, and the outside auditors—form a "three-legged stool" that supports responsible financial disclosure and active and participatory oversight. However, in the view of the committee, the audit committee must be "first among equals" in this process, since the audit committee is an extension of the full board and hence the ultimate monitor of the process.
- If a corporation is to be a viable attraction for capital, its board must ensure disclosure and transparency concerning the company's true financial performance as well as its governance practices. *Accounting games may be short-term fixes, but they are not long-term bases for financial credibility.*

---

### DEFINITION OF INDEPENDENT AUDIT COMMITTEE MEMBER

Members of the audit committee shall be considered independent if they have no relationship to the corporation that may interfere with the exercise of their independence from management and the corporation. Examples of such relationships include:

- a director being employed by the corporation or any of its affiliates for the current year or any of the past five years;

*(Continued)*

- a director accepting any compensation from the corporation or any of its affiliates other than compensation for board service or benefits under a tax-qualified retirement plan;

- a director being a member of the immediate family of an individual who is, or has been in any of the past five years, employed by the corporation or any of its affiliates as an executive officer;

- a director being a partner in, or a controlling shareholder or an executive officer of, any for-profit business organization to which the corporation made, or from which the corporation received, payments that are or have been significant to the corporation or business organization in any of the past five years;

- a director being employed as an executive of another company where any of the corporation's executives serves on that company's compensation committee.

A director who has one or more of these relationships may be appointed to the audit committee, if the board, under exceptional and limited circumstances, determines that membership on the committee by the individual is required by the best interests of the corporation and its shareholders, and the board discloses, in the next annual proxy statement subsequent to such determination, the nature of the relationship and the reasons for that determination.

- The NYSE and the NASD require that listed companies with a market capitalization above $200 million (or a more appropriate measure for identifying smaller-sized companies as determined jointly by the NYSE and the NASD) have an audit committee composed solely of independent directors.
- The NYSE and the NASD require listed companies with a market capitalization above $200 million (or a more appropriate measure for identifying smaller-sized companies as determined jointly by the NYSE and the NASD) to have an audit committee composed of a minimum of three directors, each of whom is financially literate (as described in the section of this report entitled "Financial Literacy") or becomes financially literate within

a reasonable period of time after his or her appointment to the audit committee, and further that at least one member of the audit committee have accounting or related financial management expertise.

- Audit committees should adopt a formal written charter that is approved by the full board of directors and that specifies the scope of the committee's responsibilities and how it carries out those responsibilities, including structure, processes, and membership requirements, and should review and reassess the adequacy of the audit committee charter on an annual basis.
- A discussion should take place with the company's outside auditor, not just on the acceptability of the accounting principles as applied, but also on the *quality of earnings*. The discussion should include such issues as the clarity of the company's financial disclosures, the degree of aggressiveness or conservatism of the company's accounting principles and underlying estimates, and other significant decisions made by management in preparing the financial disclosure and reviewed by the outside auditors.
- The audit committee should include a letter in the company's annual report to shareholders and Form 10-K Annual Report. This letter should disclose that management has reviewed the audited financial statements with the audit committee and should include a discussion of the quality of the accounting principles as applied and significant judgments affecting the company's financial statements, and should disclose that the outside auditors have discussed with the audit committee the outside auditors' judgments of the quality of those principles.

## Financial Analysts

Financial analysts are trained to interpret financial reports, cutting through the accounting gimmicks. The leading association for those working as financial analysts is the Association of Investment Management and Research (AIMR).

### AIMR

Founded in 1949, the AIMR serves as a global leader in educating and examining investment managers and analysts and sustaining high standards of professional conduct. Its members include more than 49,000 investment practitioners and educators in over 100 countries. Its research foundation sponsors practitioner-oriented research through funding and publishing a diverse assortment of monographs, tutorials, and research papers to broaden investment professionals' knowledge and understanding of their field.

To ensure the highest level of professional conduct, AIMR members must follow the AIMR Code of Ethics and Standards of Professional Conduct, ethical guidelines that promote integrity, competence, and dignity within the investment community worldwide (*http://www.aimr.org/*).

## Financial Media

A group of tenacious and highly trained journalists has played a prominent role in ferreting out and reporting on companies that use financial shenanigans to hide the truth. Such financial sleuthing serves to improve the quality of financial analysis. Table 16-1 lists some leading financial sleuths working as journalists.

## Lawyers Representing the Investors

One deterrent to companies using accounting tricks is the threat of crippling litigation. The plaintiffs' bar has stepped up its pres-

Table 16-1.

| Journalist | Affiliation |
|---|---|
| Diana Henriques | *New York Times* |
| Floyd Norris | *New York Times* |
| Gretchen Morgenson | *New York Times* |
| Allan Sloan | *Newsweek* |
| David Henry | *Business Week* |
| John Bryne | *Business Week* |
| Debra Sparks | *Business Week* |
| Elizabeth MacDonald | *Forbes* |
| Herb Greenberg | Thestreet.com |
| Michael Schroeder | *Wall Street Journal* |
| Mark Maremont | *Wall Street Journal* |
| Jonathan Weil | *Wall Street Journal* |

sure on companies that defraud investors. Leading academics and those who represent companies hoping to strengthen their financial reporting practices deserve mention, as well. Table 16-2 gives a list of leading attorneys.

Table 16-2.

| Attorney | Affiliation |
| --- | --- |
| Boris Feldman | Wilson Sonsini |
| Joseph Grundfest | Stanford University |
| Ira Millstein | Weil Gotshal & Manges |
| Michael Young | Willkie Farr |
| Alan Schulman | Bernstein Litowitz |
| Melvyn Weiss | Milberg Weiss Bershad |
| David Bershad | Milberg Weiss Bershad |
| Bill Lerach | Milberg Weiss Bershad |
| Norman Berman | Berman DeValerio |
| Sherrie Savitt | Berger & Montague |
| Fred Isquith | Wolf Haldenstein |
| Stuart Wechsler | Wechsler Harwood |

## How Can Shenanigans Be Prevented?

Because of the potentially dire consequences for investors and lenders who rely on misleading financial statements, actions must be undertaken to prevent shenanigans. Shenanigan prevention should involve a four-pronged attack, aimed at:

1. *Improving auditors' ability to audit.* Since investors and lenders rely heavily on the auditor catching any accounting tricks, auditor training should place greater emphasis on this skill.
2. *Improving training for users of financial reports.* Investors and lenders, who rely heavily on representations in financial reports, must be trained to search for accounting tricks.
3. *Improving the control environment within organizations.* Financial improprieties are less likely to occur in organizations with strong financial controls. Such controls include internal auditors, independent auditors, an audit committee, and independent members on the board of directors. Moreover, regulatory oversight by the SEC serves as an additional control.

4. *Restructuring managers' incentives.* Management incentives that reward honest financial reporting and punish the kinds of shenanigans described in this book would reduce the likelihood of managers using such trickery. An ethical tone must be established at the top of the organization.

## Concluding Thoughts

Despite the efforts of rule makers, internal and independent auditors, regulators, and others working in harmony to prevent, detect, and eliminate financial shenanigans, the problem continues to exist and is not likely to disappear any time soon. As a result, investors and other stakeholders must continue their search for any signs of financial shenanigans. Hopefully, with the lessons from this edition of *Financial Shenanigans*, you will be much better armed for that challenge. Work hard, be curious and persistent, and you will prevail.

# 17
# AS BAD AS IT GETS

Jack Nicholson and Helen Hunt won Oscars starring in the 1997 film *As Good as It Gets*. In 2002, Enron Corporation could be featured in *As Bad as It Gets*, a movie about duping investors.

On November 8, 2001, energy giant Enron notified investors that it would restate its financial statements for the years ended December 31, 1997, through 2000 and the quarters ended March 31 and June 30, 2001 *reducing previously reported net income by $586 million*, or 16 percent. A Special Committee of the Board of Directors was formed to investigate these matters and the investigation revealed that losses far exceeded *$1 billion*.

The noose tightened twenty days later, when several credit-rating agencies lowered Enron's long-term debt to below investment grade. This would make future borrowing virtually impossible and precipitated the quick demise of the company. Shortly after the downgrade, Enron's crosstown rival, Dynegy, terminated a hastily completed merger agreement to buy Enron for approximately $9 billion in Dynegy Inc. stock and the assumption of $13 billion in debt. Bankruptcy filing was now inevitable. On December 2, 2001, Enron filed for protection under Chapter 11 of the U.S. Bankruptcy Code, the largest such filing in U.S. history. The stock price, which had once traded at $90, crested at 25 cents.

## The Victims

Thousands of Enron employees not only lost their jobs but much of the value of their retirement savings because the company had put those funds in the now worthless Enron stock. In a bizarre and cruel twist, these employees were not permitted to sell any stock as the share price was dropping, while senior management sold nearly $1 billion worth of shares throughout the year. The independent auditors, Arthur Andersen & Co., appear to be both victims and villains in this saga. Apparently Enron duped the accountants with its cleverly created ploy to inflate profits. However, Andersen's own hands were muddied as they disclosed that they had destroyed over 1,000 audit documents. While many of the facts are not yet known and the Special Committee of Enron's board has just begun its work, many warning signs were flashing.

## Background

Houston-based Enron started as a natural gas pipeline company in the 1980s, with a stock price virtually flat for the decade. In the 1990s, Enron became a global trading behemoth and, by 2001, had 21,000 employees and an $80 billion market capitalization. The stock price grew more than sevenfold.

Enron effectively operated like Wall Street trading companies. It bought, resold, and invested in commodities future contracts, gambling on future prices and market conditions. It not only traded in natural gas and electricity contracts, but also speculated in water contracts, advertising and time contracts, complex derivatives, broadband capacity futures, and weather derivatives.

The *old* Enron generated consistent (although sluggish) revenue and profit growth from selling products to customers. It had real assets on its balance sheet that investors and creditors value. In contrast, the *new* Enron generated revenue and profits from risky and unpredictable trading and asset sales to investment partners. Moreover, the new Enron created few tangible assets. In fact, Enron's CEO, Jeffrey Skilling, boasted about the company's absence of hard assets. He described the approach as "asset lite," adding, "In the old days, people worked for assets. We've turned it around—what we've said is, the assets work for people."

Being "asset lite" meant that once Enron announced problems, there was no foundation of hard assets—real product or real value—to fall back on. Creditors braced for a big loss.

## The Strategy

An important part of Enron's strategy for growth was through a variety of investment partnerships and special purpose entities (SPEs). A Houston-based analyst at Prudential Securities estimated that there existed over 3,000 such partnerships. Enron created a series of joint ventures (many involving related parties at Enron) and excluded the results from its consolidated financial statements. As a result, Enron materially inflated its profits and hid massive debt from shareholders. (See Table 17–1 for the company's preliminary estimates.) Enron failed to disclose details of these ventures until just before the collapse.

The joint ventures used a variety of schemes to enrich senior executives, create phantom profits, and drive up Enron's share price. When the business began to implode, senior executives unloaded $1 billion in Enron stock and the chief executive suddenly resigned. The chief financial officer lined his pockets with an additional $30 million in fees from these ventures before his forced resignation in October 2001.

The partnerships were typically initially funded with Enron's own stock. Much of the bogus profits recorded by Enron came either from the continued appreciation in the company's stock or from Enron selling goods or services to these affiliated entities.

The most egregious ploys reported to date (January 2002) involved three ventures: Chewco Investments, L.P. (Chewco); Joint Energy Development Investments Limited Partnership (JEDI); and LJM Cayman, L.P. (LJM1 and LJM2). Enron inflated profits by over $500 million by choosing not to consolidate these partnerships. In a November 2001 SEC filing, Enron disclosed the following:

Table 17–1. Preliminary Restatement of Net Income and Debt*‡

|  | 1997 | 1998 | 1999 | 2000 | Mar 2001 | June 2001 |
|---|---|---|---|---|---|---|
| Net income reported ($ mil) | 105 | 703 | 893 | 979 | 425 | 404 |
| Restatements |  |  |  |  |  |  |
| Chewco and JEDI | (28) | (133) | (153) | (91) | 6 | — |
| LJM | — | — | (95) | (8) |  |  |
| Miscellaneous | (51) | (6) | (10) | (38) | 29 | 5 |
| Net income restated | 26 | 564 | 635 | 842 | 460 | 409 |
| Debt reported ($ mil) | 6,254 | 7,357 | 8,152 | 10,229 | 11,922 | 12,812 |
| Restatements |  |  |  |  |  |  |
| Chewco and JEDI | 711 | 561 | 685 | 628 | — | — |
| LJM |  |  |  |  |  |  |
| Miscellaneous |  |  |  |  |  |  |
| Debt restated | 6,965 | 7,918 | 8,837 | 10,857 | 11,922 | 12,812 |

*Source: November 2001 8-K.
‡Amounts are subject to change pending the results of the investigation.

1. JEDI recorded revenues (allocated to Chewco) that consisted entirely of *appreciation in value of Enron stock* held by JEDI.
2. Enron shifted expenses to LJM1 and LJM2, by providing administrative assistance to the general partners and office space to the partnerships.
3. In December 1999, LJM2 acquired a 90 percent equity interest in an Enron entity with ownership rights to certain natural gas reserves for $3 million. As a result, Enron recognized $3 million in revenue from an existing commodity contract.
4. In December 1999, LJM2 paid Enron $30 million for a 75 percent equity interest in a power project in Poland. Enron recognized a $16 million gain in 1999 on the sale.
5. In September 1999, LJM1 acquired from Enron a 13 percent equity interest in a company owning a power project in Brazil for $10.8 million, and acquired redeemable preference shares in a related company for $500,000. Enron recognized a $1.7 million loss on the sale of these interests to LJM1. Enron recognized revenues of $65 million, $14 million and $5 million from a commodity contract with the company owning the power project in 1999, 2000 and 2001, respectively.
6. In June 2000, Enron sold LJM2 dark fiber-optic cable for $100 million, netting $67 million in pre-tax earnings in 2000 related to the asset sale.
7. Enron recognized $20 million of income for marketing the fiber to others and other fees for providing operation and maintenance services to LJM2 with respect to the fiber.

## Warning Signs and Lessons from Enron

Investors should be wary whenever a company dramatically changes its business model, particularly from one easily understood by investors to another, far more obtuse and difficult to evaluate and monitor. Moreover, investors should assume the use of special-purpose entities, and other off-balance-sheet entities can be used to create phantom profits and hide liabilities. The absence of detailed disclosure about such entities raises additional red flags. Other warning signs in the Enron debacle include numerous

---

Accounting Capsule

## Special Purpose Entities

An SPE is an entity created to carry out a specified purpose or activity, such as to consummate a specific transaction or series of transactions with a narrowly defined purpose. SPEs are commonly used as financing vehicles in which assets are sold to a trust in exchange for cash or other assets funded by debt issued by the trust. In many cases, SPEs are used to achieve off-balance sheet treatment.

To illustrate, here is an example of how an SPE might work. A third-party investor (unrelated to a transferor) may set up an SPE for the benefit of a transferor, which is the company that transfers or contributes the assets to the SPE. The investor will control the activities of the SPE and retain the risks and rewards, like common stockholders in a "normal" corporation. The SPE will hold assets and finance them through debt and equity issued to institutional investors or public shareholders. To reduce the interest rate paid on the debt, the SPE will obtain credit enhancements (for example, guarantees or similar derivative arrangements), often from the transferor and/or other third parties. This spreading of the risk through the credit enhancements, coupled with the fact that the SPE's securities are usually liquid and easily traded, generally reduces the cost of the borrowing to a level below what it would have been had the transferor directly borrowed money from a bank or the market.

Most SPE transactions are off-balance sheet (i.e., financial information about the SPE, including its assets and liabilities, does not appear in the financial statements of the transferor.)

To achieve off-balance sheet treatment, an SPE must meet two conditions. First, the assets must be sold to the SPE (must be legally isolated from the transferor) and, second, an independent third-party owner must have made a substantive capital investment (which amounts to at least 3 percent of the SPE's total capitalization). If executed properly, the legal isolation and the control by a third party reduce the risk of the creditor. Thus, off-balance sheet treatment of an SPE involves more than just sufficient third-party equity. This equity must be "at risk" from the investor's perspective. If the investor's return is guaranteed or not "at risk," the transferor would be required to consolidate the SPE in its financial statements.

---

related-party activities and self-dealing by senior executives, large stock sales by directors and officers, and the mysterious resignation of a rather young CEO. Also, the company showed arrogance in its treatment of financial analysts who were asking probing questions about its accounting and disclosure policies.

## The U.S. Government Investigation

Enron's collapse and the mammoth investors' losses led to investigative actions by the highest branches in our government.

In January 2002, for example, the U.S. Department of Justice began a criminal investigation of Enron Corporation. This action marks a new escalation in a many-sided investigation of Enron, which filed the largest corporate bankruptcy in U.S. history. Four congressional committees, the SEC, and the Labor Department have begun separate investigations.

Congressional investigators are looking into whether Enron used the partnerships to exaggerate its revenue and conceal the full dimensions of billions of dollars in debts from failed investments in overseas power and water projects. In December 2001, Arthur Andersen CEO Joseph F. Berardino testified to Congress that the energy-trading company may have committed "illegal acts" by withholding critical financial information concerning one of the many outside partnerships.

White House Press Secretary Ari Fleischer said that, as a result of Enron's collapse, President Bush is likely to propose new federal policies aimed at protecting people's pensions and ensuring that financial reports are more revealing.

## Final Thoughts

While little can be done to restore the wealth of investors who were duped by Enron, Cendant, and others, we can learn from their experiences to be more alert for the next "big" one by being skeptical and heeding the many lessons in *Financial Shenanigans*.

# UNDERSTANDING THE BASICS OF FINANCIAL REPORTING

## Overview

This tutorial provides the basic tools for reading and interpreting financial statements. Specifically, it describes the following:

- Basic accounting principles and journal entries
- The structure and purpose of each major financial statement
- Key aspects in understanding financial statements

Financial statements summarize economic transactions and measure companies' profitability and financial condition. Companies that use financial shenanigans distort their actual profits (or net income) and financial condition.

## Accounting Is As Simple As 1-2-3

Some of you may have never taken an accounting course. Others may have taken a course or two, yet remember nothing. In either case, it doesn't matter—because in the next few pages you will learn all the formal accounting you need to know to understand financial statements. All you need to remember are three lessons.

## Lesson No. I

Accounting is really quite simple, since *all* transactions fit into one basic equation:

$$\text{Assets} = \text{Liabilities} + \text{Capital}$$

In nontechnical terms, this equation states that the total book value of the resources (owned by the entity) is equal to the book value of the claims against those resources.

*Assets* represent economic resources—such as cash, inventory, or buildings—that will provide future benefits beyond the current year.

*Liabilities* represent claims against those resources by creditors, vendors, employees, and others.

*Capital* represents the residual claim against those resources by the owners (shareholders).

The balance sheet is the formal financial statement that shows the details of a company's assets, liabilities, and capital.

## Lesson No. 2

One major component of capital is a company's profits for the current year. Profit (or net income) is computed as follows:

$$\text{Net income} = \text{Revenues} - \text{Expenses}$$

*Revenues* (or sales) are the inflows of net assets (i.e., assets less liabilities) from selling goods or providing services.

*Expenses* are the resources consumed in the process of generating revenue.

*Net income*, a measure of operating performance, is calculated as the excess of revenue earned from selling a product or providing a service above the efforts required or expended to sell the product or provide the service.

Thus, whenever a company records revenue, both net income and capital increase. Conversely, whenever a company records an expense, both net income and capital decrease.

The statement of operations (or income) is the formal statement that shows the details of a company's revenues and expenses.

### Lesson No. 3

For the equation Assets = Liabilities + Capital to hold, there must be at least two parts to each and every transaction. For example, when an asset account increases, either another asset account must decrease, a liability account must increase, or owners' equity (i.e., capital) must rise.

That's all there is to it. Everything else (as they say in the Talmud) is just commentary.

## Applying the Lessons

All the information shown on financial statements is first recorded in a series of journal entries. Let's examine some common business transactions and their effect on the accounting equation (A = L + C) and on net income.

---

#### CHECKLIST: GUIDING PRINCIPLES

1. Revenue should be recorded after the earnings process has been completed and an exchange has occurred. Similarly, gains should be recorded when there is an exchange.
2. An enterprise should capitalize costs incurred that produce a future benefit and expense those that produce no such benefit.
3. As an enterprise realizes the benefits from using an asset, the asset or a part thereof should be written off as an expense of the period.

*(Continued)*

4. When there is a sudden and substantial impairment in an asset's value, the asset should be written off immediately and in its entirety, rather than gradually over time.
5. An enterprise has incurred a liability if it is obligated to make future sacrifices.
6. Revenue should be recorded in the period in which it is earned.
7. Expenses should be charged against income in the period in which the benefit is received.

## Transaction No. 1: Sale of Merchandise

| | | | | |
|---|---|---|---|---|
| *Increase:* | Accounts Receivable | 500 | | (asset) |
| *Increase:* | Sales | | 500 | (revenue) |

Whenever a sale is recorded, assets, revenue, net income, and capital all increase. The accounting entry is usually made when a sale has taken place and the merchandise has been shipped out. If a company records revenue too early (Shenanigan No. 1, as discussed in Chapter 4) or creates fictitious revenue (Shenanigan No. 2, as discussed in Chapter 5), net income, assets, and capital have been overstated.

## Transaction No. 2: Receiving Cash When Future Services Are Due

| | | | | |
|---|---|---|---|---|
| *Increase:* | Cash | 200 | | (asset) |
| *Increase:* | Unearned Revenue | | 200 | (liability) |

This transaction increases assets and liabilities. One accounting trick (Shenanigan No. 5, Chapter 8) is to record revenue instead of unearned revenue in such a case. The result is that net income and capital are overstated and liabilities are understated.

## Transaction No. 3: Receiving Cash at Time of Sale

| *Increase:* | Cash | 900 | | (asset) |
|---|---|---|---|---|
| *Increase:* | Sales | | 900 | (revenue) |

This transaction increases assets and revenue. One accounting trick that is used when a company wants to defer some sales revenue until a later period is to record a liability initially and wait until the following year to transfer the liability to revenue. This trick, also known as setting up reserves (Shenanigan No. 6, Chapter 9), shifts income from a year in which a company may have a large profit to a later year when profits are weak. The objective is to "smooth" income over the years, eliminating the peaks and valleys.

The journal entries to set up and later tap a reserve are as follows.

This year's entry:

| *Increase:* | Cash | 600 | | (asset) |
|---|---|---|---|---|
| *Increase:* | Unearned Revenue | | 600 | (liability) |

Future year's entry:

| *Decrease:* | Unearned Revenue | 200 | | (liability) |
|---|---|---|---|---|
| *Increase:* | Sales Revenue | | 200 | (revenue) |

The result is that this year's sales revenue is recorded as being earned in a later period.

## Transaction No. 4: Estimating Probable Liability

| *Increase:* | Loss from Litigation | 6,000 | | (loss) |
|---|---|---|---|---|
| *Increase:* | Estimated Liability | | 6,000 | (liability) |

This transaction increases liabilities and reduces net income. One accounting trick (Shenanigan No. 5, Chapter 8) is neglecting to record this entry. The result is that liabilities are understated and net income overstated.

**Transaction No. 5: Recording the Purchase of an Asset**

| | | | |
|---|---|---|---|
| *Increase:* | Equipment | 10,000 | (asset) |
| *Decrease:* | Cash | 10,000 | (asset) |

This entry exchanges one asset for another. One accounting trick (Shenanigan No. 4, Chapter 7) is to record this entry when a company acquires an expense (a past benefit) rather than an asset. For instance, a company pays an advertising bill and decides to record advertising as an asset. The proper entry for recording an expense is:

| | | | |
|---|---|---|---|
| *Increase:* | Advertising Expense | 500 | (expense) |
| *Decrease:* | Cash | 500 | (asset) |

Recording advertising expense as an asset ("capitalizing" it) rather than an expense results in the current period's net income being overstated. Over the next several years, however, the cost will be transferred from the asset account to depreciation expense. Thus the net result of incorrectly capitalizing an expense is that the expense is improperly shifted from the current period to a later period.

**Transaction No. 6: Amortizing an Asset**

| | | | |
|---|---|---|---|
| *Increase:* | Depreciation Expense | 500 | (expense) |
| *Decrease:* | Equipment | 500 | (asset) |

This entry transfers a portion of the asset to an expense as the benefit is received. A company purchases various assets to use in producing its product and in generating revenue. When revenue is recognized (as a sale takes place), that portion of the assets that can be associated ("matched") with the sale should be transferred from assets to expenses. One accounting trick (Shenanigan No. 4, Chapter 7) is transferring those assets to expense too slowly, either by amortizing them over too long a period or by failing to write off worthless assets. The result of either error is to record too small an expense and thereby to shift expenses to a later period.

Alternatively, if a company is concerned that profits in the later periods will be inadequate, a strategy may be to set up reserves. As indicated earlier (Shenanigan No. 6, Chapter 9), one purpose of setting up reserves is to shift revenue to a later period. Another approach (Shenanigan No. 7, Chapter 10) is to shift future-period expenses into the current period. Simply depreciating a larger amount this year and smaller amounts in future years will give you the desired results. Another way to shift expenses to the current period is by prepaying next year's expenses.

### Transaction No. 7: Recording Gain on Sale of Assets

| | | | |
|---|---|---|---|
| *Increase:* | Cash | 15,000 | (asset) |
| *Decrease:* | Equipment | 10,000 | (asset) |
| *Increase:* | Gain on Sale | 5,000 | (revenue) |

Recording a gain on the sale of assets boosts assets and net income. One accounting trick (Shenanigan No. 3, Chapter 6) is to sell off assets, especially those with low book values, and record a gain on their disposal.

## Structure of Financial Reports

Economic performance is generally communicated to interested parties in the form of financial statements. These reports include (1) the statement of income, (2) the balance sheet, and (3) the statement of cash flows.

## The Statement of Income

The statement of income (also called the statement of operations) communicates the profitability of a company over a specified period of time. A company's profit or net income is equal to its revenues and gains minus its expenses and losses.

Table T-1 gives the Gillette Company's statement of income. It also includes common-sized information that will be helpful in doing vertical and horizontal analysis.

(*Note:* The Gillette Company is used for illustrative purposes only, *not because it committed any shenanigans.*)

Notice that there are several important subclassifications within the statement of income:

1. *Gross profit* (or gross margin, when stated as a percentage of revenues): excess net sales over cost of sales
2. *Operating income* (or profit from operations): gross profit less operating expenses, such as selling, general, and administrative expenses
3. *Income from continuing operations:* net income after taxes, but before any noncontinuing transactions (such as extraordinary gains or losses, the effects of a change in accounting principles, and gains or losses related to discontinued operations)
4. *Net income* (net income after tax, or NIAT) (or net margin, when stated as a percentage of revenue): income from continuing operations plus or minus the noncontinuing transactions

## The Balance Sheet

The balance sheet (or statement of financial position) presents a *snapshot* of a company's resources (i.e., its assets) and the claims against those resources (i.e., its liabilities and owners' equity or capital) at a specific point in time. The asset portion of the balance sheet reports the effects of all of a company's past investment decisions. The liabilities and owners' equity portion reports the effects of all of the company's past financing decisions. Capital is obtained from both short- and long-term creditors and from owners. Thus the balance sheet reflects the following equation:

Table T-1. The Gillette Company Consolidated Statement of Operations

| ($ in millions, except per share data) | 2000 | 1999 | Horizontal % | Vertical % of Sales 2000 | Vertical % of Sales 1999 |
|---|---|---|---|---|---|
| Net sales | 9,295 | 9,154 | 1.54% | 100.00% | 100.00% |
| Cost of sales | 3,384 | 3,392 | 0.00% | 36.41% | 37.05% |
| Gross profit (margins) | 5,911 | 5,762 | 2.60% | 63.59% | 62.95% |
| Selling, general and administrative expenses | 3,827 | 3,675 | 4.13% | 41.17% | 40.15% |
| Restructuring and asset impairment charges | 572 | — | — | — | — |
| Total operating expenses | 4,399 | 3,675 | 19.70% | 47.33% | 40.15% |
| Income (loss) from operations | 1,512 | 2,087 | −27.55% | 16.27% | 22.80% |
| Nonoperating charges (income): | | | | | |
| Interest income | (5) | (7) | −28.57% | — | — |
| Interest expense | 223 | 136 | 63.97% | — | — |
| Other charges—net | 6 | 46 | −86.96% | — | — |
| Income from continuing operations before income taxes | 1,288 | 1,912 | −32.64% | 13.86% | 20.89% |
| Provision for income taxes | 467 | 664 | −29.67% | 5.02% | 7.25% |
| Income from continuing operations | 821 | 1,248 | −34.21% | 8.83% | 13.63% |
| Loss on disposal of discontinued operations, net | (428) | — | — | — | — |
| Income (loss) from discontinued operations, net | (1) | 12 | — | — | — |
| Net income | 392 | 1,260 | −68.89% | 4.22% | 13.76% |
| **Income (loss) per share** | | | | | |
| Continuing operations | $0.78 | $1.14 | — | — | — |
| Disposal of discontinued operations | ($0.41) | — | — | — | — |
| Discontinued operations | — | 0.01 | — | — | — |
| Net income (loss) | ($0.37) | $1.15 | — | — | — |

$$\text{Assets} = \text{Liabilities} + \text{Owners' Equity}$$

That is, the book value of a firm's assets or resources equals the book value of the claims against those assets by creditors and owners.

The balance sheet for The Gillette Company is given in Table T-2.

**Uses of the Balance Sheet.**   An analyst, voicing frustration at using a balance sheet to analyze a company, stated: "A balance sheet is very much like a bikini. What it reveals is interesting, what it conceals is vital." Many others have also been left asking what vital information is found beyond the numbers. Is the company hiding any material information?

While the task of interpreting a balance sheet may be daunting, those who have mastered this skill often find important insights concerning problems on the horizon. One such expert, Michael Murphy, editor of the *Overpriced Stock Service* newsletter, believes that "the potential problems of technology companies always show up first on the balance sheet."

The balance sheet provides information about the company's present resource base and how those resources were financed. It provides useful information on management's stewardship of invested capital and about the solvency and liquidity of the company. A review of the liabilities and owners' capital reveals the company's financial commitments and the relative interests of the owners and creditors. Such information may have a bearing on a company's financial strength (its ability to meet its long-term obligations) and its financial flexibility.

By examining the current assets and current liabilities, analysts can judge a company's liquidity (its ability to meet its short-term obligations). Current assets minus current liabilities is called *working capital*. It is viewed as a measure of financial safety—a cushion against uncertain drains of financial resources in the future.

**Limitations of the Balance Sheet.**   The balance sheet *does not* indicate the current value (or "market value") of a company's assets, liabilities, or owners' equity. Instead, it presents the "book value" (or historical cost) of all these items.

Table T-2. The Gillette Company Consolidated Balance Sheet December 31, 2000 and 1999

| ($ millions) | 2000 | 1999 | Horizontal % | Vertical % of Assets 2000 | Vertical % of Assets 1999 |
|---|---|---|---|---|---|
| *ASSETS* | | | | | |
| Current assets | | | | | |
| Cash and cash equivalents | 62 | 80 | −22.50% | 0.60% | 0.68% |
| Trade receivables, less allowance for doubtful accounts of $81 and $74 | 2,128 | 2,208 | −3.62% | **20.46%** | 18.73% |
| Other receivables | 378 | 319 | **18.50%** | 3.63% | 2.71% |
| Inventories | 1,162 | 1,392 | **−16.52%** | 11.17% | 11.81% |
| Deferred income taxes | 566 | 309 | **83.17%** | 5.44% | 2.62% |
| Other current assets | 197 | 315 | **−37.46%** | 1.89% | 2.67% |
| Net assets of discontinued operations | 189 | 117 | **−83.90%** | **1.82%** | 9.96% |
| Total current assets | 4,682 | 4,740 | −1.2% | **45.01%** | 40.22% |
| Property and equipment, net | 3,550 | 3,46 | 1.02% | **34.13%** | 29.42% |
| Intangible assets | 1,574 | 1,897 | **−17.03%** | 15.13% | 16.10% |
| Other assets | 596 | 625 | −4.64% | 5.73% | 5.30% |
| Total Assets | 10,402 | 11,786 | −11.74% | 100.00% | 100.00% |
| **LIABILITIES AND STOCKHOLDERS' EQUITY** | | | | | |
| Current liabilities | | | | | |
| Loans payable | 2,195 | 1,440 | **52.43%** | **21.10%** | 12.22% |
| Current portion of long-term debt | 631 | 358 | **76.26%** | 6.07% | 3.04% |
| Accounts payable and accrued liabilities | 2,346 | 2,149 | 9.17% | 22.55% | 18.23% |
| Income taxes | 299 | 233 | 28.33% | 2.87% | 1.98% |
| Total current liabilities | 5,471 | 4,180 | 30.89% | **52.60%** | 35.47% |

Table T-2. The Gillette Company Consolidated Balance Sheet December 31, 2000 and 1999 *(continued)*

| ($ millions) | 2000 | 1999 | Horizontal % | Vertical % of Assets 2000 | Vertical % of Assets 1999 |
|---|---|---|---|---|---|
| Long-term debt | 1,650 | 2,931 | -43.71% | **15.86%** | 24.87% |
| Deferred income taxes | 450 | 423 | 6.38% | 4.33% | 3.59% |
| Other long-term liabilities | 767 | 795 | -3.52% | 7.37% | 6.75% |
| Minority interest | 41 | 38 | 7.89% | — | — |
| Contingent redemption value of common stock put options | 99 | 359 | -72.42% | — | — |
| Stockholders' equity | | 85 | — | | |
| 8.0% cumulative ESOP convertible preferred stock | — | | | | |
| Unearned ESOP compensation | — | (4) | | | |
| Common stock, $1 par value, authorized 2.32 billion shares; issued 1.365 billion shares (in 2000) and 1.364 billion (in 1999) | 136 | 136 | 0% | 13.12% | 11.57% |
| Additional paid-in capital | 973 | 748 | 30.08% | 9.35% | 6.35% |
| Earnings reinvested in the business | 5,853 | 6,147 | -4.78% | 56.27% | 52.16% |
| Accumulated other comprehensive income: | | | | | |
| Foreign currency translation | (1,280) | (1,031) | 24.15% | — | — |
| Pension adjustment | (34) | (30) | 13.33% | — | — |
| Treasury stock, at cost, 2,000 shares | (4,953) | (4,219) | 17.40% | | |
| Total stockholders' equity | 1,924 | 3,060 | -37.12% | 18.50% | 25.96% |
| Total liabilities and equity | 10,402 | 11,786 | -11.74% | 100% | 100% |

Also, some items that are of value of a business *may never appear* on the balance sheet because they cannot be expressed in dollars. A brand name that has attracted customer loyalty (such as Coca Cola) and an industry reputation for quality products are examples of "unrecorded assets."

A third limitation is that the balance sheet *represents only one moment in time.* Seasonal factors and unusual circumstances must be considered. Even when comparative balance sheets for several years are presented, they fail to explain *why* changes occurred, particularly those related to operations. Accordingly, the statement of income and the statement of cash flows are essential complements to the balance sheet.

## The Statement of Cash Flows

The statement of cash flows reports the net cash (inflows minus outflows) from the three principal business activities—operating, investing, and financing.

As shown in The Gillette Company example (Table T-3), there are three major sections on the statement of cash flows: (1) cash from operations, (2) cash used in investment activities, and (3) cash used in financing activities.

One key question addressed by the statement of cash flows is whether the company generates enough cash from operations by itself or must generate cash from investments (e.g., by selling off assets) and/or from financing (e.g., by issuing debt or equity issues) to meet its cash needs.

## Key Aspects of Understanding Financial Statements

Analysis of financial statements focuses on four main characteristics:

- Profitability
- Liquidity
- Solvency
- Activity (or operational efficiency)

Table T-3. The Gillette Company Consolidated Statements of Cash Flows for the Years Ended December 31, 2000 and 1999 (in millions)

|  | 2000 | 1999 |
|---|---|---|
| **Cash flows from operating activities:** | | |
| Net earnings | **$821** | **$1,248** |
| Adjustments to reconcile net earnings to net cash | | |
| Provision for restructuring and asset impairment | 572 | — |
| Depreciation and amortization | 535 | 464 |
| Other | 5 | (7) |
| Changes in assets and liabilities, excluding effects of acquisitions and divestitures: | | |
| Accounts receivable | (100) | (48) |
| Inventories | 149 | (140) |
| Accounts payable and accrued liabilities | (45) | 65 |
| Other working capital items | (136) | 97 |
| Other noncurrent assets and liabilities | (197) | (252) |
| **Net cash provided (used) by operating activities** | **1,604** | **1,427** |
| **Cash flows from investing activities:** | | |
| Additions to property, plant, and equipment | (793) | (889) |
| Disposals of property, plant, and equipment | 41 | 124 |
| Sale of businesses | 539 | — |
| Other, net | (1) | 2 |
| **Net cash provided (used) by investing activities** | **(214)** | **(763)** |
| **Cash flows from financing activities:** | | |
| Purchase of treasury stock | (944) | (2,021) |
| Proceeds from sale of put options | 23 | 72 |
| Proceeds from exercise of stock option and purchase plans | 36 | 149 |
| Proceeds from long-term debt | 494 | 1,105 |
| Repayment of long-term debt | (365) | — |
| Increase (decrease) in loans payable | (385) | 484 |
| Dividends paid | (671) | (626) |
| Settlements of debt-related derivative contracts | 279 | 42 |
| **Net cash provided by financing activities** | **(1,533)** | **(795)** |
| Effect of exchange rate changes on cash | (5) | (2) |
| Net cash provided from discontinued operations | 130 | 111 |
| Net increase (decrease) in cash and cash equivalents | **(18)** | **(22)** |
| Cash and cash equivalents at beginning of period | 80 | 102 |
| Cash and cash equivalents at end of period | **$62** | **$80** |

## Profitability Ratios

Profitability ratios measure the financial performance of a company over a period of time. There are a number of profitability ratios that analysts commonly use, including (1) gross profit margin, (2) operating margin, (3) net profit margin, (4) return on assets, (5) return on equity, and (6) earnings per share. Using the financial statements of The Gillette Company, these ratios are described as follows.

*Profitability Ratios*

Gross profit margin          = Gross profit/sales

Operating margin          = Operating profit/sales

Net profit margin          = **Net income after tax (NIAT)/ sales**

**Return on assets (ROA)**     = **NIAT/ total assets**

**Return on equity (ROE)**     = **NIAT/ total stockholders' equity**

**Earnings per share (EPS)**  = **NIAT/ number of common shares outstanding**

The Gillette Company: Profitability Ratios

|                             | 2000    | 1999    |
| --------------------------- | ------- | ------- |
| Gross profit margin         | 63.59%  | 62.95%  |
| Operating margin            | 16.27%  | 22.80%  |
| Net profit margin           | 4.22%   | 13.76%  |
| ROA                         | 3.77%   | 10.69%  |
| ROE                         | 20.37%  | 41.18%  |
| EPS (continuing operations) | $0.78   | $1.14   |

**Gross Profit Margin (or Gross Margin) = Gross Profit/Sales.** Gross profit margin measures the margin available to cover a company's operating expenses and yield a profit.

**Operating Margin = Operating Profit/Sales.** Operating margin measures a company's profitability from its main source of business.

**Net Profit Margin (or Net Margin or Return on Sales) = NIAT/
Sales.**  Net profit margin measures how much a company earns
on each dollar of sales. Thus if a company has a net profit margin
of 3 percent, it earns three cents on every dollar of sales.

**Return on Assets (ROA) = NIAT/Total Assets.**  Return on assets
measures the return on investment of both the stockholders and
the creditors.

**Earnings per Share (EPS) = NIAT/Number of Common Shares Out-
standing.**  Earnings per share measures the profitability of the company that accrues to common stockholders on a per-share basis.

**Return on Equity (ROE) = NIAT/Total Equity.**  Return on equity
measures the return on investment for the stockholders.

### Liquidity Ratios

Liquidity ratios indicate the amount of cash or short-term assets
(such as receivables and inventory) that are available to the company. If the liquidity position gets too high, then the company is
sacrificing profitability; if the liquidity position gets too low, then
the company may not be able to meet its current obligations. Some
key liquidity ratios are as follows.

*Liquidity Ratios*

Current ratio      = Current assets divided by current li-
                     abilities
Working capital = Current assets minus current liabili-
                     ties
Quick ratio        = Cash and receivables divided by
                     current liabilities

The Gillette Company: Liquidity Ratios

|                 | 2000         | 1999         |
|-----------------|--------------|--------------|
| Current ratio   | 0.85 times   | 1.33 times   |
| Working capital | $789 million | $560 million |
| Quick ratio     | 0.47 times   | 0.62 times   |

**Current Ratio = Current Assets/Current Liabilities.** The current ratio measures the extent to which the claims of the short-term creditors are covered by the company's current or short-term assets.

**Working Capital = Current Assets Minus Current Liabilities.** Working capital measures the excess of current resources over the current obligations. The greater the amount of working capital, the greater is the cushion available to meet any unforeseen cash requirements.

**Quick Ratio = (Current Assets Minus Inventory)/Current Liabilities.** The quick ratio measures the extent to which the claims of short-term creditors are covered without the need for an inventory sell-off.

### Solvency Ratios

Solvency (leverage) ratios, which reflect a company's ability to meet its obligations, indicate how the company finances its operations. If a company's leverage (debt) is too high, then it may be taking great risks; if it is too low, then it may be failing to take advantage of opportunities to use long-term debt to finance growth. Some examples of solvency ratios are as follows.

*Solvency Ratios*

| | |
|---|---|
| Debt to assets | = Total debt/total assets |
| Debt to equity | = Total debt/total equity |
| Long-term debt to equity | = Long-term debt/total equity |
| Interest coverage ratio | = Operating income/interest expense |

**Debt to Assets = Total Debt / Total Assets.** Debt to assets measures the extent to which a company borrows money to finance its operations.

**Debt to Equity = Total Debt / Total Equity.** Debt to equity measures the creditors' funds as a percentage of stockholders' funds.

**Long-Term Debt to Equity = Long-Term Debt/Total Equity.**
Long-term debt to equity measures the balance between a company's debt and its equity; a high degree of financial leverage indicates a risk in meeting the principal and/or interest on the debt. Long-term debt is computed by subtracting from total liabilities and stockholders' equity the current liabilities and the stockholders' equity.

The Gillette Company: Solvency Ratios

|                          | 2000        | 1999        |
| ------------------------ | ----------- | ----------- |
| Debt to assets           | 81.50%      | 74.04%      |
| Debt to equity           | 440.64%     | 285.16%     |
| Long-term debt to equity | 156.29%     | 148.56%     |
| Interest coverage        | 7.78 times  | 14.35 times |

**Interest Coverage Ratio = Operating Income/Interest Expense.**
The interest coverage ratio is calculated from the income statement. It measures the multiple by which the operating income exceeds the fixed interest expense that must be paid. The higher the ratio, the less chance that the company will default on the payment.

### Activity Ratios

Activity ratios indicate the productive efficiency of the company. Generally, stronger activity ratios are associated with higher profitability (as a result of high productive efficiency). Some examples of activity ratios are as follows.

*Activity Ratios*

| Inventory turnover | = Cost of sales divided by average inventory |
| Average days' inventory on hand | = 365 days divided by inventory turnover |
| Accounts receivable turnover | = Sales divided by average accounts receivable turnover |
| Average receivable collection period | = 365 days divided by accounts receivable turnover |

The Gillette Company: Activity Ratios

|                                      | 2000     | 1999     |
|--------------------------------------|----------|----------|
| Inventory turnover                   | 2.65     | 2.27     |
| Average days' inventory on hand      | 137 days | 160 days |
| Receivable turnover                  | 4.29     | 3.79     |
| Average receivable collection period | 85 days  | 96 days  |

**Inventory Turnover = Cost of Sales/Average Inventory.** Inventory turnover measures the number of times a company turns over its entire inventory during a year. The higher the turnover, the shorter the amount of time that a company must sit with idle inventory. To compute the 1999 inventory turnover, the January 1, 1999, balance ($1.595 billion) is needed. This figure can be found on the 1998 balance sheet (not exhibited in this book).

**Accounts Receivable Turnover = Sales/Average Accounts Receivable.** Accounts receivable turnover measures the number of times a company turns over all its receivables during a year. The higher the turnover, the more quickly customers are paying their bills. To compute the 1999 receivables turnover, the January 1, 1999, balance ($2.622 billion) is needed. This figure can be found on the 1998 balance sheet.

### Using the Ratios

Ratios are used to compare a company's current performance with its prior years' performance and with the performance of similar companies in the industry. Information about these ratios can be obtained from the following sources, among others:

• *Almanac of Business and Industrial Financial Ratios* (Prentice-Hall)
• *Annual Statement Studies* (Robert Morris Associates)
• *Dun's Review* (Dun & Bradstreet)

### Limitations of Using Ratios

Financial ratios must be used with caution for the following reasons.

- These ratios are merely "surrogates" for an underlying measure, such as liquidity or solvency. They should therefore be recognized as imprecise measures.
- If management is manipulating the numbers on the financial statements, then the resulting ratios will necessarily also be misleading.
- Ratios consider only information that is quantified on the financial statements. Excluded, yet often equally important, are qualitative and quantitative information that is not shown on these statements.

## The Goal of Financial Reporting

The primary goal of financial reporting is the dissemination of financial statements that accurately measure a company's profitability and financial condition. To ascertain that financial reports are accurate, investors and lenders focus on the following seven guiding principles.

**Guiding Principle 1:** *Revenue should be recorded after the earnings process has been completed and an exchange has occurred. Similarly, a gain should be recorded when a nonoperating asset is sold at above its book value.*

For most businesses, the appropriate time to record revenue from selling a product or providing a service is when two conditions have been met: (1) The earnings process is substantially complete, and (2) there has been an arm's-length exchange. Additionally, the risks and benefits of ownership of the product must have transferred from the seller to the buyer in order for a sale to be recognized.

Consider the accounting for the sale of a new McDonald's franchise. McDonald's receives a large initial payment for the various kinds of assistance it will provide the franchisee over the years. Since much of the money it receives is still "unearned," McDonald's should record only a part of the initial payment as revenue.

| Increase: | Cash | 1,000 | |
| Increase: | Revenue | | 250 |
| Increase: | Unearned Revenue | | 750 |

*Guiding Principle 2: An enterprise should capitalize costs incurred that produce a future benefit and expense those that produce no such benefit.*

Assets represent economic resources of the enterprise that are expected to provide some future benefit for the enterprise. Assets are initially recorded at their historical cost. However, if the anticipated future benefits dissipate, either gradually or suddenly, the asset account must be reduced to reflect the lower-than-expected economic benefit.

One area that may create some controversy and disagreements between management and the independent auditor is determining whether there is indeed a future benefit. This issue may arise in the following situations:

1. Initially, when a company incurs a cost (e.g., in purchasing equipment or office supplies).
2. If the initial decision is to record as an asset (i.e., to "capitalize" it), a decision must then be made as to over how long a period the benefit will be derived and what proportion will be derived each year.
3. If there is a sudden and permanent decline in the value of the asset, a decision must be made as to how much of the asset should be written off as a loss and when the write-off should occur.

If the amount of the asset is insignificant ("immaterial"), or if the benefit will be received over a short time horizon, then the cost should be reflected immediately as an expense rather than as an asset.

*Guiding Principle 3: As an enterprise realizes the
benefit from using an asset, the asset or a part thereof
should be written off as an expense of the period.*

As an enterprise realizes the benefit from using an asset, the
expired portion of the asset must be transferred to an expense
account, and, of course, the asset account must be decreased by a
similar amount. This is a common and natural process. A company acquires resources in order to produce benefits—to generate
additional revenue and profits. Over time, those resources are
used in the productive process, and revenue and profits are realized. At that point, a portion of the assets should be transferred
to the appropriate expense accounts. For example, inventory is
classified as an asset when the raw material is first acquired. When
the product is completed and sold, however, the entire cost of the
product is transferred from the inventory account (an asset) to cost
of goods sold (the corresponding expense).

| | | | |
|---|---|---|---|
| *Increase:* | Cost of Goods Sold | 500 | |
| *Decrease:* | Merchandise Inventory | | 500 |

*Guiding Principle 4: When there is a sudden and
substantial impairment in an asset's value, the asset
should be written off immediately and in its entirety,
rather than gradually over time.*

Since assets represent future benefits of an enterprise, in the
event that the benefit no longer exists, the asset should be written
off *as a loss* as soon as it becomes determinable. The term "big
bath" is used to describe large write-offs of assets whose value
suddenly declines and must be written off.

Thus, when a company closes a plant, it should make an accounting entry that records a loss and eliminates the asset account
Plant and Equipment.

| | | |
|---|---|---|
| *Increase:* | Loss on Plant Closing | 1,000,000 |
| *Decrease:* | Plant and Equipment | 1,000,000 |

*Guiding Principle 5: An enterprise has incurred a
liability if it is obligated to make future sacrifices.*

A liability represents a present obligation of an enterprise to perform some act or to sacrifice some resource in the future. A common shenanigan is an attempt to hide or "keep off the books" actual or probable liabilities. This technique is referred to as *off-balance-sheet financing.*

Going back to our McDonald's franchise, the portion of the initial payment to McDonald's that was unearned should be recorded as a liability [since future services (sacrifices) are required].

*Guiding Principle 6: Revenue should be recorded in
the period in which it is earned.*

Under the accrual basis of accounting, revenue should be recorded in the period in which it is earned rather than in the period in which cash is received.

*Guiding Principle 7: Expenses should be charged
against income in the period in which the benefit
is received.*

Generally accepted accounting principles require that expenses should be "matched" with revenue. Thus, expenses must be charged in the period in which the enterprise realizes a benefit from using assets to produce or sell its product.

# INDEX